To Barbara & Bob
My Very Best Wishes
John K. Potter

The Baker's Vault

By

John K. Potter

ISBN: 1-4107-4956-8 (e-book)
ISBN: 1-4107-4955-X (Paperback)
ISBN: 1-4107-4954-1 (Dust Jacket)

This book is printed on acid free paper.

1stBooks – rev. 11/10/03

This book is dedicated to my son, John and my daughter, Meredith, who have been my inspiration since the day they were born.

TABLE OF CONTENTS

PROLOGUE

Paris, France, December 29, 1797

Charles' eyes were red, with dark circles under them, but he was ecstatic as he carefully spread the glue onto the spine of the newly printed book. He then positioned the middle of a brown leather cover down on the spine and pressed with all his might. After a couple of minutes, he reached across the long wooden table and picked up a heavy iron bar and replaced the pressure of his hands with the weight of the bar. He carefully slid the book with the new cover next to a stack of other identical books. There were now six copies of <u>Recit de la Revolution</u>.

Exhausted, he rubbed his eyes and sighed deeply. He ached all over. He stood up and limped back over to the old press at the back of his print shop to begin the process again.

It was hard for his 63-year old eyes to see in the dim light of just the four oil lanterns hanging from their hooks on the beamed ceiling. Charles nearly stumbled over a stack of just-delivered paper lying on the well-worn wooden floor near the printing press. He was tired. Very tired. He'd been working on printing the book for nearly seventy-two hours straight. When he raised his arms to again pull the lever that brought the printing plates down on the waiting leather cover, he winced at the pain. He pulled down the printing plate with all his might. He released the lever and looked at the cover. It wasn't suitable. The gold leaf that outlined the letters was getting too thin.

He shuffled over to a cupboard in search of more gold leaf to add to the plates. It was very dark in that corner of the room, and even though he squinted, he could not find the bottle. He needed one of the hanging lanterns.

He spotted the step stool he'd used to put up the lanterns near the front window where he'd hung the last lantern. He hobbled over to the window and looked out at the cobblestone street in front of his shop.

Since it was nearly three o'clock in the morning, no one was about. All he could see were the dancing shadows from the gas street lamps. He toyed with the idea of going home to his apartment on the Rue d' Mercy and getting some rest, but he was just too excited about the book. It had been his all-consuming passion for nearly three years, and he wanted to finish the job of putting the first ten books together before he stopped.

He pulled the stool under the hanging lantern, stepped up on it, and reached for the lantern. It was just out of his reach, and he had to stand on his tiptoes to get hold of the handle so he could slip it over the hook. He managed to get it off the hook, but his tired legs simply gave out. He teetered on the stool. His arms flailed in the air as he tried to keep his balance, but it was too late. The stool tipped over, and Charles went with it.

He landed hard his left side with a loud grunt as the air in his lungs gushed out. He felt a sharp pain in his ribs and another piercing his left elbow. He lost all control of his arm and hand. Unfortunately, that was the hand holding the lantern.

When the lantern smashed onto the floor, the glass globe shattered. Flaming oil spewed out over the floor and onto the new paper. The raging fire was almost instantaneous and immediately out of control. The wooden interior was quickly consumed by flames.

Charles stared at the flames for a moment, almost in a trance. Then, he realized the danger, not the danger to him, but to his books. Even though he was in extreme pain from his three broken ribs, he pulled himself up, and walked right through the flames to the table where the six books lay. With his right hand he scooped them up under his arm. Coughing and choking from the smoke, he made his way to the front door and out onto the street.

At first he tried to yell, but the smoke he'd inhaled only made him cough more. But within a few seconds he had enough fresh air in his lungs to call out. "Fire!" "Fire!"

The call echoed through the empty narrow streets. Doors all along the street began to fly open as men, women, and children ran out to see what was happening. They, too, were horrified. Quickly they organized a bucket brigade using whatever water they could find. It was like spitting on a bonfire.

Charles limped across the street. He was nearly knocked down several times by people racing around trying to do something, anything before the flames reached their house, their shop. When he got to the other side and looked back at his shop, he was horrified. He thought he might go back in and get the other books without covers, but the shop was a raging inferno. Sparks filled the night sky, and the two shops on either side of his began to burn.

By the time the fire brigade arrived, with their teams of white horses pulling two pumpers and two huge barrel-like carts with additional water, half of the houses on the block where in flames. The firemen unfolded their hoses and began fighting the fire as best they could.

Charles sat down on the curb across from his print shop. He cuddled his small pile of books next to him and began to sob. He put his head in his singed hands and shook from both fright and pain. His working smock was still smoking from the fire.

A man, dressed in rags, came over to Charles, and using his old coat, slapped out the last spots where Charles' smock was smoldering.

Charles looked up and thanked the man. Then others came to Charles' aid. One was the owner of the shop next to the print shop. Charles broke down in tears when he saw him. "I am so sorry, M'sieur Le Roux," he said. "It is all my fault."

Le Roux started to get angry. "You, Du Pypes? You started this?" he said motioning toward the print shop.

Charles slowly nodded. He pulled the stack of books closer to him as he talked. His voice was weak and strident. "I was working. My book," then, suddenly, he was interrupted by a sharp pain in his chest. His head began to spin. The pain was numbing his left side. Everything went black. He collapsed onto the street.

CHAPTER ONE

O'Hare Airport, Chicago - April 10

"Can I get you anything before we take off, Ms Mason?" the stewardess asked.

"No, no thank you," April said as she leaned back in the comfortable leather seat of the Boeing 747. There was no one in the seat beside her. First class, she thought, Julian must be desperate. She peered out the window and saw the empty waiting area. Only a year ago it would have been full of well-wishers, friends and families seeing people off, but now with the new travel restrictions no one but passengers were allowed into the terminal waiting areas.

Suddenly, April couldn't help herself. She giggled. Out loud. She quickly glanced around to see if anyone noticed, but her secret was safe. She'd just remembered the scene at the security area.

April had just put her tote bag and purse on the conveyer belt, stepped through the metal detector, without setting off the alarm, and picked up her things off the conveyer belt. She looked back. There they stood in a neat row, her mother, Louise, her father, Frank, and her publisher, Julian Maxwell. Each was smiling and waving like a bunch of Stepford people. She returned their waves and tried to imagine just what each was thinking as they waved. Her mother was probably thinking, "Poor dear, headed off to Paris alone without a man. Please let her be safe and not get mugged." Her father was most likely thinking, "If only I'd have had the chance to see Paris before I got married. What a time I'd have had." And Julian was undoubtedly thinking, "Find a man! Find him fast and get back to writing! I need a new book for next fall."

April's daydream was interrupted by the stewardess. "Excuse me, Ms Mason, but could you autograph this copy of your book for me?" She held the book right in April's face.

April looked at the paperback. It was her fourth book, Lovely Corpse. "Of course," she said taking the offered book and turning to the title page. "Your name?"

"Cynthia. Cynthia Travis, Ms Mason."

"Please just call me April," she said with a smile and then wrote, "To Cynthia, The best Flight Attendant ever." She signed the book and handed it back.

The stewardess thanked her and started to leave but instead bent over and picked up an envelope from under April's seat. "Excuse me again," she said and showed April the envelope. "Is this yours Ms. I mean April?"

April immediately recognized it as the one Julian had given her a few minutes before she boarded the plane. "Yes, thank you very much. It must have dropped out of my coat pocket." April took the envelope. The flight attendant rushed forward to show the autograph to her flight mates.

April opened the envelope and read the short note from Julian. "April, dear, I told you that I'd have someone meet you, but I wasn't sure who it would be. Now I'm sure. His name is Kevin O'Connor. He should be at the gate when you arrive in Paris. Unfortunately, however, Kevin is, shall we say, somewhat unreliable. Don't be surprised if he is late. Have a wonderful vacation. Julian."

April reread the note, then laughed at the line about the vacation. Oh, sure she knew Julian had said it was a gift from the publishing company, but she knew that Julian was very concerned about her writer's block. She was certain this "vacation" was some kind of ploy to get her back to the computer.

She scanned the note again. Then it occurred to her, what part of Julian's scheme was this Kevin O'Connor was going to play? Was he to be a man Julian was trying to fix her up with, or was Mr. O'Connor simply a guide? Well, she'd find out in seven hours or so. She looked at her watch. It was eleven P.M., time for take off.

Villa, San Tropez - April 11

It was six A.M. at the old, run down villa high above the pretentious village of St. Tropez on the French Riviera. A violent thunderstorm was raging. Lightning streaked the sky and the rain poured down in long sheets of water.

The kitchen in the villa was dark except for the brief moments when a flash of lightning would light up the room with an eerie blue light. The rain pelted hard against the window over the kitchen sink. The villa was nearly a hundred years old, and it smelled a musty odor when it rained.

The smell was especially strong in the kitchen. The kitchen was nearly thirty feet long and fifteen feet wide. There was a large fireplace in the center of the back wall. A heavily scared wooden table, which seated sixteen people, was in the center of the room. Several ladder-back chairs were placed along each side of the table. On the long wall opposite the fireplace, was a sink, a refrigerator and a stove lined up in a row with wooden cupboards on either side of each of the appliances. Everything in the room was an antique.

At one end of the long, narrow room were French doors which led out to a large terrace. At the other end, an arched doorway led to the other rooms in the house.

Seated in the dark kitchen, at the end of the table facing the French doors, was a middle-aged man, Andre Du Pypes VII. He had a full head of grey hair, even though he was only forty-one, and deep furrows across his brow. In the light of a lightning flash his long thin face and hawk nose created striking angular shadows which hid his bloodshot eyes. Andre sat at the long, well-worn, kitchen table and stared at an old, tattered book, lying open in front of him. Beside the book was a wine glass partially filled with a cheap Merlot, a nearly empty bottle of wine, and a revolver. In his drunken stupor he glared at the old book, slowly shook his head, and drank the last sips of wine from the glass. Andre poured another glass, but it was only half full when the bottle was empty. He sat the bottle down, put his elbows on the table and his head in his hands. He ran his hands through his hair and shook his head slowly from side to side.

Each time the lightning flashed, the stark blue light entered the room from the French doors and cast eerie shadows against the long walls. The loud thunder claps which bounced off the nearby hills seemed to echo through the room getting louder and louder. Andre never flinched.

Silently, he cursed his ancestor, Charles Du Pypes, the author of the book that had brought damnation to the Du Pypes family for nearly ten generations. Andre was certain that the book, published in 1797, and its story of the treasure of the baker's vault which made the book so famous, was the cause of all his family's troubles. This book was supposed to contain the key to finding a treasure. Instead, it was a curse.

The curse had begun the night the first six, and only, six copies of the book were printed. Charles died of a heart attack that night as he watched his print shop burned down. When he died, he had only one copy of <u>Recit de la Revolution.</u> The other five copies of the book were seen being carried away from the scene of the fire by a man in a long coat. Charles's son, Jean, pried the book from his dead father's hand. No one in the family knew where the other five copies were. Andre was certain the curse was on anyone who owned a copy of the book.

The copy in front of him had been in the Du Pypes family for more than two hundred years. The curse had visited each generation.

Each subsequent male heir was accosted, some killed, others ruined, others beaten when they could not tell whomever it was who wanted to find out, the exact location of the vault. In more than two hundred years, however, no one had ever found that infamous vault. Andre was certain no one would ever find it.

The curse fell upon Andre at an early age. His father, Jorge was killed by a fortune hunter in their front yard as Andre watched in horror. He was five. When he was seven, he was reading the book under a large tree. Suddenly, for no apparent reason, a huge branch broke off and fell on his leg. It crushed all the bones in the leg and left him a cripple.

The past thirty years had been uneventful. Partly, he supposed, because he had become a recluse, and partly because he had accepted that he was cursed and simply learned to live with it.

Lately, however, he felt the curse coming nearer again. A man had sought him out, pretended to be his friend, but Andre knew, he knew well, that the man wanted the book. It was only a matter of time before the man would strike.

Andre pulled the book closer to him with a trembling hand and tapped lightly on the open pages. How many? he wondered, had died because of this book? How many lives were ruined? How many more would die?

30,000 Feet Over the Atlantic Ocean - April 11

After the plane had reached its cruising altitude, and the seat belt light was turned out, April reached in her tote bag and took out her paperback book, her crossword puzzle book, and a pen.

After putting the paperback in the pouch on the seat in front of her, she put the tote bag under her seat and settled back in her seat. She opened her new crossword book to the first puzzle and looked at the clue for one across, "mausoleum." Five letters. She pondered the clue. It could be "grave" or "crypt." What else, she asked herself. Instinctively she looked at one down. The clue was "unprotected" - ten letters. Vulnerable? she asked herself. If the first letter down was "v" then the first letter across had to start with a "v". Then her eyes lit up. "Of course, one across is 'vault'."

CHAPTER TWO

Book One

Of the six books Charles Du Pypes printed in 1797, five ended up in the hands of various people.

The books were stolen by Gerard Cavette, a vagabond in the city of Paris on that fateful night. He saw the fire as he was preparing to bed down in a corner of a nearby stable. Curious, Gerard walked to the street and saw the fire raging. He also saw Du Pypes, coughing and choking as he dragged himself across the street and away from the fire in his print shop. He saw that Du Pypes was holding on to six books under his arm, and wondered why the books were so precious to the man who was almost burned up by the fire.

Du Pypes' clothing was smoldering, and Gerard took off his greatcoat and used it to smother the few remaining flames. As he did this, many other people were racing into the street to help fight the fire. A few came running over to help Du Pypes. During the commotion, Gerard managed to slip five copies of the book under his greatcoat as he left Du Pypes to others more capable of helping him. He disappeared into the shadows and was gone.

The next day Gerard went to a bookshop far away from Du Pypes' print shop and sold all five copies to Marcel, the book seller. Gerard didn't need them. He couldn't read.

The next day, a young naval officer, Lieutenant Carlos Lamont, came into Marcel's book shop looking for something to read as he was about to go on a long voyage. He spied a copy of <u>Recit de la Revolution</u> and thought the title seemed interesting. It would be a good diversion.

Lt. Lamont was assigned to a frigate that was to leave for the Indian Ocean the next day. He put the book in his knapsack and headed to his home port of La Havre.

Unfortunately, on his voyage, Carlos was very busy and the book went unread until nearly a year had passed.

Carlos had just been relieved as the watch officer and went to his small cabin. His hat had become smeared with grease and he opened his footlocker to find a new one. The book was on the bottom of the footlocker with the hat. He picked it up and decided to read for a while and laid down. He only got through the forward of the book when a cannon ball from a pirate ship smashed through the hull and into his cabin killing, him instantly.

The book went down in the Indian Ocean with the ship.

CHAPTER THREE

St. Tropez Bay, April 11

The sun had been up for two hours and yet steam drifted up from the streets still wet from the early morning storms. It was unseasonably hot for early April.

The few commercial fishermen left in this tourist-filled village had sailed out of the bay hours ago, and now the streets were starting to fill up with people from all over the world who came here to see and be seen. Several crowded the outdoor café's and bistros on the waterfront. As they sat at their tables drinking their coffees, many glanced out at the bay teeming with expensive yachts.

One such was the "Se Soulever" out of Algiers. A two hundred and twenty-foot, sleek white yacht. Her fan tail was covered with a bright blue canvas awning. She rolled softly with the waves. Aboard the yacht was the owner, Francois Duer, his two bodyguards, his crew of five, and the early morning's guest, Pepe Duvall.

Everyone was gathered under the awning on the fantail. The two bodyguards, dressed in black, kept a constant vigil. They were tall, muscular, and wore darkly tinted sunglasses. To those on shore they looked like ordinary men, but just below the gunnels nearly at their fingertips were two AK-47 assault rifles, and under their black sport coats, in canvas shoulder holsters, were their Glock .45's.

Francois sat at a large, round table filled with a sumptuous array of exotic foods. He was a large man, heavy set, and balding. His face was round, and puffy, and his deep-set black eyes were nearly hidden by his bushy eyebrows. He was dressed in a freshly pressed white suit making him appear even larger. He picked at his food carefully as he studied the man standing in front of him.

When the crewman finished serving Francois his coffee, he dismissed him with a flick of his wrist. He wiped his chin and looked up at his guest. "So, Pepe, you've come to me again," he said with a smirk. "What is it this time?"

Pepe Duvall was a short, wiry built man about thirty with a long, thin face and huge nose. He was sweating heavily, and kept wiping his face with a handkerchief frequently. His white suit was rumpled and looked as if it hadn't been cleaned in a month. As he talked, Pepe shifted from one foot to another. "I came to you, Monsieur Duer, because I knew you'd be interested. You have a great reputation for collecting that which others cannot."

"And, you, Pepe, have a reputation for failure," Duer said staring him right in the eye.

"There were reasons, unforseen problems, but I have accomplished a lot," Pepe said and shifted again. "I just had a few bad times. I'm not perfect like you."

"Please," Duer said holding up his hand, "Let's not have any of that. Now, you told my man something about a book. A rare book?"

" Yes. The rarest. It is called <u>Recit de la Revolution</u> and it was written in 1797 by a Frenchman, Charles Du Pypes."

Duer's eyes flashed. "I have heard stories about this book. Something about a treasure?"

"Yes, that is the one. It has a story about a treasure hidden in the sewers of Paris during the French Revolution."

"Yes. I recall. But this treasure was never found."

10

"True, but they say this book contains clues to the treasure's hiding place. It is just that there is only one copy of the book left, or so they say."

"You have this book?" he asked trying to contain his excitement.

"Well, yes and no," Pepe said fidgeting openly now.

"Which is it, yes or no?"

"Well, I don't have it, but I know where I can get it, but."

"But?"

"But to get it is very risky."

"By risky, do you mean expensive?"

"I mean there are, shall we say, risks and expenses."

"I see. Do you have an estimate of these - expenses?"

Duvall was now rocking in place as he became more and more nervous. "Yes. A good estimate."

Suddenly, Duer slammed his fist down on the table causing food and silverware to fly everywhere. The two bodyguards reacted instantly by drawing their Glocks and pointing them at Duvall. Duvall threw up his hands and stood there shaking.

"Put those guns down," Duer barked at the two bodyguards. "And you," he said pointing at Duvall, "Stop that incessant rocking and tell me what you want!"

Duvall slowly put his hands down. The bodyguards returned their guns to their holsters. It was deadly quiet. Duvall gulped and said, "Twenty-five thousand Francs."

Duer stared at him for a moment, then burst out laughing. "Francs? You want Francs? Where have you been? It's Euros now." He laughed again.

Duvall crinkled up his face, then eked out a smile. "Yes, I mean Euros."

"When can you deliver this book, Pepe?"

"A few days, I think."

"Five days, Pepe," Francois demanded. "And you will deliver it to me in Paris where I am going this week. Five days."

"Yes. Five days."

"The price is ten thousand. Half now, and half when you deliver the book."

"But?"

"End of discussion. Get your money from the captain on the bridge. Now get out."

Duvall wanted to protest, but he knew it was no use. He gave a little bow and started for the bridge.

"And Duvall," Duer called out stopping Duvall in his tracks. "Failure is not an option," he warned.

Duvall gulped, and continued on.

31,000 Feet over Shannon, Ireland

April, her sleep mask somewhat askew, was sound asleep. The crossword book was open on her lap. She was dreaming of being rescued by a knight in shining armor that spoke with a thick French accent. She was smiling as he rode toward her on his white steed with a silver saddle. Suddenly, the knight screeched to a stop. He raised his visor on his glistening helmet and said, "Good morning ladies and gentlemen," the voice said, but it was distinctly feminine, with only a hint of a French accent. "We are just passing over Shannon, Ireland."

April awoke with a start. Because her eyes were still covered with the sleep mask, she had no idea where she was. She looked around but saw nothing. Then she remembered and pulled off the mask. She pulled up the window shade and let the bright morning sun stream in. It nearly blinded her, and she quickly covered her eyes.

"Our estimated time of arrival in Paris is one hour and sixteen minutes. Breakfast will now be served."

As the voice repeated the announcement in French, April got her bearings and looked around. The other passengers were in various stages of waking up, too. She yawned and sat up in her seat. She stretched her arms and crooked her neck to help her wake up. She looked out the window and saw Ireland disappear as the plane began to cross the English channel.

After she finished her breakfast, April still felt very tired and decided to go back to sleep until they arrived.

CHAPTER FOUR

Book Two

In April of 1807, Andre Val Dumon, a history professor at the Sorbonne, was the next person to purchase a copy of <u>Recit de la Revolution</u> at the original bookstore where all five copies were taken. Andre was an avid reader as well as a historian. He read the book quickly and immediately became fascinated by the thought of finding the baker's treasure.

He went to find the bake shop the minute he finished the story of the baker's vault. However, it was no longer where it was supposed to be. He went to the city hall and looked up the bake shop's address only to find that the baker had been arrested by the Committee for Public Safety in July 1794, only a few days after the young aristocrat had seen the treasure being buried. The baker was executed by the guillotine one month to the day after being discovered. He took his secret to the grave.

Andre looked high and low for the bake shop. He thought he had found it on an old map of the city. But the fire that fateful night had destroyed not only the print shop but many shops on that street, including, ironically, the bake shop beneath which the treasure lay. The fire also spread to the surrounding area and destroyed nearly six city blocks. The area had been rebuilt and everything was changed, including the street names.

Andre became obsessed. He spent all of his money and time looking for the treasure. He read the story over and over looking for a clue to the whereabouts of the treasure. Every day he went down into the sewers and looked for the markings of the vault, and each night he returned home late smelling frightful.

Soon, his wife, Marguette, became concerned about his sanity and began nagging and begging him to give up the search for the treasure and return to his work at the university. He could not be swayed.

Finally, completely fed up with his behavior, Marguette, in a fit of anger at her husband, threw the book into the fireplace and laughed as it burned. Andre killed her that night, and killed himself.

CHAPTER FIVE

The sudden clank as the wheel wells opened and the whirring screeches of the wheels being lowered on the giant 747 jolted April out of her restless sleep. Her eyes darted around the cabin to help her get her bearings. She'd been flying for nearly eight hours and felt stiff and groggy. She sat upright and tried to shake the cobwebs from her mind. She took her silver compact out of her purse, opened it and gasped. She didn't like what she saw in the mirror. Oh, god, The Wicked Witch of the West, she thought as she quickly rifled through her purse to find her hair brush and lipstick.

After a couple of minutes of what she called "damage control," she tossed the hair brush back in her purse, put on her lipstick and rechecked the mirror of her compact. That's as good as it gets, she said to herself as she put her compact away.

"Ladies and gentlemen, we are approaching the beautiful city of Paris. Please fasten your seat belts and return your seat backs to the upright position for landing," the steward announced and then repeated the instructions in French.

April looked out her window. It was a bright, cloudless day, and she could see the entire sprawling city spread out before her. The Eiffel Tower was off to her left far in the distance, and she saw the Seine winding its way through the center of the city. Wow, she thought, it's breathtaking!

April sat back and smiled to herself. She was leery of coming to Paris at first, but now that she was there, she was happy she'd changed her mind. She took the note from Julian out of her purse and reread it. "April, dear, I told you that I'd have someone meet you, but I wasn't sure who it would be. Now I am sure. His name is Kevin O'Connor He should be at the gate when you arrive in Paris. Unfortunately, however, Kevin is, shall we say, somewhat unreliable. Don't be surprised if he is late. Have a wonderful vacation. Julian."

April wondered what this Mr. O'Connor would be like. Probably an older man, she surmised. Julian always had older friends. She decided on a grand fatherly man, a bit plump with white hair and crinkly eyes. She looked at her watch. It was 10:45 Paris time.

At that same time, Kevin O'Connor was lying on his bed in his small, cluttered, one room flat on the Right Bank of Paris. His clothes were thrown over chairs and piled in the corners. The ever-present dirty dishes were stacked high in the sink. He was reading <u>Mysteries of Love</u> by April Mason. He was still in his pajama bottoms. He began rubbing the stubble on his chin. Suddenly, a frown crossed his face. He sat up. "You can't do that," he said to the book. "Any burglar in his right mind would wear gloves!" He threw the book across the room.

Disgusted, he got up and shuffled into the bathroom. He looked at himself in the mirror. "You can write better than that, O'Connor," he said out loud. He turned on the faucet and picked up his watch off the shelf under the mirror. He stared at it in disbelief. "Holy, shit," he exclaimed. "Eleven ten! Her plane gets in at noon!" Kevin grabbed his washcloth.

Fifteen minutes later, Kevin ran out of his flat, down the two flights of stairs, and out into the street. He stopped and scratched his head. Where had he parked? The sidewalk was crowded. He jumped up and down to see if he could see his car, but it was nowhere in sight. Then it dawned on him. He took off in a dead run around the corner and there, a block

17

away, was his car, one wheel on the curb. He ran to it, and pulled on the door, but it was locked. He fumbled around for his keys. Not there. "The dresser," he said and took off running back to his apartment.

After the 747 made a smooth landing, the flight attendant made her usual announcement, "Welcome to Paris! The local time is 11:43 A.M.."

Kevin's grey, banged up, 1990 Citron flew down the N-7 highway. He was cursing himself as he wove in and out of the traffic. All he needed, he thought, was to be stopped by the police for speeding. "What the hell," he said and pushed the accelerator to the floor. The car jumped in response. Its powerful engine roared. It wasn't like other Citrons.

Horns honked, tires squealed, and drivers cursed him as he cut in front of three of cars to barely make the turn off for Aeroport d'Orly. He had to stop at the stop light. He tapped his feet and looked at his watch - 12:22. He was sweating and anxious. When the light turned, he sped off.

April looked at her watch - 12:22. She looked at the line of people ahead of her waiting to go through customs. Only three more people to go, she thought. It was still going to be a while. She was getting excited now. She pulled out Julian's note and scanned it again. "Kevin O'Connor," she said to herself. "Why can't I remember that?" She began to tap her feet in nervous anxiousness.

Kevin pulled onto the ramp leading to the terminals. He searched the signs for the right terminal. He had to slow down to read them. Then he saw it - United Airlines, Terminal 3. He saw the cut off and roared onto the terminal ramp.

"You are from Chicago, Miss Mason?" the gruff looking customs official asked as he scanned her passport.

"Yes," she said cheerfully.

"I see. Business or pleasure, Mademoiselle?" he said looking at her passport.

"Both I hope," she said.

"Ah, yes," he said. "Have you anything to declare?"

"No, I don't think so."

"I see. Is this your first time in Paris?"

"Yes."

"I thought so," he said as he stamped her passport and handed it to her. "You will find your luggage in the next room." He gestured toward the battered metal doors in back of him.

Kevin slowed down to look over the crowd of people standing on the curb in front of Terminal 3. He had a mental picture of her from the picture on the back of her book. No April. "Damn," he said and moved over in the parking lot lane. He sped into the huge parking structure. Not a place to park! Finally, he saw a couple heading toward a car. He waited, tapping his feet, until their car finally pulled out of the space. He parked, jumped out of the car, and took off running toward the terminal.

April stood waiting with her two bags in the baggage check out area. The room was filled with long, metal tables. The customs officers were examining the bags very carefully. She wondered if she had packed anything that might upset them. She decided she had not. She had a large green Samsonite suitcase with wheels on it and a smaller matching bag. Both were heavy.

Finally, a straight-laced, officious looking officer motioned to her to put her bags on the table. The table was high, and she struggled to get them up on it. The officer didn't make any attempt to help her. "Anything to declare?" he said in a monotone tinged with boredom.

"No, I don't think so."

"Any furs, jewelry?"

"Just my everyday diamonds," she said with a bright smile. He didn't get the joke.

"Open this bag, please," he said pointing out the big bag.

April fumbled with the locks for a moment then managed to get it open. He rummaged around for only a few seconds.

"You may go," he said, turning away from her to the next person in line.

She strained to get the bags off the counter then grabbed the handle of the big bag on wheels with her right hand and dragged it along carrying the other bag and her purse in her left hand. When she got out the door, she saw a long ramp leading up to the next floor. She wished she'd packed lighter as she began hauling the heavy bags up the ramp toward the door.

Kevin was going full speed now as he ran into the terminal and spotted the international arrival board. The plane had landed nearly an hour ago! He checked the board for the gate number and headed for it. When he arrived at the gate, he saw passengers emerging from the door to customs and coming up the ramp. He slid to a stop. He was out of breath. April was nowhere in sight. Had he missed her? Had she missed the plane? No, Julian would have called him. Where in the hell was she?

April, exhausted, finally reached the next heavy metal door and pulled it open. She tugged her rolling suitcase inside, reached for her other bag, pulled it inside and looked up at another long ramp.

Kevin recognized her immediately from her picture on the back cover of her novel. He watched as she struggled with her bags and began to trudge up the ramp toward him. He leaned on the wall near the iron gate.

Using the last of her strength, April managed to up the ramp with her bags and through the metal gate. She stopped and looked around. No little old man. She started to pick her bags up, when she heard a voice call out, "Miss Mason?"

April turned and saw a handsome blond-haired young man in jeans and a tee-shirt that said "I Want You" across the front of it, running toward her. She smiled and held out her arms, but he ran past April, grabbed a girl behind her and swung her around. As she watched a couple kissing, she felt a twinge of envy. She heard the voice again, this time behind her. "Miss Mason?" April turned and saw an incredible hunk standing not two feet away. He was at least six feet tall, sandy hair, deep blue eyes, a warm open face, and a terrific smile. He wore a brown tweed sport coat, blue button-down collar shirt and chinos. He looked like a page out of GQ.

"Mr. O'Connor?" she said, hoping he was the right man.

Kevin nodded. He looked her over. Thirty maybe thirty-two he guessed. She was much more attractive than her picture on the back cover of the book. Good body, too. I'll have to be careful, he reminded himself.

"Please, call me Kevin, Miss Mason. Julian asked me to meet you," he held out his hand and shook hers briefly. His grip was firm. Their eyes met, and they both swallowed a little too hard. "Let me help you," he said.

As was her habit, April quickly looked for a wedding ring. None. "Thank you," she said, putting on her best smile.

Kevin took the suitcase that rolled, leaving her to manage the other bag and her purse. "Welcome to Paris," he said as he began moving swiftly toward the exit.

"Have you been waiting long?" she called out, trying to keep up with him.

"A little over an hour. I should know these things take time," he said moving in and out of the sea of people.

April had a hard time keeping up with him. "I'm sorry you had to wait," she called out.

"No problem."

April lost him in the crowd for a second, then spied him up ahead. "Mr. O'Connor," she yelled.

Kevin stopped and turned. April was behind a family that was more interested in talking than moving. He waited. "Sorry," he said as when she caught up with him, "I'm used to the crowds." He waited while she caught her breath, then took off again.

By the time they reached his car, April was exhausted. Kevin put her bags on the rear seat.

Nice buns, April noted.

Then, he began taking old clothes, papers, candy wrappers and various things from the front seat and throwing them in the back.

Obviously a bachelor, April thought as she watched him carelessly throwing things in the back and cleaning up around the front seat. Why do single men always used their cars for storage? she thought shaking her head.

Kevin held the door open as April climbed in the car, then he got in on the driver's side.

After he pulled out of the parking space, April asked, "Is Julian a close friend?"

"Not really," Kevin replied. "He handles some free lance articles in the States for me."

"So you're a writer, too."

"Of a sort. Mostly articles for the Paris Gazette, but I've got a couple of books in the works." How many times had he used that line? he wondered. He paid for his parking and pulled out into the traffic. "I understand this is your first time in Paris."

"Yes. I'm very excited. Actually this is the first time I've ever gone abroad. It's kinda scary."

"Well, we'll try to make you comfortable. It's a great city. Do you speak French?"

"Not really. I studied French in high school, and I got some tapes and stuff to refresh myself, but it's still all Greek to me."

"Ah, a sense of humor. Very good," he said as he gave April a winning side glance. "It's important that you try. The French, even though they'd never acknowledge it, appreciate those who try to speak their language. How long do you plan to stay?"

"A month. At least that's my plan right now."

"Good. I've found a nice apartment in Place Vendome that rents month to month. Julian said I should book you for a month, but I put a hold on two more."

"Oh, I can't stay that long. I have to get back to work."

"Well, you never know."

"True," she said.

Kevin drove back toward Paris on the N–7. April sat quietly watching the countryside pass by. I wonder if I'll like it here alone? She thought. She was getting more and more excited with each mile. Kevin pointed out various sites and places of interest as they approached the city.

As they came into the heart of the city, Kevin turned off the N–7 and headed up the Boulevard Saint Michael toward Ile De La Cite.

April was fascinated by the sights. "Oh, look," she said sitting up and pointing to her left. "Isn't that Notre Dame?"

"Yep, and if you look over to your right, that bunch of buildings is the Sorbonne."

"Really?"

"Trust me."

April laughed. "Dumb question."

"You'll get to know your way around. It took me a while."

"How long have you lived in Paris, Kevin?"

"Since 1992. I had to come here on a trip, liked the place, and so, I stayed."

"Ever thought of going back to the States?"

"Not really. Oh, I'm sure I will some day, but right now I'm having too much fun."

"Sounds like a true ex-patriot."

"No, just a guy who likes doing things his way."

Kevin pulled over when they came to an intersection. He pointed straight ahead. "That's the Palais of Justice to the right just over the Seine. Don't miss it. Take the tour."

"I plan to. There's so much I want to see. My parents were here years ago, and my mother gave me a whole list of things I should see."

"Since you're only going to be here for a month, I hope that list is short."

"Six pages."

"Double spaced?"

"Single. Both sides of the paper."

Kevin laughed.

He has a great laugh, April noticed. A very good sign.

Kevin turned left onto the Quai des Grands August and headed West. As they drove along the Seine, he pointed out other points of interest, the Pont Neuf, the Louvre, the Museum d'Orsay, and then turned right and crossed over the Seine on the Pont de la Concorde and into the Place de la Concorde. He pulled over and stopped. "This is the Place de la Concorde." He let her drink in the size of the huge square filled with people milling around. Then he pointed to a tall stone monument. "That obelisk was given to the French people by an Egyptian viceroy in 1833. Take a good look around. This is a great starting point for getting to know the city. It's right in the heart. This is where the French guillotined the aristocracy during the French Revolution. Then it was called the Place de la Revolution."

April shivered at the thought. Little did she know just how important this place was to become.

Kevin sat back so she could see as he motioned toward April's right. "Over there are the Tuilleries, the gardens that front the Louvre. It's a great place to have a sack lunch, look at the flowers, and think. Your apartment isn't too far from here."

"Where do you live?"

Kevin motioned in back of himself, "On the Right Bank, just off the Boulevard Du Montparnasse. I can't afford the Left Bank. Well, let's get you settled."

Kevin gunned the car and turned right onto the Rue de Rivoli. "This area is called St. Honore, where all the boutiques

and expensive shops are. You can shop till you drop -
providing you have the money - lots of it."

As usual, a typical man, April mused, he's driving too fast
for me to see the stuff in the windows. When they neared the
Louvre, he turned left onto the Rue de Richelieu. "This is the
theater district of Paris," he said, "where the 'Comedie
Francaise' puts on some of the best plays I've ever seen. Up
ahead is the famous Paris Opera House and over there on your
right is the Palais Royal. They have very good tours of the
Palais. Don't miss that either."

Kevin turned left onto Rue Danielle Casanova then two
blocks later turned right through a set of double steel doors
into a courtyard. He stopped in front of a dark blue canopy.
"Here we are, 75 Rue Danielle Casanova. Your home away
from home."

"Casanova? The Casanova?"

"Could be."

April climbed out of the car and looked up at the six story
grey stone building surrounding the courtyard. It was old and
seemed to reek of history. She sighed. It was very impressive.

Kevin got the bags out of the car, and this time he carried
both suitcases as they went in through the French doors into a
very small lobby filled with antiques. He pressed the button
for the elevator. "They say Victor Hugo once lived in this
building," he said as they got on the elevator. He pressed six.

When they got off, she followed him down the long narrow
hallway. They stopped in front of a door marked 75D. He put
the key in the lock, turned to her and said, "Okay, close your
eyes."

"What?"

"Close your eyes. You won't get the full effect if you don't."

April closed her eyes. Kevin opened the door and led her
into the foyer, down two steps and into the center of the living
room. He turned her so she faced the French Doors on the far
side of the room. "Don't open your eyes yet," he said as he

opened the doors to the small terrace. "Okay, you can open them now."

April opened her eyes. She was staring directly at the Eiffel Tower in the distance. She gasped. "Oh ... Oh, my," she managed to say. "It's ... it's wonderful."

"Paris, mademoiselle," Kevin said bowing. She walked past him and out onto the terrace. "And just below, the Place Vendome." April looked down. The huge circular square was surrounded by identical buildings all built in a circle. "The square is home to many famous jewelry shops, and the Ritz Hotel there in the square just across the way."

April was awestruck. She stood holding on to the iron railing and stared at the city spread out before her. "It's magnificent."

Kevin was also staring - at the sun shining through her thin skirt. Nice legs, he observed.

April finally turned, went inside and looked around at the apartment. The living room had high ornamented ceilings and was tastefully decorated with a combination of antiques and contemporary furniture. There was a long overstuffed couch facing the fireplace with two Queen Anne chairs flanking it. An antique desk was in one corner near the French doors, and a sitting area with three chairs and a small table in the other corner. The fireplace had a huge mantel lined with candle holders of all shapes, sizes and description. Three large Renaissance paintings completed the tasteful decor.

"Oh, Kevin," she said, "this is more than I could ever have hoped for."

"There's a small kitchen over there," he said, pointing to a door on the left side of the room. "And this," he said as he walked to a set of tall, ornate double doors, "is the piece de resistance." He opened the double doors.

The first thing that caught April's eye was the massive canopied bed in the middle of the room. She gasped. He laughed.

"Nice playpen," he said.

April just stood there dumbfounded. "What?" she asked.

"Never mind," Kevin said as he wandered into the bedroom. April followed him. To their left were two floor-to-ceiling windows draped in heavy velvet. He opened the drapes and let the sunlight fill the room. A ray of sunlight fell directly on the bed. Was this a sign? April wondered.

"There aren't any closets in these old places, but this armoire should be adequate - unless you do a whole lot of shopping." He walked to a door beside the armoire and opened it. "This is the bath. I'm sorry the shower is one of those things you have to wrap a curtain all the way around, but as least you have a shower. Most places only have tubs."

April walked over and peered into the large bathroom. The centerpiece was the long, footed bathtub with a shower curtain ring over it. There was the commode, a bidet, and a large pedestal porcelain sink. The entire bath was white, with a white tiled floor and white fixtures. A long, full length mirror was attached to the far wall.

As they walked back into the living room, April said, "I . . . I don't know what to say. It's all so elegant, so ... so ...."

"Homey?" Kevin said.

April looked at him and chuckled. "No. No, I don't think 'homey' is the right word at all! I'd say ... Tres magnifique!"

"Bon," Kevin said.

"This must cost a fortune."

"A small one, but we both know Julian can afford it."

"How did you ever find this place?" April asked.

"Just luck. It used to belong to some friends of mine, but they're getting a divorce, and neither could afford it any longer."

"A divorce? Why?"

"Why does anyone get a divorce?" He gestured to the bedroom. "Only the bed knows for sure."

"Cynic."

"Realist," he said as he wandered toward the front door. "Well you must be tired from your trip, so I'll let you get settled in. I thought we might have dinner tomorrow night if that's all right with you."

April followed him to the door and opened it. "It would be delightful. How can I ever thank you?"

"All part of the service, ma'am," he said as he bent in a mock bow. "By the way, there's a market just down the street on your right as you go out the main entrance, and I recommend the bistro on the corner." He handed her his card. "Call me tomorrow at the office and we'll work out dinner."

April came up to him, threw her arms around him and planted a kiss on his cheek. "Thank you so very much."

Kevin looked down into her big brown eyes and was tempted to return the kiss, but he could hear Julian's voice, "And for Christ's sakes stay away from her!" He pulled away. "You're welcome," he said. "Oh, one more thing," he said. "You'll find a map of the city and some brochures on the desk. I recommend Paris Visions for a quick tour to get the layout of the city. They're not far from here. Well, got to get to the office. Enjoy." Kevin closed the door behind him.

April walked back out onto the terrace and stood gazing at the city. She was excited about the view, the city, and Kevin O'Connor.

CHAPTER SIX

Book Three

Ivan Illyvanic, a Russian patriot, and loyal follower of Czar Nicholas, was also a long time friend of the royal family. He had helped design two of the Faberge eggs given the Czar's family at Christmas time.

His wife, Tatyana, was born in France of Russian parents. Her mother died in childbirth and Tatyana came to Russia after her father committed suicide by hanging himself in 1900. She married Ivan in 1910.

They lived on an estate outside Moscow. Tatyana brought with her, from France, many things, among them her father's extensive collection of books. This collection was in the library of the manor house. Among the books in this collection was a copy of Recit de la Revolution.

Ivan had been classically educated, and read French very well. He often took a book from the library to read when he went to bed.

In 1917, the Russian Revolution was in full swing, and those close to the czar were all in danger. Ivan was one of those people who protested the arrest of the czar and his family. That put him on a very special list.

On a cold, spring night in March 1917. Ivan and Tatyana were upstairs in bed reading. He was reading the story of the baker's vault. Tatyana was cold, and so Ivan rang for the butler to get a hot water bottle for her. The usually very prompt butler did not come. Ivan called out. No answer. He was getting angry. He got out of bed to go see why the butler did not come. But when he tried to open the door, it was jammed. He pushed hard on the big double doors, but they were securely locked from the outside.

As he turned to say something to Tatyana, she screamed and pointed to the window. He could see flames from down stairs licking at the window. Then he saw smoke coming in from under the door. He ran to the window and was nearly hit by a bomb thrown from below. Ivan ran to Tatyana to protect her from the bomb. It was too late. The bomb exploded and blew everything in the bedroom in thousands of tiny pieces. Tattered pages of the book fluttered to the floor.

CHAPTER SEVEN

Kevin walked into the offices of the Paris Gazette, a daily English language paper. As he walked through the sea of desks almost touching each other in the general press room, he had to dodge the reporters and copy people who were scurrying around like worker ants. He greeted several people as he passed through, past the city desk, and went into his glass-enclosed cubicle at the back of the room.

He was immediately accosted by his boss, George Lavalle, editor-in-chief, a short stocky man with a curly head of black hair, and a pudgy nose that always seemed to stick up in the air. He always looked rumpled, even in a freshly pressed suit, and his tie was always mismatched to his suits. George was known to his friends and cohorts as the "most nervous man in print."

"So, what's she like?" George asked anxiously.

Kevin sighed. "Just another tourist, George," he said.

"Come on, kid."

Kevin hated it when George called him "kid." He hesitated for a minute. "She's cute, she's built, and she's a drag. Okay?"

"Think she'd do a piece for us?"

Kevin was surprised. "A piece?"

"You know," George said, "'My First Time in Paris' - something like that."

"You want me to ask?"

"Yeah. As a matter of fact, I do. I'd like to meet her, too."

"Really?"

"Yeah. Is it a problem?"

"Not mine. I'll get you her phone number."

"Good."

"Fine," Kevin said powering up his old computer to finish an article on the best bars in hotels in Paris.

"Oh, by the way," George said, nervously shuffling his feet, "you had a call."

"From?"

"Julian."

"Oh, shit. What did he want?"

"He wanted to know if you got to the airport on time, and if she was comfortable. All that stuff."

"And you said?"

"'I'll have Kevin call you.' He left his home number."

"He wants me to call him now?"

"I believe that's what he had in mind." George reached over and picked up a note pad off Kevin's desk and jotted down the number. "I've got it memorized. It was easy, it's my secretary's measurements," George said handing Kevin the pad and walking off in the direction of his office.

Kevin looked at the number, "36-23-36 +1 in Chicago." He shook his head, sat down and pulled the phone to him. He did not want to make the call. It was a drag, but he knew he had to. He dialed.

Julian answered on the first ring. "I hope this is Kevin," he said.

"It's me. Reporting in. She is safely ensconced in her apartment and seems happy as a lark. Satisfied?"

"Were you late?"

"Nope. Surprise. Anyway, I'm taking her to dinner tomorrow night. Any objections."

"Kevin, seriously I don't want to be a nuisance, but she is very important to us, and I'm sorry if I seem a bit uptight about all this, but you understand, don't you?" Julian said in his upper crust English accent.

"Yeah, I understand, Julian. I'll take good care of her, and I'll get her fixed up so she'll get back to writing."

"Thank you. As I told you earlier, we will definitely honor our commitment."

"I'll keep my end of the bargain too. Bye Julian."

"Good evening, Kevin."

Kevin hung up and chuckled to himself. "Julian, you may be very surprised by the end of the month," he said out loud. "Very surprised."

The next evening, when Kevin rang the doorbell of April's apartment, he was not prepared for who opened the door. She looked like April, sounded like April, but this woman was a knockout! April looked stunning. She wore a low-cut, black silk sheath dress that fit her perfectly proportioned body as if it were sprayed on, a single strand of pearls, and six inch black satin pumps. Her black hair was styled in a page boy and shone brightly in the overhead light. Her big, brown eyes were accented by soft blue shading and her lips were a deep red. He was awe struck. When she walked over to get her silk wrap off the couch, all he could think of was this woman could move, really move. Her walk was sensual and smooth. He stood there with his mouth wide open.

April was somewhat caught off guard, too. Kevin looked absolutely handsome in his tailored blue suit and red tie. The suit fit his long, trim body perfectly. He had that same warm smile and an air of control. She liked that. Paris was going to be fun! she thought.

"You look terrific," Kevin said. "Great dress."

"Like it?"

Kevin nodded, "Very much," he said meaning the whole package, not just the dress.

April chattered away in the car as they drove to the restaurant. She was bubbling over with stories of her quick tour of Paris. Kevin was amused by her enthusiasm, charmed by her presence, and excited by her sensuality. April Mason was a real beauty.

They pulled up in front of Le Grand Vefour's just in time for their reservation. Kevin had had to pull a lot of strings to get them into this, one of the most famous restaurants in Paris. It would cost Julian a fortune, he mused.

April took his arm as they entered. The Maitre'd greeted them in the small alcove. "Bon Soir, Kevin," he said extending his hand. Kevin shook it then motioned toward April.

"Louis, this is Miss April Mason, an American author," he said gesturing toward April.

"Good evening, Miss Mason. Welcome to Le Grand Vefour." He kissed her hand lightly and motioned for them to enter.

April smiled and put her arm in Kevin's. "Thank you," she said.

Louis led them into the sumptuously decorated main dining room with its ornate, mirrored domed ceiling and gold painted glass panels. The waiters, dressed in tuxedos, were all gathered at a row of tables in the center of the room. These tables served as a service bar.

Kevin noticed that April's appearance turned several men's heads as she passed through. They were seated in a banquette in the far corner of the room.

"The Grand Vefour opened in 1777. It was the first, and only, I believe, restaurant in the arcades of the Royal Palace. They say Napoleon used to sit over there," Kevin said as he pointed to a table against the wall in the center of the room.

"It's so grand," April said as she looked around at the sea of elegant people dressed to the nines.

"It's one of the great restaurants of Paris. Lots of politicians, rich people, and a few tourists manage to get in, even though it's kind of out of the way here in the Arcades."

"You come here often?"

Kevin laughed, "No. I'm afraid not. I've been here a few times, but it's a little rich for my blood. But, Julian's paying, so we can just enjoy. I can't think of a better place to spend his money."

"How long have you known Julian?" she asked.

"Six years. I met him at the office, and we hit it off." He was going to add "at first," but decided against it. "You?"

"Oh, Julian has been my editor for the last twelve years, since my first novel. He does a wonderful job for me. I owe him a lot."

That does it, Kevin said to himself, no knocking Julian.

"He's a great guy," Kevin said swallowing his tongue.

"So, you enjoyed the Paris Visions tour."

"Yes, very much. It was well worth it. We didn't stop long at anyone place, but like you said, it gave me a great overview of what I should go back and see. Thanks for recommending it. Oh, did I tell you I tried speaking French?"

"How did it go?"

"You were right, the people at the market and even on the tour seemed to appreciate my trying, even though I stumbled a lot. I'm thinking of taking some lessons."

"Good idea."

The sommelier came to the table, and while Kevin was ordering a bottle of wine, April drank in the atmosphere. The room was the epitome of the word "elegant". The people sitting at the other tables seemed right at home in this very famous restaurant.

When the waiter returned with the wine, April was impressed with his choice. She'd heard of it from her father. When it was served, she raised her glass, "To Julian."

"To Julian," Kevin managed to say. They both sipped the wine but never took their eyes off each other. She was even more beautiful than yesterday, he thought.

April raised her glass again, "And, of course, to you Kevin. Thank you so very much." He's so good looking, April thought as she downed the wine.

"So, you getting settled in?"

"I haven't even unpacked. I was too excited. I went out for a walk last night. It was fascinating watching the people strolling down the Champs Elysees. Just like in the movies."

"Paris is a terrific night city."

"Yes, it seems so full of life and romance." April gave him a look over the top of her eyes that made Kevin very uneasy. Was it a come on? He wasn't sure. He knew one thing. He couldn't blow this "assignment".

The menus came, and while April looked hers over, Kevin tried to decide how to handle this delicate situation. Even though he was very attracted to her, he knew that there were other considerations, not the least was his other "assignments." He couldn't afford to get involved with anyone right now. Besides, Julian wanted him to fix her up with someone, and he'd made it clear that that someone was not to be him. To escort April once in a while was okay, but the rules were clear. Kevin had made a pact with himself to not let himself become emotionally involved. But, as he watched her, he had the feeling that pact was in real danger as each minute went by. She was growing on him, and that was a real problem.

After they ordered, April asked him questions about the city and told him about her shopping trip that day - "so many shops, so little time." She was charming and funny, too.

When they finished dinner, Kevin ordered brandy. Suddenly, April sat upright, leaned over and peered into his eyes. "So, what's your duty, Mr. O'Connor? Are you supposed to watch over the crazy lady?"

"Crazy lady?"

"Julian thinks so."

"Really? He didn't say that to me."

"Oh? Just what did he say?"

36

Kevin was caught off guard. He hemmed and hawed for a moment, then said, "Well, he didn't say you were crazy."

"And ...."

"And, he said that you were having a little problem. Writer's block?"

"And, did he say why?"

"This is very embarrassing."

"Oh, come on, Mr. O'Connor."

"Kevin, please."

"Okay, Kevin. Give it to me straight. Did he tell you why I have writer's block?"

"Okay. Yeah, he did. He said you sort of stressed out because you broke up with your boyfriend and that was affecting your writing."

"Well, that's partly true. Anything else he told you that I should know? After all, I should know what you do, don't you think?"

"That's it. Unless."

"Yes. Unless."

"Unless you have something you want to explain in your own words."

April downed the brandy in one gulp. She tipped her head to one side and looked at Kevin out the corner of her eye. Slowly, a smile crossed her face. "Yes. Yes, I guess I should tell you everything. Could I have another brandy?"

Kevin ordered two more brandies, and sat back. "I'm all ears."

April nodded. "All right, here goes. It's true I'm having a bit of trouble getting my next idea to pop up in my head and into the computer. And it's true that I've always been in love each time I've written a novel."

"With the same man?"

"Not quite, six different men."

"Six different novels."

"That's also true. But, I want to change that. I mean, I admit I did go a bit overboard this last time with Bob."

37

"Bob?"

"Yes. He was the last one." The brandies were served, and April downed hers quickly and motioned to the waiter for another. "Bob was two-timing me. Not that he thought about it that way. Stephanie drove him to it. She'd drive anyone over a cliff. Anyway, when he told me he was marrying her, I sort of went off the deep end."

"You killed him?" Kevin asked cautiously.

"No, I just kidnaped him. Only until I finished my novel, mind you, but I did tie him up for a while." She smiled to herself recalling the incident.

"You're kidding."

"I kid you not. You wanna hear about it?"

"Sure," Kevin said leaning back in his chair and cupping his brandy sniffer to warm the brew. He was getting a big kick out of April's candor.

"Well, it all began when he told me he and Stephanie were getting married. Now, I knew that was a possibility, but not so soon, I'd hoped. Anyway, I was just on the last chapter of my book. I needed him to be there, physically, until I finished it. I don't know why I feel that way, but I do, so I tied him up."

"With a rope."

"And duct tape. He wasn't going anywhere. Then I went into my office and finished the book. It was morning when I finished."

"Wait! Back up. How did you manage to tie him up?"

"I told him I wanted to tie him up so I could write the final scene more accurately - you know, from the point of view of the killer. I said I'd never tied anyone up before."

"And he bought that."

"You don't know Bob. He's a pushover for anyone in a bikini. So I tied him up and put him on the couch."

"Bikini?"

"My good luck bikini. White. I always write in it. So anyway," April sipped from the new glass of brandy and without missing a beat went on. She described what happened next.

"I finished the book. I had only a few pages left anyway. Bob slept. Well, I felt great. Like I do every time. But then the same old thing happens, I stare at the screen for a long time, then the tears begin. See, 'The End' also means something very different in my case. It means pain." April sat quietly for a moment. She was almost in a trance, then she stiffened her back and seemed to wake up. She began telling the story as if she were writing it.

"Anyway, I got up from my desk and walked to the floor-to-ceiling windows in my study which is twenty-two floors above the city. It was almost dawn, and the Chicago skyline was partly obscured by low clouds and falling snow. As I stared out the window, I didn't even feel the tears for a long time. I was happy I'd finished the novel but sad because it meant the end of another relationship. Why does it always end this way? I asked myself for the thousandth time. Not having an answer this time either, I walked back into the living room. Bob was still sound asleep. The ropes that tied his hands and feet were showing from under the blanket I'd thrown over him a few hours before. He looked so peaceful, so innocent. His day-old beard was only fuzz which didn't mar his handsome, square-jawed face. Poor dear, I thought as I glanced at the perfect square knots. He didn't know what hit him.

"I sat down cross-legged on the floor beside the couch and stared at him. There was less pain this time, but it hurt nevertheless. Another relationship finished. It was just like all the times before. A little more dramatic maybe, but in the end the result was the same.

"I had such high hopes this time. Bob was so perfect. Our romance had begun so gloriously. The afternoons on Lake Michigan in his powerboat, the car trips to Lake Geneva, and the cute little cottage by the lake where we made passionate love on a big, old featherbed. And there were the candlelight dinners, the Sunday afternoons reading the papers in bed and lying naked in front of the fireplace in his apartment. Bob was the ideal man, rich, handsome, and in the beginning very thoughtful. The summer had been wonderful - until I started working on my novel.

"Then, the little irritations began, the nagging about how much I worked, his insistence on my meeting his obnoxious parents, his mother's calls to remind me of every little thing. I always felt his parents didn't approve of me. And those boring dinners at his folks' which I had to attend just when my ideas were flowing so great. And finally, the last straw, Bob's petty jealousy of Julian. Bob seemed to feel Julian was coming between us in his zeal for me to finish my book. That was uncalled for.

"Each day as we drifted further and further apart. I always felt I could stop the deterioration, but in the end it was Bob's father's nasty tactics to get Bob to go out with the dreaded "Stephanie - The Perfect" that drove the stake into our relationship. I hated the fact that his ploy worked. I should have seen it coming, but ... no.

"Well, anyway, as I began to untie Bob's legs, he began to stir. I quickly untied the knots on his legs and untied the rope leading to his hands so he could sit up. He was awake by now, and the fire in his eyes was raging. He glared at me.

"Sit up," I said and helped him roll over and sit up on the couch. "Turn around."

"Bob turned around, and I began to untie his hands. I admit I was wary because I didn't know what to expect. Bob waited patiently until his hands were free, then rubbing his wrists, he tried to speak. But the duct tape across his mouth only allowed a muffled grunt. I did not want to pull off the tape.

"Bob reached up and pulled on the tape very gently. It was still stuck tight. I reached down to help him, but he held up his hands and pushed me away. He pulled harder and then, finally, in one quick motion, he ripped the tape off his mouth. You should have heard the scream."

By now, Kevin was almost doubled up with the pent-up laughter he just couldn't release.

"Then Bob tried to stand up, but his legs were too weak from being tied up for a such long time, and he fell back on the couch. He sat there, rubbing his mouth, not saying anything, just staring daggers at me. I was terrified.

"Finally, he said, "You finish that goddamned book?"

"Yes," I said timidly.

"I see. And that's it?"

"Yes...I suppose."

"You 'suppose'? Is there something else?" he asked as he reached down and massaged his aching legs.

"I'm sorry I had to tie you up," I said.

"I'll bet," he said as he slowly got up, stamping his feet to restore the circulation. He rubbed his wrists and squeezed his fingers to get the numbness out.

"You want some breakfast?" I asked.

"No, I don't want some breakfast. I want to go, now!" he said. I could see the anger rising in his throat like heartburn.

"You're mad," I said.

"Mad? Mad? Why should I be mad?!" Bob said incredulously. "I'm not mad. I'm furious! And you know why?"

"Because I tied you up?"

"Because I was stupid enough to get involved with you in the first place! I should have known that night you told me about this, this obsession you have about not being able to write unless you're in love. But no, I was too damned dumb, too much in love with you! And then, that, thing about your wearing your 'writing bikini!' God, what an idiot I was!"

"I can't help it. I'm, just compulsive," I pleaded.

"Compulsive? Compulsive! You're not compulsive, you're a nut! As soon as you started that fucking book, all you wanted to do was write and make love! Then, after we made love, it was always right back to the book! We had no social life. We had no lazy Sunday afternoons. All we had was writing, writing, writing!"

"But you don't understand, when I get going on an idea, I."

"You go into a coma," Bob interrupted. "Look this isn't going anywhere, I'm outta here." He got up and hobbled toward the door.

I started to reach out to him.

"Don't," Bob held up his hand as if to push me away as he passed by me. "Don't say another word."

He opened the door then turned back to and gave me this terrible look, "Do me one big favor, April. Don't call me. Don't write to me. And for God's sake, don't come to my wedding!" Bob stalked out and slammed the door. The end.

When she finished telling the story, April was feeling no pain.

Kevin was in tears laughing. "And he left?"

"Yep, with duct tape stuck to the heel of his shoe."

Kevin couldn't hold it in any longer and burst out with a big guffaw. The others in the room immediately gave him a withering look, but he could not stop laughing.

April looked at him over the top of her eyes as she finished the last of her brandy. He was so cute!

"And there is a kicker to this story," April cut in. "He married Stephanie, and she ran off with the gardener three weeks later!"

They both broke up. They were laughing so hard that everyone in the room was staring at them. When they regained control, they noticed the others in the room and quieted down. They did let out a chuckle or two while Kevin paid the bill.

Kevin walked, or rather, almost carried, April to the door of her apartment. It was very late. She was more than tipsy, she was at that dangerous point when she could do or say anything. Kevin recognized it. He propped her up against the wall and fumbled in her purse to find the key to open the door.

April watched him through the alcohol fog. "Don't you want to come in?" April said with a hint of pleading.

"I can't. I've got to go to work tomorrow. You can sleep in, but I can't."

"Oh, a poor baby," April said, touching his cheek. She wanted him to kiss her and held her head up to his.

He was tempted, but instead he said, "Gotta go." He opened the door and helped her over the threshold.

"I'm sorry you have to go," April moaned. The disappointment oozed from her puckered lips.

"I hope you had a good time," Kevin said slowly backing away.

"I had a wonderful time," April said.

"Well, goodnight," he said.

"Goodnight," she said.

Neither moved. They just looked at each other.

Kevin finally broke the spell. He backed away, waved and began walking toward the elevator.

"Night," April said.

"Night," he said as he punched the button for the elevator.

She watched as the elevator doors closed behind him, then April closed the door and walked into her bedroom and switched on the lights. She looked at the canopied bed. "I guess it's just you and I," she said to the bed.

Kevin sat in his car for a long time thinking about April. He didn't believe in love at first sight, but if it could happen, she'd be a real contender. He sat up and started the engine. "Come on, O'Connor," he said out loud, "get a hold of you. Do what's right. Just see that she finds a man." He gunned the engine and drove out of the courtyard. His mind was made up - temporarily.

CHAPTER EIGHT

Book Four

Eddie Hobson was a spy. His parents were French from Montmartre and came to America in the 1920's. Eddie was born in the Bronx and raised in a tough part of the city. At home, Eddie listened to his parents conversing in French and wanted to learn the language, so when he was six they began to teach him. By the time he was twelve, Eddie read and spoke fluent Parisian French.

Eddie was smart and got into Columbia University at the age of nineteen. He was studying to be a lawyer when his talent for speaking French came to the attention of one of the deans who in turn called one of his friends in the OSS. On September 2, 1943, Eddie was approached by "Wild Bill" Donovan, the head of the Office of Strategic Services, the forerunner to the CIA. Donovan reported directly to President Roosevelt. He recruited Eddie that day.

Eddie graduated from spy school a top student. In addition to his language skills, he was very adept at the other skills, including killing people.

Eddie parachuted into France on May 1, 1944, to help organize the French Resistence for D-Day. He walked into Paris whistling a tune his mother had sung to him as a child. Eddie was very self-confident, too self-confident for his own good. He was captured the second day he arrived in France by the Gestapo. He was rescued the same day, when, by accident, one of the leaders of the Resistence, Louis Trebec, recognized Eddie as he was being arrested. Louis had met Eddie in the United States at his parent's home in 1939. The rescue cost Louis his life, but Eddie was safe, chagrined, and immediately much more careful.

Eddie did his job well, and by D-Day the Resistence was ready. Eddie had fallen for Michelle, a lovely operative, and spent much of his time with her at her apartment in the Latin Quarter. One evening they heard an explosion nearby. Since they knew it wasn't an action of the Resistence, they put out the lights and looked out the window overlooking the street below.

They watched as an entire company of German soldiers waited for the smoke from the explosion to clear before racing into a home a block away. An old man and his wife were dragged out of the house and shot.

Curiosity got the best of Eddie, and after the soldiers left and the bodies were taken away, he and Michelle decided to go into the house to find out why the people were killed. Inside, they found a smashed two-way radio on the floor of the living room. They looked around and saw nothing else that intrigued them except a wall safe, which was open. Inside was an old book. Eddie took it with him.

Eddie read Recit de la Revolution from cover to cover, and decided that he'd look for this baker's vault. Since a lot of their secret movement was in the old sewer system, Eddie decided he would look for the vault as they moved around.

One night Eddie stuffed the book in his coat and left for an assignment. He and two others were to blow up a telephone exchange that night. Unfortunately, one of the other two was a turncoat, and when they arrived at the rendezvous, the Germans were waiting.

Eddie managed to escape, but only momentarily. He was running down the lane next to the river when he was shot in the back of the head. He fell into the Seine, and he and the book sank silently into the swirling water.

CHAPTER NINE

The bright morning sun burst though a crack in the drapes and headed directly for April's eyes. She was snuggling a pillow and dreaming about Kevin. She was smiling in her sleep and talking out loud, "I love you, too, Kevin."

At that moment, the sunbeam hit her right in the right eye. It was like a flash of lightning. She rolled over as fast as she could. She rubbed her eyes and lifted her head off the pillow. Suddenly a stabbing pain enveloped her head. "Oh god," she said and flopped back down. The hangover struck full force, headache, queasy stomach, dizziness, and cotton mouth. I want to die, she thought as she tried not to move. Sleep. I need sleep. She rolled over only to have the sun beam catch her square in the eyes again. Quickly she rolled back over on her other side. This was not going to be a good day.

At the same time, Kevin was in his office trying to concentrate on an article on Paris restaurants, but the memories of April the night before haunted him. He kept seeing her, laughing, eating, smiling and, of course talking a mile a minute.

Each time he recalled the night's festivities, a bigger smile crept across his face.

"What you're working on?" George asked as he walked into Kevin's cubicle and looked over his shoulder.

"What?"

"You seem to be getting a big kick out of what you're writing. Can I see?"

"No. I mean yeah. It's coming along great."

"Hey, didn't you take April Mason out to dinner last night?"

"Yep."

"Well?"

"Well, what?"

"How'd dinner go?"

Kevin spun around in his chair, put his hands behind his head, and leaned back. "Frankly, George, I was somewhat disappointed."

"Oh?"

"Well, one of the shells for the Oysters Rockefeller was cracked, the soup was a bit tepid, one of the panties on the lamb chops fell off."

"No." George interrupted. "You know what I'm talking about - April Mason. How'd it go?"

Kevin thought a minute then said, "Well. Actually very well. She's interesting. Very bright. Talks a lot though. It was okay."

"Okay? There you go with that 'okay' stuff. Be specific."

"She's five foot six, black hair, brown eyes, slim, about 110."

"And?"

"And she's nice."

"Sexy?"

"Yeah, somewhat."

"Somewhat? Come on. You sound like you're describing half the women in the world. What's she really like?" George asked waving his hands and pacing back and forth nervously.

"Ah, the newspaperman's favorite question. I just told you. She's interesting, but -"

"Not your type?"

"Right," Kevin said turning back to his computer. "Now, look, if you want this article today, let me write it. Okay?"

George shrugged, his shoulders sagged, and he dropped his head. "Okay." He slowly walked out of the cubicle. He stopped and turned. "I still want an article from her."

"I'll ask," Kevin said. As soon as George was out of earshot he mumbled, "Like hell I will."

April re-awoke at noon. She carefully, slowly, opened one eye. No pain. She opened the other. There was a dull ache, but the stabbing pains had gone. The room was in heavy shadows the sun having moved enough so the rays of light fell on the foot of the bed. April laid back on her pillow and stared at the ornate ceiling.

A smile grew slowly as she thought about Kevin. He was so gallant last night, she murmured. As she sat up, her mind began fuzzing out. She couldn't remember if he had asked her out again. She wanted him to, that was for sure.

She moved to the edge of the bed and put her legs over. They felt like lead weights.

She decided to call Kevin and apologize for drinking so much - just as soon as she came back to life.

Kevin couldn't get April off his mind. Finally, about three o'clock in the afternoon, he reached for the phone on his desk, but before he could pick it up, it rang.

"Kevin O'Connor," he answered.

"Thank you," the voice on the other end of the phone said.

At first, Kevin didn't recognize the voice. It was a woman, but who? "April?"

"I think so," she replied.

"You sound - different."

"I know. I feel awful."

"Are you sick?"

"No. Not that kind of sick. I think it was the brandy. What was that in that brandy?"

"Alcohol as I recall. A lot of it."

"Funny, it didn't taste like it. It tasted wonderful, but this morning..."

"I should have warned you. My bad. Can you forgive me?"

"There's really nothing to forgive. I just called to say I had a terrific time. Everything was so perfect." She wanted to say "including you" but stopped short. "How can I make it up to you?"

"No need to do that. I had a great time, too." He meant it.

"I want to do something. I know, let me take you out to dinner."

"April, you don't have to take me out."

"Please?" she asked softly.

She sounded on the verge of tears, Kevin thought. He hated it when women cried. He was always a sucker for tears. He knew he shouldn't take her up on her offer, but he did. "All right. When?"

"When can you get away?"

He laughed to himself. He didn't want to seem to be a pushover. "Tomorrow night?" he asked, knowing full well he could go anytime.

"Terrific! Where shall we go?"

Kevin thought for a moment. "Chez Benoit." He agreed to make the reservation, and he'd pick her up at seven. When he hung up, he shuddered. He was asking for trouble - nice trouble - but trouble nevertheless.

April felt a lot better when she hung up. She felt so good that she knew exactly what she was going to do - go shopping!

Pepe Duvall sat in his seedy hotel room on the waterfront in St. Tropez. He was frustrated. He'd tried to have drinks with Charles Du Pypes for three days, but each time Du Pypes was busy. Pepe had promised Duer he'd deliver the book to him in Paris in five days. Time was running out. He slid open the drawer in his bedside table and took out his steel blue Beretta. He checked the chamber and made sure it was loaded, flicked the safety on, and put the gun in his coat pocket. He put on his coat and left. He had to get that book.

CHAPTER TEN

Book Five

Marcel, the book seller who originally purchased the five books, became an old man, and in 1818, he was forced by illness to close his shop. He donated his remaining books to the Bibliotheque Nationale, the major library in Paris. His last copy of <u>Recit de la Revolution</u> was among the books he donated.

This copy languished in the back shelves of the Bibliotheque Nationale for over 150 years. Then it was stolen.

The thief was Nathan Turlow, a distant relative of Andre Val Dumon. A distant cousin of Nathan's, Pierre Le Bosc, had just died and left him the writings of his ancestors which the cousin had spent years compiling. Among the writings were the notes and ravings of Andre Val Dumon.

Like Andre and Pierre, Nathan was a scholar. He was also a professor at Eton in England.

Nathan was the first in his family to read the ravings of his ancestor in more than one hundred and fifty years. What he read fascinated him, especially Dumon's writings about the baker's vault and the book the story came from - <u>Recit de la Revolution.</u>

He began a search for the book. After two years of inquiries, he was surprised to find a copy at the Bibliotheque

Nationale in Paris. The trouble was he could not check the book out because it had become classified as an antique. He could read it only in one of the reading rooms, and he had to stay in the room and return it before he left the library. He read the book twice. Like his ancestor, Nathan was sure the book contained a clue to the whereabouts of the treasure, but the hassle factor at the library was getting to him. It took hours just to have the librarian find it and assign him a reading room. He became more and more furious about this, and one day he brought with him a book the same size as Recit de la Revolution. He returned the fake book and stole the original.

After rereading the book several times, Nathan began his own methodical search. In the course of his search, he described the clues to the whereabouts of the treasure to many other people in both England and France. And, as a result of his telling a lot of people about the treasure, in 1979 several people began to scramble to find the treasure. Many people searched the sewers not even knowing what they were looking for. The clues Nathan let out were accurate, but time had changed everything. The streets weren't the same, most of the ancient sewer system had either been destroyed or remodeled, and even those sections that remained were encrusted by the ravages of time.

After the burst of public enthusiasm for the search subsided two years later, Nathan remained convinced he could find it. He compared all of the clues, maps and guesses and came to his own conclusion. He was sure he knew where the vault was. He waited until late at night, then climbed down into the sewer and began looking. It was morning before he came to the spot marked on his map. He didn't go any further because just at the moment when he thought he saw the opening, bulldozers on the street above caused the sewer to collapse. Nathan was buried alive in the cave-in.

No one knew he was down there, of course, and his body and the book in his pocket were never found.

CHAPTER ELEVEN

Kevin and April arrived at Chez Benoit, one of the last of the traditional bistros in Paris, precisely at seven thirty. April wore a green suede suit which she'd purchased that afternoon. She looked elegant. Kevin was proud as he escorted her though the sea of diners to a table in the corner. He ordered cocktails for them, and they scanned the extensive menu.

As they waited, he looked at her as she scanned the room. Her big brown eyes were glistening from the light from the small lamp on the table. He hated the fact that his heart was beating too fast. When the drinks came, Kevin raised his glass, "To you, Ms Mason. Welcome to Paris."

April looked him right in the eye and raised her glass, "To you, Mr. O'Connor, and to Paris, the City of Love."

Kevin felt a small lump in his throat. "Right. To love," he repeated. They clinked glasses and drank. They maintained eye contact as they sipped their drinks.

April looked at the menu, but she wasn't reading it. She was thinking of how blue Kevin's eyes were, and what a great smile he had. She was also impressed by his manners. He was American, but he behaved like a European - at least what she thought Europeans behaved like. Chivalry and all that. It was old fashioned, but she loved it. When she looked up, she saw his eyes quickly dart back to the menu. She'd caught him looking at her, and she was flattered to say the least.

Kevin had given this night a lot of thought. To escort April around town once in a while was all right. But that afternoon he'd made a pact with himself not to become emotionally involved. It wouldn't be fair, to her, to him, or them. He'd come to that decision on his way to pick her up. He was certain it was the right thing to do, but now, sitting across from her, he wasn't sure.

He also knew that every minute he delayed invoking "Ploy 601" increased the jeopardy. There was no time for women in his life. Besides, it was too dangerous. The last time he got seriously involved with a woman, he ended up getting shot.

April peered over her menu once again. Kevin seemed to be lost in thought. She was having wicked thoughts about the two of them and that big canopied bed in her apartment. The corners of her mouth turned up as she visualized the bed.

Kevin sighed. He put down his menu just as April did. Timing, he knew, was everything. He'd wait for just the right opening to invoke 'Ploy 601'.

"So," April began, "I told you everything about myself the other night, now it's your turn to tell me all about Kevin O'Connor. Who is he and what does he want?"

"When you find out, let me know," Kevin said with a smile.

"Come on, Kevin. I'm serious. I want to know all about you."

Kevin shrugged. "Okay, but I warn you - it's very boring."

All through dinner Kevin mixed fact with fiction. He was born Stamford, Connecticut, dad in civil service, mom too (actually both were in the CIA), no brothers or sisters, etc. He told her about his family (mostly true). He said his childhood and college days at NYU were normal (again, mostly true). Some of his anecdotes made her laugh, and he told other stories which were ones he'd heard from others. Sometime during his history, they ordered wine and dinner.

Then he came to the present. He talked about his job at the Paris Gazette, how he joined the paper when he came to Paris on another job and stayed (generally true). He still hadn't yet found the right time for 'Ploy 601', but curiously enough April opened the door.

"And what about the women in your life?" April asked coyly.

"A few," he said and left it at that.

April looked at him out of the corner of her eye and said firmly, "What's 'a few'?"

"More than three."

"Well, don't just sit there with that smug look on your face, tell me all about them. All of them. All 'few'."

"Including high school?"

"And college and right up to today."

He couldn't have asked for a better cue. Time for 'Ploy 601'. "Well, I've only had three meaningful relationships. Jenny, my first, in many ways, was the hometown girl I was going to marry. She left for college, and I never saw her again. Then, in college, there was Lisa. She was voluptuous, tall and beautiful. We were pinned in my Sophomore year at NYU. That was when I learned the meaning of the word 'torrid'."

April arched an eyebrow. "Oh, ho."

"Anyway, that lasted until my senior year when she posed nude for Playboy. I never saw her in the same light again, but a hell of a lot of others did."

April burst out laughing. He joined in.

She took a sip of wine and looked at him with baleful eyes, "And the third?"

He knew it was time for Ploy 601. "My wife. Suzette. I'm sorry she couldn't join us," he said, lightly. "She's in Nantes working on an exhibit at the antiquity's museum."

April's heart thudded into her stomach. He was married?! Kevin kept on talking about his wife and something about her being somewhere, but April was too distraught to pay any attention. As he went on about 'her', April tried to gather her wits about her. She should have known someone that attractive would be married. She steeled herself and tried to listen. Finally, she tuned back in.

"...so what with her job taking her all over France and mine being right here, we just don't get to see each other much during the year."

"Oh, that's too bad," April heard herself say.

"Well, it goes with the territory. Let's get back to you. I understand that you just finished another novel. What's it about?"

April suddenly felt very tired. She sat back in her chair and braced herself for a long night. "A woman who finds herself living with a killer," she said. Did she sound as bored as she felt?

All through dinner April felt as if she was being interviewed. He asked the same dumb questions every reporter asked her. She couldn't enjoy the meal even though it was delicious. As the waiter was clearing the table, she glanced around and saw a tall, thin, dapper man, about 35, approaching the table.

"Kevin, what a surprise," he said with a rich French accent. "I didn't expect to see you here."

Kevin looked up. His stomach muscles tightened. "Jean Pierre," he said with little enthusiasm.

"How's Paris's crack reporter?" Jean Pierre asked. There was no mistaking the sarcasm in his voice.

It didn't take a genius to see that there was no love lost between these two men, April thought. She imagined she saw smoke coming out of Kevin's ears.

Jean Pierre glanced down at April (or was it April's breasts?). "And who is this lovely lady?"

Kevin bit his tongue, stood, and introduced them. "April Mason, I'd like to present Jean Pierre Demain."

April looked up at Jean Pierre. He had an angular face, with a straight, roman nose and thin eyebrows, but his green eyes fascinated her. They were both warm and impish. Sexy.

"Enchante," Jean Pierre said taking her hand and kissing it.

"Very nice to meet you," April said with a renewed sense of energy.

"Jean Pierre is a lobbyist," Kevin said.

"A representative," Jean Pierre interjected, "for the tourist industry."

"Oh, really," April said in her most charming voice. "How exciting?" She gave Jean Pierre a very friendly smile.

Kevin looked at April. He didn't know her well, but he was certain she was putting it on very thick.

"What, may I ask, is such a beautiful American woman doing here in Paris with -- Mr. O'Connor?"

"Oh, we're just having dinner," April said.

"I see. Just dinner?"

"Yes. Just dinner," April said as if she'd been bored all evening which inferred a lot.

"And are you visiting or do you live here in Paris?"

"Just visiting. Actually, I'm staying for a month or so. I may do some work, as well."

"Oh?"

"She's an author, Jean Pierre. A mystery writer," Kevin interrupted.

"Most fascinating. I'd like to hear more about your work. Miss Mason is it?" Jean Pierre said, his eyes now firmly fixed on April's bosom.

"Yes, please call me April," she said. She saw where Jean Pierre's eyes were focused, and she saw the disapproving look on Kevin's face. She liked both looks. "I'm sure Kevin could arrange it. Couldn't you, Kevin?" April asked, the venom oozing from her lips.

Kevin's eyes narrowed. What the hell was she up to? "If that's your wish."

"Is Mr. O'Connor your keeper?" Jean Pierre asked.

"Oh, no," April turned her face to Jean Pierre, "it's just that Mr. O'Connor has been given the task of showing me around."

"A task? Like a guide?"

"You might say that," April said giving Jean Pierre that look that said, 'Let's dump Kevin and go off somewhere.'

"How very kind of you, Kevin," Jean Pierre said, biting his tongue to keep from laughing out loud. He wished April would stand so he could get the full effect, but she sat there looking up at him. He looked down. This time he looked at her face.

"Nice seeing you, Jean Pierre," Kevin said, and sat down - indicating this conversation was over.

Jean Pierre knew Kevin wanted him to go away. He hated being brushed off, but this was not the place to make a stand, and the woman looked too delicious. "Yes." Jean Pierre nodded to Kevin then turned to April. "May I give you my card, Miss Mason? Perhaps we can enjoy a lunch sometime soon." He pulled a card from his coat pocket and handed it to her.

"Thank you," she said giving Jean Pierre a warm smile. "I would enjoy lunch very much."

"Until then, Mademoiselle," Jean Pierre said bowing slightly first to April then to Kevin. "Au revoir."

"Jean Pierre," Kevin said evenly.

"Au revoir," April said brightly, flashing yet another smile.

After Jean Pierre left, Kevin asked, "What was that all about?"

"What?"

"That phony smile bit."

"I was just trying to be nice to your friend."

"He's no friend of mine. Let's get out of here," Kevin said starting to rise.

"I want desert," April suddenly demanded. "After all, as you said so often, Julian is paying."

Kevin sat back down. April was turning ugly.

Pepe Duvall sat in his car a block from Du Pypes' villa and waited. He knew that Andre had visitors. This was no time to intrude. He checked his gun once again and put it back in his pocket. He would wait this out. He had all night.

59

As he drove April home, Kevin was sorry that he had come on so directly. He could have told her he was married in a better way, although he couldn't think of one right then. He was just following his instincts. She was getting to him. He was sure he did the right thing for both of them, but he also knew he had hurt her.

From the moment he told her he was married, she had changed drastically. She was cold and aloof all during dessert. If looks could kill, he was dead and buried.

April seethed. Inside she was boiling mad, hurt, shocked and disappointed. She didn't know what to say so she said nothing. Actually she was afraid to speak for fear she'd scream. All she could do was sit there and churn.

The silence in the car was deafening.

When Kevin pulled in and parked in front her apartment house, April didn't give him time to get out, go around and open the door for her, she just got out, said a curt good night, and disappeared inside.

Kevin sat there for a moment and tried to assess the situation. April was a big girl, he reminded himself. She would get over him.

Suddenly, his eyes opened wide. "Julian," he said in a hush. What was he going to tell Julian? He was supposed to take care of her. More to the point, what was she going to tell Julian? He rubbed his hands across his face. He felt the cold sweat. He had to call Julian right away, but first, he had a more important errand to run.

April slammed the door of her apartment and threw her purse on the couch. She felt like crying and screaming. "Married. Why didn't I see it? What's happened to my feminine intuition? It must be the water!" she said to the walls as she spun around and sat on the floor. Tears were streaming down her face. "I'll get him," she vowed. "Somehow, somewhere, I'll get him!"

Kevin made his way down the passageway near Gare de
Est to the Brasserie Flo. He was on a mission. As he entered
the restaurant, he scanned the spacious room looking for his
prey.

He spotted Jean Pierre sitting at a table near the back under
a huge stained glass window. Jean Pierre was sitting with two
beautiful young women. They were huddled in animated
conversation laughing and having a good time. Kevin made a
beeline for the table.

"Why Kevin, what a surprise," Jean Pierre said as Kevin
stopped in front of the table and glowered at him. "What
brings you here?"

"I was looking for you."

"And here I am. Please, sit down. I believe you know my
friends, Simone and Lizette?"

Kevin nodded toward Simone, a very exotic looking black
girl with her hair pulled back, and then to Lizette, a pretty,
stately young woman with long, flowing blonde hair and more
than ample breasts.

"Kevin, mon ami, I have missed you," Lizette said. "Sit by
me," she said patting the chair next to her.

"Would you ladies mind excusing us for a couple of
minutes?" Kevin said staring directly at Jean Pierre.

"Oh, oh, he sounds serious," Simone said with a mock
frown.

"Yes," Lizette said, and the two began to giggle. "This
won't take long," Kevin said, not taking his eyes off Jean Pierre.

"Ah, Kevin, must we?" Jean Pierre asked.

"Yes."

Jean Pierre sighed with frustration. "Shall we humor him?"
he asked the girls.

The two young women stood up. Simone was dressed in a
tight fitting white dress that revealed every sensuous curve.
Lizette was taller and wore a form-fitted black suit. "Come on,
Lizette," Simone said. "Let's let the boys have their fun."

"Don't be too long, Kevin, I haven't had my drink yet," Lizette said as she kissed him on the cheek and winked at Jean Pierre at the same time.

As they walked away, all the men in the room followed them with their eyes. Well aware of the attention they were getting, the two put on a show for everyone as they ambled away.

"Kevin, you're causing a scene. Please sit down," Jean Pierre chided. Kevin slowly sat down across from Jean Pierre so he could look him straight in the eye.

"Now, what is this all about? The young American woman, Miss Mason?"

"Stay away from her," Kevin demanded.

"Oh? Are we in love?"

"No. Just stay away."

"That's it? No explanation?"

"I didn't like what I saw tonight."

"I did."

"I know. I've seen that look before. She doesn't need your type."

"And what 'type' is that?"

"Hustler."

"And you're not?"

"Touche. Look, Jean Pierre, she's very vulnerable right now, and I don't want to see her get hurt."

"Vulnerable? All women are vulnerable, Kevin. You'll have to do better than that."

"Let's put it this way, it's my job to protect her, and neither you nor anybody else it going to...."

"Your job? You? A protector of women? Please, do me the courtesy of not assuming I'm a complete idiot. Your reputation precedes you. As does, I suppose mine."

"Okay, so I'm not lily white, but this time I'm serious. I don't want you getting involved with April."

"I see. You want her all to yourself. What about your wife? Or are you no longer married?"

"Leave her out of this."

"Really. How odd it is that you feel so strongly about Miss Mason and yet don't want to talk about your wife."

"Look. I promised her publisher I'd find someone suitable for April."

"I think I'm suitable."

"Not a chance."

Jean Pierre sensed something was wrong. Kevin wasn't being Kevin. He was too serious about this woman. "Kevin, my friend, I have never seen you so, so protective. Could there be more to this perhaps?"

"Not that concerns you. Besides, it's none of your business. Just do us both a favor and stay away from her."

"Or?"

"You don't want to know."

The two men sat facing each other. Each was concerned about what the other would do next. Neither man wanted to back down.

"We're back," Lizette interrupted.

Kevin looked up at the women. "One more minute."

"I don't think so, Kevin," Jean Pierre said firmly and stood up.

Kevin glared at him. The two women were hovering over the table. He got up. "Remember what I said. Stay away." Kevin said. He stared at Jean Pierre for a moment then turned and left the restaurant.

The two girls were intrigued. Both started to talk at the same time, but Simone won out, "What was that all about?"

"A challenge, ma cherie," Jean Pierre said as he watched Kevin go out the door. "Actually, a very interesting challenge."

It was a warm, balmy night. The moon was full and reflected brightly off the bay at St. Tropez. Pepe hid in the shadows and watched as two men and a woman left Du Pypes' villa. He waited until he saw their car pull away, then he

63

checked the chamber of his pistol once again then stuck it back in his coat pocket. He walked up to the door and knocked.

Andre opened the door, took one look at Pepe and said, "For the last time, Duvall, I have no intention of selling you the book!"

"Then you leave me no choice," Pepe said in a low, menacing tone. He pulled his pistol out his coat pocket and trained it on Andre. With a flick of his wrist Pepe motioned for Andre to go inside. Pepe followed and closed the door behind them with his foot.

"Get out!" Andre demanded.

"Where is the book?"

"I don't know."

Duvall smashed Andre across the face with the barrel of his gun. Andre reeled backward and fell against a bookcase. Then, he slumped to his knees. Blood streamed down the left side of his face. "The book," Pepe demanded. He put the barrel of the gun directly between Andre's eyes. "Now," he shouted.

Andre turned his head slightly to the right and indicated with his eyes, "In the cupboard."

"Get up," Pepe said still pointing at his head. Andre struggled to his feet, went to the cupboard, reached in and got the book.

"Put it on the desk," Pepe ordered. Andre did as he was told.

Pepe looked down at the book to make sure it was the right one. "There," he said, "That wasn't so hard was it?"

Andre began shaking his head, but the movement stopped the moment the bullet entered his brain and shut down his life. He fell back across his desk. Duvall walked up to the desk, pushed the body aside and picked up the book. He looked around in the desk and found some brown paper. He carefully wrapped the book. He checked to be sure Andre was dead. "You should have listened, Andre," he said. "I don't like people who don't listen."

A few moments later, Duvall emerged from the villa with the book under his arm. He looked around to see if the noise of the gunshot had alerted anyone. Satisfied it hadn't, he walked down the wooden steps to his car parked on a narrow street a block away. He carefully laid the old book beside his train ticket to Paris on the front seat, got in and drove off toward the train station.

CHAPTER TWELVE

April spent most of the morning seething and pacing, pacing and seething, over Kevin's marriage situation. She couldn't figure out why her hadn't seen it from the beginning. Had she lost her female intuition? She used to be able to spot a married man a block away. She finally came to the conclusion Kevin was more wrapped up in his work than in his marriage. This would account for the casual way he talked about his marriage. Poor woman, she thought. But it still hurt.

Her thoughts were interrupted by a call from Jean Pierre. He invited her to a VIP tour of Notre Dame that afternoon, and then, only a few minutes later, Professor Montrer, of the Sorbonne, called. He had a change in his appointments and could see her right away.

Thirty minutes later, April climbed the old stone steps and entered the side door of the language arts building of the Sorbonne. She was looking forward to meeting the professor whom she'd heard a lot about. She walked slowly down the long hallway lined with old paintings and lithographs. She stopped and studied a few. When she came to room number 27, she knocked politely.

"Entre," came a small, thin voice from inside.

April entered. Sitting at a battered metal desk piled high with papers was an old man with pince-nez glasses. He sported a white goatee and wild, bushy white hair. He pulled his glasses off and stood as April entered. "Miss Mason?"

"Yes. Professor Montrer?"

"Yes."

"We spoke on the phone this morning?"

"Yes. You said you wanted to refresh your understanding of our language?"

"Yes, I do. I want to be able to speak with some degree of confidence. I think it's important since I'm going to be here a while."

"Are you planning on living in Paris?"

"No, not really, but I am staying a month, and I thought I'd have a better time if I spoke the language."

Professor Montrer tilted his head and rubbed his chin as he thought about her answer. Finally, "I suppose that is possible, but I've found that even those who've studied for some time can have a good time without talking," he smiled.

April liked him from that moment on. "True. Words don't necessarily mean understanding."

"So you've made up your mind have you?"

"Yes, and you know, I'm not sure why, but something in the back of my mind tells me I need to do this."

"Ah, I see. Well, I learned long ago never to doubt the instinct of a woman, so shall we begin?"

Francois Duer came up the ramp from Customs. His plane from Algiers had been ten minutes early. As he neared the top of the ramp, he saw Paul LeMieux, his Paris "aide," waiting. Paul LeMieux was a short, rather slender man in his late 30's. He had an oval face with small, somewhat slanted eyes. He wore a nicely-fitted pinstripe suit. Paul came down the ramp to meet and help Duer with his carrying case.

"Good morning, Paul," Duer said, handing him the case. "Is everything in order?"

"Yes, sir. We went over the apartment with a fine-tooth comb and could find nothing out of the ordinary."

"Excellent. I can always count on you."

"Thank you, Monsieur Duer. I trust your flight was satisfactory?"

"Yes, quite."

They walked through the terminal toward the exit where a limousine waited. They did not notice the man in the grey suit carrying an empty suitcase following at a discreet distance.

April and Jean Pierre crossed the huge courtyard in front of the Notre Dame Cathedral. April stopped and turned back to admire the magnificent structure once again. "Jean Pierre you're such a wonderful guide," she said as she turned back to him. "Thank you so much for giving me the VIP Tour. It was fascinating. What history."

"My pleasure. Besides, what good is having connections if one does not use them?" Jean Pierre said.

"A point well taken," she said with a warm smile. "And, I was very impressed. You seem to know every nook and cranny of the grounds," April said, taking his arm. "I can't wait to tell Kevin how kind you've been."

Jean Pierre stopped and turned to April. "I wouldn't do that if I were you, April."

"Why not?"

"It's a long story."

"Oh? I want to hear all about it."

"Perhaps over lunch?"

"Sure."

Jean Pierre hailed a taxi, and they drove to a small outdoor café on the Champs Elysees. They were seated outdoors at a table with a good view of the people passing by. After they ordered, April asked, "So what's the story with you and Kevin?"

Jean Pierre sighed. "Well, Kevin and I have been rivals for some time. Usually, over women."

"But Kevin's married."

"So it seems."

"Seems? Is he married or not?"

"Yes. He is, and she is very striking, but . . . "

"But," April said, hanging on Jean Pierre's every word.

"But, frankly, she doesn't seem the academic type at all."

"Why not?"

"Well, to be candid, she looks more like a lady of the evening than a scientist. Not that she isn't attractive, mind you, but a bit trashy."

"Trashy?" April's curiosity was peaking, and she wanted to know a lot more about Kevin's wife, but she stopped herself. Jean Pierre might take her interest the wrong way.

"For lack of a better word. And this running all over the country to various museums seems very strange."

"Frankly, I find much about Kevin strange. I'm sorry. You were telling me about this so-called rivalry."

"Well, it began when we were both single at the time. Kevin was working for that rag, The Paris Gazette. We met at a few functions and found ourselves attracted to many of the same women. Too often, for Kevin, the women were more attracted to me. He's never forgiven me for winning the 'admiration' of those women. He can be very jealous."

"Well, I'd think that when he got married that ended the rivalry."

"One would think that, but Kevin can be very difficult. In fact, he asked me not to see you."

"Really?"

"Yes. Something to do with protecting you?"

April began to laugh. "Oh! I didn't think he was taking it that seriously!"

"May I ask just what his connection with you is?"

"Well, Kevin was asked by my publisher in Chicago to find me an apartment and sort of look after me, but I didn't think he'd interpret that to mean he was to be my bodyguard! I've got to talk to him."

Jean Pierre reached across and took April's hand. "April, my love, I'd really rather you keep me out of this. Kevin can be very, shall we say, dangerous."

"You think so?"

"I know so. Let's just keep our meetings secret for a while."

"All right. But I am going to talk to him about trying to run my life."

"Of course. Speaking of meetings, shall we have dinner soon? I know just the place. It's full of history, and many say romance."

April thought the last part of the invitation sounded a little oily, but shrugged. "You'll call?"

"Of course."

"Great."

During lunch, Jean Pierre regaled her with stories about the history of Paris and his exploits in the tourist business. April enjoyed every minute. When they finished and Jean Pierre paid the bill, they got up and walked to the street where Jean Pierre hailed a taxi. April told him she wanted to walk for a while before going home.

Just before he got into the cab, Jean Pierre said, "By the way, tomorrow is Sunday. You said you wanted to get a good feel for the city. May I suggest you stroll along the Seine. On Sundays many of the artists and books sellers have stalls there. You can often find bargains, and the people are fascinating."

"I will, thanks," April said and waved as the taxi pulled away from the curb.

That afternoon, Kevin sat in his cubicle and listened intensely to the voice on the other end of the phone. He scribbled a note on a scrap of paper "Mr. X is back" and frowned. "I understand Inspector," he said and listened again. "115 Boulevard Saint Germain. I know the place." He hung up.

As he started to get up, George, dressed in his ever-present rumpled suit, came sauntering in. "I thought you didn't work on Saturdays."

"I had to make notes from my dinner at Benoit last night. Why are you here?"

"I forgot Louise's package she left yesterday. Oh, yeah, one other thing. I lost it."

"You're always losing things. What now?"

"The phone number for April Mason."

Kevin rolled his eyes then wrote the number on the scrap piece of paper and handed it to George.

"So, how's she doing?"

"I don't know," Kevin said gathering up his coat from the back of his chair.

"Why not, don't you see her?"

"You call her," he said not wanting to get into the whole story. He brushed past George.

"Where're you going?"

"Out," Kevin said as he ran down the aisle of desks and out the door.

"Out? That's what my kids say. Out." George said as he stared at the swinging doors.

He looked at the scrap of paper with April's phone number. He started to put it in his pocket when he noticed writing on the back. It read "Mr. X is back." "Who's Mr. X?" he said aloud.

Francois Duer was in a pensive mood as he sat behind the ornate Louis XIV desk in the library of his Paris apartment. The pendulum of the gold clock over the mantle of the fireplace chimed. It was six o'clock. He checked the time with his pocket watch. He stood up, walked to the window behind the desk and peered out on the Boulevard Saint Germain below. He was concerned because things were going well, too well. That always made him nervous. His thoughts were interrupted by a knock on the library door. "Come in," he said as he turned to face the door.

Paul LeMieux entered. "You sent for me, sir?"

71

"Yes, Paul. Please come in," Francois said as he seated himself again behind the desk. "Have you heard from Duvall?"

"He called this morning. He has it."

"Good. What time may we expect him?"

"Early tomorrow afternoon."

"I see. Very well, bring him straight to me. Oh, and Paul, have we heard from Snooky?"

"I talked with her yesterday. She says things are going well, but it will take some time."

"Good. I think I'll stay in tonight, Paul, so you may do as you wish. I will see you at breakfast."

Paul nodded and left.

Kevin walked up the steps of the Palais de Justice, on the Ile de la Cite. The huge, 15th Century building with its stone columns in front was an imposing structure. Kevin entered the building and walked down the marble lined halls to the Paris Division of Interpol. He was immediately directed to the office of the head of the Paris Division, Chief Inspector Marcel Le Pluete. They greeted each other as old friends. Marcel was seated at a well-worn wooden desk with a phone, a pen set and a pad of paper in the center. He was a stern looking man, lean and gaunt with deep-set eyes and a pointed chin. His shirt was neatly pressed but his tie was pulled down. He flipped though files as he talked with Kevin.

"Duer? Francois Duer? Are you sure?" Kevin asked.

"Yes. We are quite certain he is back in Paris. He arrived early today and is staying in an apartment on the Boulevard Saint Germain," Le Pluete said as he rocked back in his chair.

"I thought he was killed in that raid in Athens last year."

"Obviously not. Our people identified him when he went through customs at the airport using a fake passport. They weren't completely certain it was he at the time, but one of my men alertly managed to get his fingerprints. It was Duer."

"Why didn't you have him arrested?"

"He's too big a fish to arrest for the simple use of a false passport. We want to get him on more serious charges."

"Wasn't he involved in that murder in Athens last year?"

"Yes, we believe so, but unfortunately, we can't prove it. Kevin, I'm very curious as to why he came to Paris. He knows we want him, yet he's willing to take this risk."

"That's not like him, unless the stakes are very high." Kevin pointed out.

"Yes. That's why I am giving you the assignment to find out why he's here. After all, you are the best undercover man we have." Le Pluete got up from his chair and sat on the edge of the desk only a few feet from Kevin. "Kevin, my friend, I have a hunch he's up to something very big. I don't know what it is, but my instincts tell me that if we play our cards right, we can, at last, put him away for a long time."

Le Pluete crossed back behind his desk and picked up the thick file folder and held it out. "This is the latest information we have on Duer. I'd like you to read the file, but it must stay here. I'll leave you to your reading." Le Pluete walked to the door. "You may take notes, but be careful with them."

After Le Pluete left, Kevin sat down at the desk and began reading. Much of what was in the files was information Kevin already knew - Duer had been implicated in several international crimes: smuggling, murder, espionage, etc., but there was no direct proof of his personal involvement. He always had a person who acted as a buffer to take the responsibility if something went wrong. Duer had the reputation of being one of the most cunning masterminds of international crime. He also had never been arrested or put on trial by any country in Europe or Africa.

Duer had arrived in Paris from Algiers and was staying in a large apartment at 115 Boulevard Saint Germain which was owned by an Italian bicycle corporation. His passport was German under the name of Henrich von Dure (not a very clever alias, Kevin thought). The apartment was being watched 24 hours a day by Interpol. He had not left the apartment since he arrived. "Not much to go on," Kevin said aloud.

CHAPTER THIRTEEN

Duvall sat in a coach compartment with several other passengers. He felt good that he had gotten away cleanly from St. Tropez. Now all he had to do was give the book to Duer and get his money, then he would be rich. As the train slowed for a stop at Orleans, the other passengers in his compartment got up to get off the train. Duvall noticed that one man's wallet dropped to the floor. Duvall couldn't resist. With his foot, he slowly pushed the wallet under his seat. He picked up his newspaper and began reading. The man did not seem to notice his wallet was missing, and when the train stopped, he got off. Duvall waited until the train started again before reaching down and putting the wallet in his coat pocket. Pocket money, he mused.

It was a cool, crisp, Sunday afternoon. It looked as if it might rain, so April wore her raincoat and a floppy hat she loved.

As she walked along the crowded street, April shifted her tote bag from one shoulder to the other. There were several booksellers' booths and artist displays set up for the day along the street that ran parallel to the Seine River.

She was in a good mood even though occasionally she was jostled by the large number of people who crowded along the Quay near the Pont Neuf. The book sellers had their books all neatly set out on tables, and the artists had their paintings and sketches prominently displayed. She looked at her watch. Nearly two. She decided to keep looking for another hour.

Duvall stepped off the train at the Gare De Austerlitz station in Paris and looked around. He carefully tucked the book wrapped in brown paper into his coat pocket and began walking toward the exit. The station was crowded. He was anxious to get rid of the incriminating evidence of the murder of Andre Du Pypes.

When he emerged from the train station, he went to the taxi stand, pulled out the wallet he had 'found', and began taking the money out of it.

A policeman standing near the taxi stand looked over at Duvall. He frowned and pulled a flyer he'd been given that morning out of his coat. It had a picture of Duvall and a headline that read "Wanted for Questioning" He looked at Duvall. He was sure it was the same man. Duvall saw the policeman looking at him and jumped into a taxi. The policeman yelled, but the cab had already pulled away from the curb.

It took only a few moments for the policeman to call for help. Within minutes, a patrol car had spotted Duvall's taxi. With sirens screaming, they began to chase the taxi. Hearing the sirens, Duvall's driver wanted to stop, but Duvall pulled out his gun and held it to the driver's head. "Just drive." He said. The driver pushed the accelerator to the floor.

As the taxi and the two police cars approached the Pont Neuf bridge, the traffic became congested. The police were gaining on Duvall's taxi because traffic moved aside to let them through.

Suddenly, Pepe ordered the driver to stop. He jumped out before the cab came to a complete halt.

Pepe ran across the street and into the crowd of people walking along the quay.

Seconds later, two police cars were beside the cab. The driver pointed to the direction Pepe had gone. Three policemen got out of the cars and started racing across the street in pursuit of Duvall.

Pepe ran through the milling crowd, pushing people aside. A crowd was gathered around a painter's booth watching him draw. They blocked the entire path. Pepe burst into this crowd, and pushed several people down as he forced his way through. Once past this crowd, he slowed down and tried to mingle with the people, but the police were shouting and people were moving aside. He had to start running again.

April paid the book seller and took the small book, wrapped in brown paper, from him. As she turned to walk away, a man came from out of nowhere. He was running right at her! She tried to avoid him, but they collided. Her tote bag, her book, Duvall's book, April and Duvall all went flying head over heels. April crashed into a display of paintings. Duvall ran into the corner of a book stall. Books came crashing down on him. Duvall got up quickly. He saw the package wrapped in brown paper, picked it up and continued running.

April was helped to her feet by a few passers by. She wasn't hurt, but her hose were torn and the contents of her tote bag were strewn everywhere. She began picking them up. Others helped out, too.

She grabbed her purse first, thankful that someone hadn't taken off with it. People everywhere gathered up her belongings and helped her put them into her tote bag. The bookseller saw the book wrapped in brown paper lying on the ground and put it into her tote bag.

Moments later, the police came running by and nearly ran over April again. She got out of the way just in time. She brushed herself off and decided to go back home.

LeMieux ushered a sweaty, bedraggled Pepe Duvall into Duer's library. Duvall's coat was torn and he was out of breath.

Duer looked up. "What happened to you?"

"It is a long story, Monsieur Duer."

"Well? Out with it. Do you have the book or not?" Duer demanded holding out his hand.

Duvall reached inside his coat and pulled out the book wrapped in brown paper. He put it on the desk in front of Duer.

"As promised, Monsieur Duer," he said happily.

Without another word, Duer opened the package and stared at it. "What is this? Some kind of a joke?" Duer barked and held up the book in front of Duvall. Pepe, completely exhausted from escaping the police, just stood there staring.

Duer read the title of the book - "<u>Authentic Recipes From the French Countryside</u>?!"

Duvall went pale as Duer threw the small book at him. He began shaking.

April tossed her coat and the tote bag on the bed and went into the bathroom to clean up. The book, still wrapped in brown paper, tumbled out of her tote bag onto the floor.

CHAPTER FOURTEEN

April was just finishing her make-up when the doorbell rang. She came out of the bathroom, and as she was pulling her dress over her head, her foot kicked the package in the plain brown wrapper under the bed. "I'm coming Jean Pierre," she called as she looked at herself in the full-length mirror and straightened her clinging black cashmere dress that was cut low, but not too low she felt. She fluffed up her hair. Not perfect, she thought, but it'll have to do. She greeted Jean Pierre at the door.

"You look magnificent," he gushed. April turned to get her purse when something caught Jean Pierre's eye. "Except, my darling, you forgot to zip up your dress."

"Oh, sorry. Would you mind?" she asked

"Not at all," Jean Pierre said as he came up behind her. She had a marvelous back, he observed, as he pulled the zipper up slowly. He really wanted to pull it down, but it was too soon.

"Where are we going?" she asked.

"Café de Flore. A charming little café on the Left Bank. Somewhat touristy, but they say Jean-Paul Sartre and Simone de Beauvoir met there to discuss existentialism. I think you'll enjoy it."

The black Rolls Royce pulled up to the entrance of Café de Flore on the Boulevard St. Germain. Francois Duer climbed out followed by his shadow, Paul LeMieux. They strolled into the restaurant officiously.

A block down the street, Kevin pulled his Citron to the curb. "Oh great, he's going there for dinner. It'll take four hours," he said in a low voice. He settled down for a long wait.

Twenty minutes later a taxi pulled up in front of the restaurant. Jean Pierre got out and helped April out. As he paid the taxi fare, April looked around at the activity on the boulevard.

Kevin sat up straight in his seat. "What the hell is she doing there with that son-of-a-bitch Jean Pierre?" he said aloud. "I told him to stay away from her!" Kevin watched as April took Jean Pierre's arm as they entered the café. Smoke was coming out of Kevin's ears.

April and Jean Pierre passed by Duer's table. He was talking quietly to Paul. "I won't tolerate it, Paul. Tomorrow morning I want you to go with Duvall to find this woman he bumped into."

"But Francois, he doesn't even know what she looks like. For all we know she could have been a tourist who left town."

"I know, but my instincts tell me when she finds out she has the wrong book, whoever has it will return to the stall where she bought the recipe book. I am seldom mistaken about people's behavior."

Kevin seethed in his seat. He wanted to go into the restaurant and confront Jean Pierre, but he was afraid he might miss Duer. That was his target tonight. Jean Pierre would have to wait.

April sat back in her chair. The dinner had been fabulous, and Jean Pierre was the perfect host. He chose the right wines with each course, his knowledge of the history of Paris was extensive, and he told several fascinating stories about the city and its people.

"And what have you been doing? Did you go to see the book sellers and artists yesterday?"

"Did I! What a time that was."

"Oh?"

"Yes, I got knocked over by some guy running through the crowd and nearly ruined several paintings. Luckily I fell the wrong way."

"I don't understand."

April explained what happened. Jean Pierre was concerned.

"Were you hurt?"

"No, just some torn pantyhose. It was nothing really. Enough about me. Jean Pierre, this dinner has been delightful. I'm very impressed."

"I, too, am impressed."

"Oh?"

"Your grasp of the French language is excellent. You ordered perfectly."

"Well, I must admit I have been working hard on it. I have a marvelous tutor from the Sorbonne. He's a real taskmaster, but he's a fascinating old fellow. Do you by chance know Professor Montrer?"

"No. I don't believe so."

"Well, you seem to know most everyone else."

"It 'goes with the territory' as you Americans say."

"I'm planning to go to the Musee D'Orsay tomorrow. I understand they have a collection of Monet on display. I love his paintings."

"Why go to the museum? Why not visit his home in Giverny?"

"Is it far?"

"It's just outside Paris a few miles. I go there frequently. Would you like to go?"

"You bet! When?"

"Well, I am tied up for the next few days, but we could go on Thursday."

"That'd be wonderful," April said as she put her hand on top of his. "Let's drink to Monet."

They raised their glasses and April drained her glass. She was feeling no pain, and Jean Pierre was completely aware of her condition. Just a few more toasts and things might get very interesting.

Duer pulled the napkin out from under his chin and pushed back his chair. "How is Snooky doing?"

"She should have the delivery ready by early next week."

"Good. At least one thing is going right. Get the car, Paul," he ordered. Paul got up quickly as Duer drained the last drops from his wine glass. I will get that book, he thought, one way or another.

Kevin watched the Rolls pull away from the curb and started his engine. He crept out in traffic and followed at a discreet distance. The Rolls didn't go far until it turned the corner. Kevin was right behind. But to his dismay, only a few minutes later they were back at Duer's apartment. This was a bust. His replacement had arrived early and was parked across the street. Kevin motioned to them that he was going home.

April felt a little more than tipsy when the night air hit her as she and Jean Pierre waited outside the restaurant for a taxi. She began to sway, and he caught her. "Oops," she said. "Sorry. I think it was the last brandy."

"Yes," Jean Pierre said quietly, thinking that it was probably the three before that. She did have expensive taste. He would have to move fast, but no too fast.

By the time he got her to her apartment, however, April was feeling much better. She reached in her purse, pulled out her key and handed it to Jean Pierre. She was happy, at least for the moment. Jean Pierre opened the door. April stepped inside and turned and kissed him. "Tonight was fun, Jean

Pierre. I can't wait to see Giverny." She kissed him again. He was beginning to be aroused when she abruptly stopped, stepped back, said good night, and closed the door.

I'll never understand women, Jean Pierre thought as he walked toward the elevator.

April wobbled over to the French doors and opened them. It was a cool night, and she shivered when she stepped out on the terrace. She looked out over the shining city and took a deep breath. It was almost too much for her. She stumbled backward and ended up sitting on the floor looking at the view through the wrought iron railing. She smiled, crossed her legs, and sat there mesmerized by the city lights.

Kevin climbed the stairs to his apartment. He was tired and angry that his tailing of Duer didn't pay off. When he got to his door, it was open a crack. He was immediately suspicious. Carefully, he pulled his Glock .38 from the holster in the small of his back and with one foot, he carefully pushed the door open. A woman was bending over the bed pulling things out of her suitcase. From behind, Kevin knew instantly who she was. The long shapely legs and marvelously rounded hips were no secret to him.

"Suzette?" he said as he quietly closed the door. "What are you doing here?"

Dropping the clothes in her hand, Suzette slowly turned around. "Good evening, Kevin," she said in a low husky voice. She flipped her long, Beaujolais-colored hair back away from her face. Her green eyes seemed to penetrate the wall behind him. She was even more beautiful than he last remembered her. She wore a black jersey skirt and a white form-fitting short sleeved sweater both of which revealed every sensuous curve, even in the dim light.

She made no effort to go to him. "Put down that gun, Kevin, you can be so dramatic sometimes."

Kevin had forgotten he had it. He jammed the gun back into its holster. "So what brings you to my low rent hovel?"

"Inspector Le Pluete called me in on the Duer thing."

"Why?"

"Maybe he thought we should be together again. I am your wife, aren't I?" Suzette took a step toward him.

"That was only a cover."

"Still, we make a great team. At least we used to."

Suzette flashed a crooked smile and took a step toward him.

"Until you got me shot!" Kevin took a step - backward.

"That wasn't my fault. If you'd have listened," she said as she kept coming toward him.

"You were the one who didn't listen, you just kicked the fucking door in, and --," he said backing away.

"I thought you were in back of me!" she interrupted.

"How could I have been in back of you when you pushed me in?" he said now holding his ground.

She sidled up to him. The two now stood nose to nose. Neither spoke. Neither took their eyes off the other's eyes. The game was afoot.

The staring contest. It was the old days all over again.

The silence was deafening. I won't let her get the best of me this time, Kevin vowed to himself.

Suzette smiled to herself, I got him! She mused.

Kevin heard it, but he didn't see it.

Suzette saw it, but she didn't move.

The fly looked for a safe landing place. He circled around behind Kevin, then suddenly swooped over Kevin's head and made a perfect six point landing on his nose. His eyes peered directly into Kevin's.

Kevin fought to restrain himself, to keep the staring contest going.

Suzette struggled to keep her composure.

The fly had an itch and shuffled his legs.

Beads of sweat broke out on Kevin's forehead. It tickled. He swallowed hard.

Suzette just couldn't contain herself any longer. With one swift movement, she flicked the fly off Kevin's nose and broke out in convulsions of laughter. Kevin quickly rubbed his itching nose, then, he too, had to laugh. "Gottcha!" he said triumphantly.

"Do you know how silly you looked?" Suzette said as she backed up and flopped on the bed. "Your eyes crossed!"

"But I kept my self control."

"Is that what it was? I thought you were going to keel over."

"It itched."

Suzette snickered, "I'll bet," and she laughed even harder.

"All right. All right. It wasn't that funny," Kevin said as he pulled off his jacket and threw it on the chair by the window.

"Yes, it was," she said with tears running down her soft cheeks.

"You never change," he said sitting on his coat.

"You always do. That's what makes you so interesting."

Kevin took the gun and holster out of the small of his back and dropped it on his desk. "Okay, so what's the plan?"

"You tell me. I just got here. Who is this Duer? And what are we supposed to do about him?" she said sitting up. Her skirt was up to her navel revealing her high cut thong panties of black lace.

Kevin's heart raced, but he wasn't about to say anything. It was a good view. "I'm surprised you don't know about him. Francois Duer is a big time, international crook. He has his hands in a lot of things, and has for a long time. The problem is neither the police nor Interpol has ever gotten anything on him that would stick. He's very careful."

"So what are we supposed to do?"

"Catch him in the act."

"Of what?"

"I don't know."

Suzette frowned. She stood up, pulled down her skirt and began to pace. "Great. So let me get this straight. We have a perp, but we don't know what he's up to? Our job is to catch him in the act, but we don't know what act. Sounds screwy to me."

"Le Pluete is convinced he's up to something big or he wouldn't be in Paris, he'd be back home in Algiers," Kevin explained.

"Algiers?"

"That's where he is supposedly headquartered. He was born there."

"Nothing else to go on?"

"Nope. Oh, he came in on a phoney passport and calls himself Dure. A lousy alias if you ask me. Anyway, he's set up in an apartment owned by an Italian bicycle company that has connections with the Mafia."

"He's working for them?"

"I don't think so. He's always been a loner. I think he just called in a chit for the apartment."

"Is he alone?"

"No, he has a bodyguard, Paul LeMieux, who is also staying at the apartment."

"What do we know about him?"

"Not much. He is a small time crook, B&E, theft, assault. He served a year for beating a guy. That was seven years ago. Since then he seems to be clean."

"So where do we begin?"

"We keep an eye on him."

"That's it? Kevin. There is no case, no starting point. I think this is a waste of time."

"Could be, but you know Le Pluete. Once he sets his mind, we have to go along."

Suzette threw up her hands in disgust and returned to her unpacking.

"What are you doing?"

"Unpacking, obviously," she said as she took some of her clothes and went to his small closet and began moving his clothes around.

"You can't stay here."

"I have to. We have to keep up the cover. I understand you've kept it up."

"I just didn't bother to tell people I'd gotten a divorce."

"So we're still married. At least everyone thinks we are," she said taking the last of her underwear out of the bag and squeezing it into one of his drawers. "God, I wish you'd get a bigger place." Suzette closed the bag and put it on the floor and began to take off her clothes. "I need a shower. The train from Marseilles was hot and crowded."

He watched as she slipped her skirt off, then pulled her sweater over her head revealing two perfect breasts which were stuffed into a white lace bra at least two sizes too small. They looked as if they were anxious to get free. Suzette unhooked her bra, and they burst forth in all their glory topped off by two very pink nipples. They never ceased to amaze Kevin. She pulled off her lace thong panties and threw them on the bed. "Join me?" she asked with a hint of a smile which Kevin didn't see because his eyes were focused elsewhere. Suzette turned and walked into the bathroom.

"Damn her," Kevin said as he began to unbutton his shirt.

CHAPTER FIFTEEN

The drop of dew clung desperately to the eave. Below it was a woman sitting on her terrace. At last, the dewdrop could hold on no longer and fell on the bridge of the woman's nose.

April woke up with a start. She was still sitting in the same position she had been when she fell asleep the night before, outside on the terrace floor, her legs were crossed and her back was supported by the door jamb of the French Doors. Dawn was breaking and she could see the long shadow the Eiffel Tower threw across the city at 5:45 A.M.. She tried to get up but her legs were stuck. She pulled with all her might and finally freed her left leg. Then she pulled on the right to straighten it out. It was numb! She tried to stand up but she couldn't. Oh, god, she thought, I'm paralyzed.

It took nearly five minutes of rubbing to get the circulation back in her legs. Then she slowly stood up. Her knees were weak, but it was the pain in her ankles that killed her. She hobbled into the bedroom and flopped down on the bed. She wasn't sure she'd ever be able to get up again.

Kevin slowly opened one eye. All he could see was Suzette's hand across the bridge of his nose. She must've rolled over during the night, he thought. He gently pulled her hand off his face and placed it where it should be, on her face.

Suzette stirred, rolled over, and put her backside up against Kevin's. He was almost pushed onto the floor. I need a bigger bed, Kevin thought. He rolled over on his back and stared at the ceiling. His mind always began the day before his body was ready. He thought about the article he was writing, Suzette, what Duer was up to, April's behavior at dinner, Jean Pierre, Julian, and his stomach in the next hour.

Finally, at 7:30, he slid out of bed, made coffee on the hot plate, and took a shower. Suzette was still sound asleep when he left for the office.

April stared at the ceiling. Her mind was racing, too. She couldn't believe Kevin was married, but he was. She thought of Jean Pierre. He was nice, but. Finally, she decided to visit the Musee D'Orsay anyway, even if she was going to Giverny with Jean Pierre. She got up, took a long hot shower and washed her hair. She felt a lot better. She dressed and then looked for her other shoe. She got down on her hands and knees and looked under the bed. There was her shoe, and her recipe book, still wrapped in the brown paper. She put on her other shoe and took the book into the living room and laid it on the desk. She'd have plenty of time to look through it later.

She was just about out the door when the phone rang. She crossed to the desk and answered, "Hello."

"Miss Mason, this is Kevin O'Connor."

April's face dropped. Not him! "Yes?" she said icily.

"I was just checking up on you. Is there anything I can do to make your stay more enjoyable?"

April wanted to say 'get lost', but she controlled her emotions. "No, thank you. I'm managing quite well."

"Perhaps we could have lunch today."

"I'm afraid that's out of the question. I'm going to the Musee D'Orsay for the day."

"All right. But, please don't hesitate to call if you need anything."

"Thank you, Mr. O'Connor. I'll remember that. Goodbye." And 'good riddance' she wanted to say as she hung up.

Kevin frowned as he put the phone down. She was icy, he thought. He picked up the cable that had arrived from Julian that morning. He reread it. "Have you found a man for April yet? It's very important, you know. Get back to me soonest. Julian" Kevin sighed. He had more irons in the fire than a blacksmith. Not only that, but he didn't get much sleep the night before, Suzette was very "hungry."

Well, first things first, he told himself, and went back to writing his article for the afternoon edition. Suddenly he stopped in mid-sentence. He had an idea. He walked into George's office.

"Hey, George," Kevin called as he entered the office.

George was staring out his window half asleep in the warm morning sun. Kevin startled him. He nearly fell out of his chair.

"When's that big to do for the American Ambassador?" Kevin continued.

"What?" George said as he regained his balance and turned in his swivel chair.

"You know that fancy dress ball for the American Ambassador."

"Oh, that. Tomorrow night. Don't tell me you want to go."

"Suzette got back in town last night."

"No wonder you look like hell," George said with a twisted grin.

"Thanks. I thought maybe I should take her out some place fancy to celebrate. Any chance you could arrange it?"

"Perhaps. But only if you do a piece on it, too."

"Might make a good story. Thanks." Kevin started out the door and then stopped and turned back. "Hey, I just got an idea, why don't you and your wife invite April Mason? I think she'd like it, and Julian would appreciate it, too."

"Good idea."

"Great." He started out again, but George stopped him.

"Only one problem. I lost her phone number."

"Again? Why am I not surprised?" Kevin crossed over to George's desk, grabbed a piece of paper, and wrote her number on it. "Now don't lose this one. Oh, I just talked to her, she's going to a museum today, so you'll have to call early this evening."

"Got it."

Kevin smiled to himself as he walked back to his office. She'll never refuse George, he mused.

Suzette strolled into the bistro as if she owned it. Heads turned as the stunning redhead in the tight white dress wormed her way though the crowded tables toward Kevin's usual booth in the back.

Kevin was in a heavy conversation with Victor Lizst, a handsome, oily looking man, with arched eyebrows and sunken cheeks. He was in his mid-thirties, thin and well-dressed. "So it's a deal?" Kevin asked.

Victor eyed Kevin cautiously. "I want half now."

"I thought you might," Kevin said as he put an envelope on the table.

Victor quickly opened it and counted the bills. "All right. It sounds like fun."

"Tomorrow night. The ticket will be at the door. Be there at seven sharp."

Victor stood up and nodded to Kevin. "Seven. I'll be there."

As Victor walked away, Suzette saw Kevin sitting alone and waved. As Victor walked past Suzette, she turned and stared after him, then shrugged and joined Kevin at his booth. Victor stopped at the door and looked back at Suzette. He had a quizzical look on his face as he went out the door.

"Don't I know that guy?" Suzette asked.

"No," Kevin said emphatically. "Let's eat. I'm starved. I'll tell you all about it during lunch."

"It's hopeless, Monsieur Duer," Paul said as he crossed to the desk. "I managed to find the book seller, but he couldn't even describe the woman Duvall knocked down. She was wearing a raincoat and a hat. All he could say was she was an American with dark hair."

"What about other people?"

"A couple saw the collision, but no one knows who she was."

"All right, Paul. I still think she'll come back to the book seller's stall this weekend. Stake it out. Perhaps we'll get lucky."

"Very well."

"And you say that Snooky will have the money ready in a week?"

"Yes. She wants to make one final check, and print a few samples for us to see," Paul said. "I'm to call her this afternoon at three."

"Splendid. At least one thing is going well. It's always good to have variety in your life. You know?"

Paul smiled, "Yes. Personally, Monsieur Duer, if I may speak bluntly, I think this book thing is a farce. People have been looking for this so-called treasure for more than two hundred years. I believe that if it actually existed, someone would have found it by now."

"Ah, Paul, you are such a pragmatist. Perhaps you are right, but I am a dreamer, and I still want to pursue it. If the book cannot be found, that is what fate intended, but I have a funny feeling that we will triumph."

"I can't go against your instincts, Francois. You have never been wrong before."

"I always listen to my heart. How is Duvall?"

"Very unhappy. He wants to leave."

"We may need him. I think we'll be his host for a while longer."

"As you wish."

"When you talk to Snooky, make sure she is on schedule."

"Yes, sir."

Paul went out. Duer turned his chair around and looked out the window. He was feeling very sure of himself. He had had this feeling many times before when he was on the verge of a big score. It was a good sign.

"You're a babysitter?" Suzette said a little too loud.

"Not exactly. I'm doing Julian a favor," Kevin said meekly as he picked at his food. "I need to keep him happy. I still want to get a book published."

"Why don't you give up this book writing thing? You never work on your 'books' anyway."

"I do. Just not all the time."

"I think you're nuts. You always have to have twenty things going at the same time. Now you're a babysitter?! Come on, Kevin."

"It's not going to interfere with anything. Besides, I don't think she likes me. She's strange."

"Strange because she doesn't like you? That makes a lot of people strange."

"Look, I promised I'd help, and I'm gonna keep my promise. We're going to this affair, and you're going to be a good little girl and help me."

"I have a bad feeling about all this."

April returned to her apartment with her arms loaded with packages. It wasn't fun going to a museum alone, so she had decided to do some shopping at the boutiques. It cost her a fortune, but she had a great time. She wanted to share her enthusiasm with someone, so she decided to call Jean Pierre. He wasn't in, and wasn't expected for another day or so. She had forgotten he was going out of town for a few days. The girl at his office wouldn't give April his home phone number. Disappointed, April hung up.

She looked at her packages and smiled. "Time to give myself a fashion show." She began unwrapping the boxes.

Michelle "Snooky" Jardin bent over her architect's drawing table and peered through a powerful magnifying glass at a large lead plate fastened securely to the table. Beside the plate was a wooden case which held a wide array of metal instruments with tiny sharp edges. She swivelled around on her stool to another architect's table at the same height and looked into another magnifying glass at the Algerian 1000 Dinar note expertly pinned to the table. She smiled to herself and swivelled back to the other table. She selected a small etching tool and looking again through the magnifying glass, painstakingly, artfully, made a tiny change to the lead plate beneath the glass.

She sat back, stretched, got off her stool and walked to a counter nearby. She poured herself a cup of coffee. She added one cube of sugar, and stirred three times.

Michelle was a very petite woman in her late thirties. Her long, black hair was piled high on her head in a tight bun. Her horn-rimmed glasses hid a pair of deep blue eyes, and she wore no make up. Still, she was very attractive, even if she didn't think so. For a small woman, she was perfectly proportioned, a figure most women would envy.

Her laboratory, as she thought of the secret room beneath her antique shop, was as immaculate as an operating room. Everything was in its proper place. The walls were painted white and spotless. The window high on the wall was painted over but still managed to emit some natural light. It was a very sterile environment.

Michelle walked through the only door to the room into the next room which was almost an exact duplicate of the lab. The only things in that room were an old, very polished, cast iron printing press in perfect working order anchored in the center of the room, and a tall, wooden cabinet in the corner.

She passed through that room and through a door which led to a flight of stairs. When she got to the top, she pressed a button, and the wall swung open revealing her office. She went in, turned and reached for a book in the bookcase beside the opening. As she pulled it out, the opening closed. It matched the other bookcases perfectly. It was impossible to see where the hidden door began or ended.

Like her laboratory, her office was meticulously kept. She sat down at her polished teak desk and placed her cup of coffee on a coaster. She opened a file drawer and took out a manila folder. She scanned the papers inside. Satisfied, she closed the file and put it away. She looked at her watch. It was time. She waited. Then, precisely at three, the phone rang. "Paul?"

"Yes."

"You may come at one o'clock one week from Monday. They will be ready," she said in a soft but firm voice. She hung up the phone and sipped her coffee. This would be a very good year.

April slipped her new dress off over her head and hung it on a hanger in the armoire. She put on her terry cloth robe and went into the kitchen. She poured herself a glass of Chardonnay, and went into the living room. She saw the book, still wrapped, on the desk. She picked it up, sat down on the couch and pulled her legs under her. She sipped the cool wine, put the glass on the coffee table and looked at the book. But, before she had a chance to unwrap it, the phone rang. She went to her desk and picked it up, "Hello."

"Miss Mason, this is George Lamont of the Paris Gazette. I'm a friend of Julian's."

"Oh, yes, he spoke of you. How nice of you to call."

"Well, I've been meaning to call earlier, but you know how things are."

"Of course," she said, not knowing what he was talking about.

"I was wondering if you had plans for tomorrow evening. My wife and I would like to treat you to a rather special affair."

"Why, that's very nice of you Mr. Lamont."

"George, please. Anyway, there is a big reception and dinner for the American Ambassador at the Meurice Hotel tomorrow evening, and I, we, thought you might enjoy it."

She knew she had to be good to Julian's friends, and Jean Pierre wasn't due back until Thursday so they could go to Giverny. She decided to go, after all it might be fun. "It sounds wonderful," she said brightly.

"Great! It starts at seven, what say we pick you up about six-thirty?"

"That's good for me. Oh, tell me, is this a formal affair?"

"Black tie. I hope that's all right."

"Well, I don't have a thing to wear, but I will have," she said with a chuckle. "It'll be a good excuse to go shopping."

George laughed. "You sound just like my wife."

April cringed.

"I'm sure looking forward to meeting you. Julian has said some pretty great things about you."

"Oh, he's just a dear."

"Sure is. Well, see you tomorrow night at six-thirty. You're at?"

"Oh, yes. 75 rue Danielle Casanova. I'll be waiting in the lobby."

Great. See you then. Bye"

April hung up and smiled. He sounds like a real loser, she thought, but it isn't every day you get to meet the American Ambassador to France. It'll be an adventure, she decided.

She curled back up on the couch, and began unwrapping what she thought was her new recipe book.

CHAPTER SIXTEEN

The moment she began to unwrap the book, April knew something was wrong. The book inside the brown wrapping paper was not her recipe book. It was an old, very old, book. The leather cover was coming apart, and the pages were thin and brown with age. They were very delicate. Carefully she finished unwrapping the book. As she opened the first page, a small piece of the page crumpled in her fingers. Slowly she turned to the next page. In the middle of the page was the name of the book <u>Recit de la Revolution</u>, (Tales of the Revolution) and near the bottom of the page was a date, 1797.

April painstakingly carried the book, still in its wrapper, to her desk and turned on the lamp. She carefully laid it on the desk and sat down. She could see that even though the pages were fragile, the print was still legible. It was written in French with a very old typeface. The next page looked like a dedication. She slowly translated the passage. After a half an hour she thought it said, "*To the People of Paris and the World. These are my recollections of the events of the Reign of Terror so all will know the horror of those times.*" Below was the author's name, Charles Du Pypes.

Her first instinct was to take the book back to where she bought it. The book seller had obviously made a mistake. It seemed to be a very rare book. Little did she know that it was the last remaining copy. But her curiosity overcame her instinct, and she turned to the next page, the Table of Contents. Four stories were listed: *Marie Antoinette and the Committee for Public Safety, Robespierre's Followers, Girondists and the Guillotine,* and *The Aristocrat and the Baker.* She was hooked.

April turned to the first page and began reading. She found the text very difficult, for not only was the book in French, but many of the phrases and words were archaic. Her small French-English dictionary was simply not adequate, and she decided to purchase the best dictionary she could find the next morning. It took her nearly four hours to translate the first ten pages, but what she read, she found fascinating. She could hardly sleep that night.

Suzette was dog-tired when she got back to Kevin's apartment the next morning. She'd been assigned to watch Duer's apartment all night. Kevin was shaving when she walked in to the bathroom. She stood behind him and made faces to mimic Kevin as he shaved. He smiled, turned to her and came toward her, his face covered with shaving cream, his lips puckered as if he was going to kiss her. She quickly backed off.

"Chicken," he said as he returned to his shaving.

"I can wait," she said as she flopped down on the bed.

"Anything happen last night?" he asked.

"Yes. The bathroom light went on three times during the night. He must have a bladder problem."

"That's it?"

"It's all in my report," she said holding a single piece of paper so he could see it in the mirror. "Be a dear and drop it off at Le Pluete's office before you go to work," she said, throwing the report on his desk beside his shirt and sitting down on the bed.

Kevin walked out of the bathroom and began putting on his shirt. "It's too quiet."

"I know, I feel that too," she said.

"However, Duer is reported to be infamous for keeping everything to himself. Unfortunately, that seems to be the secret to his success."

"Are you finished in there?" Suzette asked. "I want to take a shower and sleep for three days."

"All yours," Kevin said as he came out of the bathroom and finished buttoning his shirt. "But don't forget, we're going to that reception tonight," he said as he put on his tie.

Suzette slowly got up from the bed and began taking off her clothes. "Do I have to go?" she asked.

"Got to keep up appearances. Besides, George is looking forward to seeing you."

"Oh, no. George is such a bore. He's always leering at me and making cryptic remarks about how he needs a mistress."

"He's harmless."

"That's just the trouble. I'd like to see his face if I told him I'd go to bed with him. He'd faint," she said as she dropped her bra on the bed and walked up to Kevin. "Would you be jealous?" she asked as she put her arms around him.

"Of George? You've got to be kidding."

"How about Jean-Pierre?"

Kevin's eyes narrowed. "That's none of your business," he said pulling out of her embrace and grabbing his jacket off the chair.

Suzette pulled off her panties and stood with her hands on her hips. "You'd give up all this?"

Kevin looked at her and smiled. "You're subtle. Very subtle. I'll be back at five. Try and be ready on time for once."

"Don't forget my report," she said as she grabbed it off the desk and handed it to Kevin. "Oh, and you'd better call at four and wake me."

"If I think of it," he said taking the paper and opening the door. "Sleep tight." Kevin closed the door.

April's French class went well, and afterward, she asked the meaning of some of the words she'd copied down from the old book.

Professor Montrer raised an eyebrow, "I haven't seen these words in quite some time, Miss Mason. Where did you come across them?"

"In an old book."

"It must be very old. Let me see that list again." He scanned the list. "Many of these phrases haven't been used for at least a hundred years." He translated most of the words for her as she wrote down the meanings. "I have no idea what this is," he said pointing to a word on her list. "May I keep this? I'll try and find the answers to the others."

"Sure. By the way, what is the best French-English dictionary for ancient phrases and words?"

He wrote down the name, "You'll find it at the bookstore just behind the Musee d'Orsay on the rue de L'Universite."

Outside, April went down her 'to do' list for the day. She wanted to get a formal dress for the reception, the dictionary, and a book on the French Revolution. This was more than causal reading. Was it research for a new book? She looked at herself in the store window. She liked what she saw. She smiled at her reflection, nodded, and strolled off with a new spring in her step.

Kevin was lost in thought as he ambled down the street. The Duer case, if there was one, was nothing at this point. There were no clues as to what to look for or what to do. Le Pluete was convinced something was up, but he didn't have the slightest idea of what it was either. The surveillance reports revealed nothing. Duer was just staying home most of the time. He'd go out with his henchman, Paul LeMieux, for dinner once in a while, but they didn't talk to anyone or make any suspicious movements. The only thing that led Kevin to believe something was up being that Duer always seemed in good humor. Laughing crooks are always up to something, he thought to himself.

He stopped at an outdoor café for a cup of coffee. He sat down and the waiter took his order. While he waited, he looked around. The weather was nice and everyone was out walking. It was warm for this time of year, and people were taking advantage of the fresh air. Then, just when the waiter was approaching with his coffee, he saw her. He debated as to whether or not to approach her. Finally, he made up his mind. He took the cup of coffee from the waiter and ambled toward her table.

April was putting several small packages into a large shopping bag as Kevin approached.

"Do you mind if I join you?" Kevin asked.

April looked up. She didn't know what to think.

"I need to talk to you," he said.

She was still thinking when he sat down.

"Shopping, I see," he said cheerfully. Secretly he was wondering what she was thinking. She hadn't said a word.

"Very observant," she said coldly.

"I had to get out of the office. The phones were ringing off the hook. How is your stay in Paris?"

"Fine."

Kevin sensed the bad vibes and steeled himself. "Frankly, I have this feeling you're trying to avoid me. I don't understand why."

April looked into his blue eyes. They seemed to be pleading. He looked like a little boy who thought he'd been bad. Maybe she had been a little hard on him. He couldn't help it if he was married. "I'm sorry," she said, "I don't know. I guess I was just a little disappointed."

"What did I do?"

"Nothing really. I just was surprised."

"About?"

"Look, I know this is silly, and the more I think about it, the sillier I feel. When we first met, frankly, I was attracted to you. You are rather good looking you know."

"Thank you."

"And, I guess I sort of built up this fantasy and let it take over."

"Fantasy?"

"You know, about you and me." She began to talk faster, "Kevin, I let my emotions take over all the time. It's just a fault of mine, I guess. Anyway, I had built this whole thing up in my mind about us and Paris, and there we were in this fancy restaurant, and it was so romantic, and then you told me you were married, and it threw me. I don't know why, but I was hurt, and I guess I lashed out at you. Please forgive me. I mean why I thought that you were single. I don't know. I mean how could you be? Every good looking man is married. I know that. I just went off the deep end."

As she was talking, Kevin watched her hands flailing around, her big brown eyes darting back and forth, trying to avoid his eyes and then going back to them. He felt something drop in the pit of his stomach. He felt sorry for her? No. That wasn't it. He felt pity? No. He felt like reaching out and holding her. Yep, that was it. But he couldn't. He knew he couldn't. But he wanted to.

"Please forgive me," April went on, "I acted like such a fool."

Kevin took her hands. "April, please. It's all right. I forgive you," he said looking into those adorable eyes and stifling every emotion he felt.

"You're sure?" she asked.

"Positive."

"You don't hate me?"

"No. Of course not. I should have told you right off the bat. It's my fault."

"No, it's not. I was the one."

"Truce," he said holding up his hands in mock surrender. "Let's just forget it ever happened. No harm no foul?"

"No harm, no foul," April lied. He had harmed her, at least a little. She decided to try and forget the whole thing. April reached across and took his hand. It was like an electric current racing through him. "Friends?"

"Deal."

April sat back and sipped her coffee. "You know, Kevin, I didn't drink coffee until I came to Paris. But I like this café noir."

"Paris has a way of changing people."

"It's such a fascinating city."

"So what have you been doing?"

She wanted to tell him about her dates with Jean-Pierre, but she remembered Jean Pierre's warning. "Well, I'm brushing up on my French at the Sorbonne with a private tutor, and I've been to a couple of museums, and shopping, of course."

"So I see," he said with a smile that caused a small, but powerful, twinge somewhere in April's heart.

"And guess what," April said recovering from the twinge. "Your boss, George?"

Kevin nodded.

"He and his wife invited me to a reception for the American Ambassador at the Tivoli Gardens tonight."

"Why that old son-of-a-gun, he didn't tell me. I, or rather we, are going to be there, too."

"We?"

"My wife, Suzette is in town for a few days."

"Oh," April felt the disappointment in her voice. Did Kevin notice?

"I want you to meet her," Kevin said.

"That would be wonderful," she said marveling how she covered her insincerity. She looked at her watch. "Oh, look at the time. I have to run. I still have to buy shoes," she said as she quickly got up and began picking up her packages.

Kevin stood up and helped her. "See you tonight, then."

"I'm looking forward to meeting Suzette," she said as she hurried away.

Once on the street, April fought back her tears. Why does he do that to me? I'm a complete idiot! Why can't I accept the fact that he's married? She chided herself. She stopped in front of a store and looked in the window. Shoes, she thought, new shoes, that'll help.

Kevin watched April disappear into the crowd. That feeling in the pit of his stomach was back. I can't fall in love, he told himself, I don't have time.

Kevin's old Citron pulled up at the curb in front of the stately Meurice Hotel. The doorman, in his well-tailored uniform, opened the door for Suzette. When she got out, he gulped. She stood there in a red sequined dress slit up to her hip. It looked like it had been spray painted on her. Every curve said "I wear no underwear." The doorman missed the handle on the door twice, as he watched her approach. When she walked in her red high heels, her hips swayed in a rhythm that every drummer would die for. Her gown was cut very low and her breasts seemed to be floating inside. Walking behind her, Kevin just shook his head as he watched the doorman fumble.

Inside the lavishly decorated ballroom the nearly one hundred guests, decked out in they're finest, milled about with cocktails in hand. Some were already seated at their tables. Kevin stood at the door with Suzette's arm in his. "Remember the plan. We have to make this meeting look like an accident."

"Where is this woman you're babysitting?" Suzette whispered.

"I am not babysitting," Kevin said through clenched teeth.

"Yeah, sure."

Kevin saw Victor talking with two young men and motioned for him to come over. Victor held up one finger, then shook hands with the men and came over to them. He looked very dashing in his perfectly tailored tux. Victor whispered into Kevin's ear. "Zee Tuxedo is extra."

Kevin nodded. "It had better be worth it. Did you read the books?"

"Yes. Well some of them. There were so many."

"Okay, you two, time to play." Suzette interrupted. Kevin introduced Suzette to Victor. They both stared at each other. Both were trying to figure out where they'd met before. Kevin led Suzette and Victor through the crowd. The women clucked.

The men eyed Suzette like some exotic desert. They were stopped several times on their way across the ballroom by people who knew Kevin. He worked the room like a real pro.

Finally, Kevin saw George's table. George was talking April's ear off. His wife Madeline looked bored. There were two empty seats. Kevin grabbed Suzette and the three of them made a beeline for the table. George saw them coming and stood up.

"Kevin, Suzette, how good to see you," George gushed as he came to greet them. Suzette noticed George had already made a mental note of her geography. George gave Suzette a big hug and copped a feel, which he always did. Kevin saw the look of jealousy in April's eyes as she sat there examining Suzette. Madeline got up and hugged Kevin. Kevin introduced Suzette to April.

Suzette held her gloved hand out to April who shook it briefly. "Miss Mason, you are much more than Kevin led me to believe," she cooed as she fought the surprise of April's beauty.

"And you are much more than he led me to believe also," April said. All she could think of was "cheap thrill."

"George, you remember Victor Lizst. He's with the office of international affairs," Kevin said.

George had no idea who Victor was, but he wasn't about to say so. "Why, yes, Victor. It's been a while."

Victor shook George's hand lightly. "Yes, Monsieur Lamont, I believe it was last year at the reception for General Du Shays."

"Right," George said quickly.

"Victor is here by himself tonight, and I thought if you didn't mind, he could sit with us," Kevin interjected.

"Yes. Of course," George said, "I'll have them set another place." He motioned to a waiter.

"Oh, and Victor, I'd like you to meet our distinguished visitor from the United States, this is the author, April Mason," Kevin said stepping aside.

"Enchante, Miss or is it Missus Mason?" Victor said taking her hand and kissing it gallantly.

April was amused. "Miss."

"How fortunate," Victor said, "for all the single men in Paris."

April was intrigued by the handsome man in his tailored tuxedo. Victor was just what she had imagined French men looked like. He was tall, slender, his black hair was brushed back with a small "widow's peak." His Roman nose complimented his thin face and strong jaw line. "Thank you," she said giving him a small nod and big smile.

The waiter returned with a chair which Kevin had him place beside April's and they all took their seats. Kevin and Suzette sat across from April and Victor.

After they had ordered drinks, Victor asked April, "I beg your pardon, Miss Mason, but are you the author of those wonderful mysteries? <u>A Lovely Murder</u> for example?"

"I am. Thank you for asking." April was surprised he knew about her writing.

"I enjoy your writing very much. I am very lucky to meet such a talent."

Kevin saw the look in April's eyes. She was having a good time. Thank God.

Suzette leaned over and whispered to Kevin, "She's quite attractive, but a bit older than I imagined. You must like babysitting her. Do you rock her to sleep?"

"No. And you know damned well what I'm doing. Victor is perfect for her."

"Victor is a putz."

"Look, you promised to help. You know I have to get her fixed up so she'll write again. Victor will come through and that'll be one less worry. Now be supportive for once."

"You and your crazy schemes."

"Suzette," Kevin chided.

"Oh, all right," she said rolling her eyes.

All during dinner Victor and April were deep in conversation. He was charming and complimentary. April was attentive, and found herself laughing out loud on several occasions. She thought he was a little too attentive, but he was a wonderful conversationalist. He seemed well-educated, and told wonderful jokes. By the end of dinner she was captivated by his wit and intelligence.

Victor, on the other hand, was sweating bullets beneath his facade of composure. He worked hard to come up with stories and anecdotes. Whenever he was in doubt as to what to say next, he complimented her or talked about one of her three books he'd scanned. Those ploys always worked. He had to admit she was beautiful in a country sort of way. Bedding her would not be an unpleasant task. The very thought of a long-term relationship, however, had him scared. But, he reminded himself, the money was good, very good.

After dinner, the orchestra began playing, and the dance floor was quickly crowded. April and Victor and George and Madeline got up to dance. When they left the table, Kevin sat there with a smug look on his face. Suzette shook her head, "Pretty proud of yourself aren't you?"

"Perfect. This is going to work out perfectly," Kevin proudly.

Jean Pierre arrived at the reception very late. He'd been in the country and the traffic back into the city was terrible. He went directly to the bar for a drink.

As he stood there looking out at the dance floor he spied April - with Victor Liszt! He was surprised and confused. How did he and she get together? His confusion was quickly cleared up when the music stopped. He watched April and

Victor go back to their table and greet Kevin! So, Kevin was behind this. Jean Pierre arched his eyebrows and grinned. This was going to be a fun evening!

A few minutes later, Kevin kicked Suzette under the table. She kicked him back and stared at him. He nodded toward the other side of the room. Suzette nodded. She'd remembered the plan. She shrugged, rose and dutifully asked April if she wanted to go to the powder room. April grabbed her bag and the two women headed across the dance floor.

Victor and Kevin huddled together. "How's it going?" Kevin wanted to know.

"Bon. She is a magnificent woman, and a wonderful challenge. I like that."

"Great. Keep it up. You two are perfect together."

Victor smiled. "I believe I will enjoy this woman. I know I will enjoy the money."

"Victor, I'll make you a deal. If you get her back to writing and stay with her until her book is finished, I'll double the money."

"Oh, never has one heard such a beautiful promise. I will make you proud, Kevin."

Jean Pierre watched as Kevin and Victor talked. Something was up. He didn't trust Kevin. But why Victor? Then like a bolt of lightning, he burst out laughing. Of course, he said to himself. Kevin is being the 'protector'. How noble.

Both April and Suzette eyed one another out of the corner of their eyes as they stood in front of the large mirror and repaired their make up. It was like two fighters sizing up the competition.

"So, how do you like Victor, Miss Mason?" Suzette cooed.

"Victor is -- very interesting."

"That's all? Interesting?"

"Well, frankly, Suzette, at first I thought he was a bit on the slick side, but I think he was just nervous. Once he calmed down, he was very charming."

"And attractive?"

"Yes, and on the dance floor, sexy."

"Sexy? Victor? Well, well."

"I know. I was surprised, too. So, how long have you and Kevin been married?"

Suzette winced. Here it comes, she thought. "Four years."

"Isn't it hard for you to be working all over France and leaving Kevin alone?"

"Yes, it's hard on both of us, but our reunions are well worth it," Suzette said with a smile that meant only one thing.

April felt a pang of jealousy. Why did she feel that way?

April's hesitation did not go unnoticed by Suzette who wondered why April was thrown. Could it be April was interested in Kevin? She'd put a stop to that right now. "Of course, my work is only temporary. I am hoping to get a position at the Louvre in a few weeks. And, of course, Kevin and I want to settle down and have a family."

April's heart sank. Not only was Suzette beautiful and very sexy, but she was deeply in love with Kevin. Whatever thought she might have had about a relationship with Kevin went right out the window.

Suzette knew that would do it. The kid thing always worked, she mused. One look at April and she was certain.

When April and Suzette returned to the table, Kevin noticed that April seemed different. He'd watched as she crossed the room, her shoulders sagged. Then as she approached the table, she seemed to pull herself up, and put on a phony smile. What had happened in the powder room?

April took Victor's hand and led him out on the dance floor. She was determined to have fun and to hell with Kevin O'Connor.

She held Victor tight and whispered in his ear. He pulled back and laughed. She laughed, too, a little too loud.

Kevin pulled his chair up tight to Suzette's. "What did you two talk about in the powder room?" Kevin asked.

"Oh, just girl talk. Nothing interesting. Oh, she did say she thought Victor was sexy."

"Sexy?"

"Very sexy."

Kevin nodded, "A perfect match. The plan is working."

"Let's dance," Suzette said, pulling him up. She took his arm, and dragged him out onto the dance floor. When she spotted April, she put her arms around Kevin and pressed her pelvis in tight. "I love it when you hold me," she said biting his ear making sure April had a good view.

April watched Kevin and Suzette over Victor's shoulder. In reaction to Suzette's bite on Kevin's ear, April pulled Victor closer and snuggled her head in tight. Victor was having fun.

Suzette spun Kevin around so that April could see her put her hand on his butt.

April saw, and she did the same to Victor who jumped with both surprise and delight. Suddenly, the music stopped. April made up her mind. She whispered in Victor's ear, "Let's get out of here and go some place fun."

"I know just the place," Victor said. "Tres romantic!"

"Perfect," April said.

Jean Pierre watched the antics from behind a pillar. He saw April and Victor go back to the table, get April's purse, shake hands with George and Madeline, then Kevin and Suzette. They were leaving. He put his drink down and went out the front door. Several people were milling around and he blended into the crowd just as April and Victor came out and hailed a taxi. The doorman helped them in the cab and it sped off. Jean Pierre sidled up to the doorman, flashed a 100-Euro Note, put it in his hand, and asked, "Where was that last cab going?"

"The Ritz Club."

"Merci. A taxi please."

Jean Pierre arrived at Ritz Hotel and headed for the posh Ritz Club. On his way, he made a phone call. He was almost giddy as he stepped out of the phone booth.

Jean Pierre had a membership to the private club and was greeted by name by two lovely hostesses, one of whom escorted him to the small bar. He looked for an advantageous spot to watch the fun.

"But why are we following them?" Suzette asked as she and Kevin stepped out of the taxi in front Ritz Hotel a few minutes later.

"I'm just curious. And, I've got a lot invested here."

Jean Pierre ducked back behind the curtains near the bar when heard Kevin and Suzette coming down the stairs. They were shown to a table in the corner of an alcove near the small, dance floor.

It was quiet time in the trendy club. The room was smoke-filled and crowded. The music played softly as lovers danced to the cool jazz. Victor held April close. "Isn't this much better?"

"Much," April said, her eyes stinging from the smoke.

"I am curious. Is everything you write from your own imagination or your real life?"

"A little of both. Why?"

"Frankly, as a man, I find your love scenes extremely graphic. I find myself envying the men in your books."

"Envying?"

"Yes, your descriptions of your characters' lovemaking are so, how you say, imaginative, yet so real. I can almost feel the rhythm of their bodies, smell their perspiration, taste the woman's lips. I never knew such passion could be put on paper."

"Why thank you, Victor. That's one of the nicest compliments I've ever had."

"Tell me, ma cherie, does that come from the experience of April Mason the woman, or from the mind of April Mason the author?"

April looked up at him, and gently kissed him on the lips. "Like the taste?"

"Just as I imagined it to be, sweet, yet hungry."

"Famished," she said, pulling him close and pressing up against him. They swayed in rhythm to the music, looking deeply into each other's eyes.

"What did I tell you. It's a perfect match!" Kevin whispered to Suzette as they watched the couple from their table in a dark corner.

Victor looked down into April's eyes. This was actually working he thought. He slowly moved toward her lips. "I, too, am famished," he said as he kissed her passionately.

In mid-kiss, a hand reached out from the crowd, grabbed Victor's shoulder and roughly spun him around. April flew out of Victor's embrace.

Victor was face to face with a tall, muscular, handsome, blond, Germanic young man with blue eyes that were hard as steel.

He held Victor's shoulder in a death grip.

"You bitch!" the man screamed. "You whore!"

Victor went paler than his white shirt. Sweat popped out on his forehead, and he stared in horror.

"I go out of town for just three days and look what you do to me! A woman!" He pointed at April. "A woman for god's sake!" The man slapped Victor hard across the face, but Victor just stood there stunned.

"But Gunther, my sweet, you don't understand!" Victor managed to say.

"Gunther?" Kevin whispered to Suzette.

"I don't have to understand. I can see with my own eyes," Gunther said, pointing at April who was by now cowering from Gunther's finger. A hush fell over the club.

"I wasn't cheating on you! It was just a job!"

"A job?" April said.

"Oh, shit," Kevin mumbled.

"I keep you in everything. If you wanted money you should have asked me! What is it to be, me or her?" Gunther yelled again pointing at April. She backed away further.

112

Victor turned and looked at April then back at Gunther, then back to April. "Sorry tart," he said.

Gunther turned on his heels and started toward the stairs. Victor chased after him. "I'm sorry, Gunther. Please forgive me."

Kevin jumped up and approached Victor, but Victor held his hand up as he was running toward the stairway, "Kevin, I'm sorry. Wait, Gunther!"

Kevin threw up his hands.

As Victor and Gunther passed the bar, Jean Pierre was hunched over a small table laughing so hard tears were rolling down his face. "I'm sorry Gunther," he giggled as Gunther went out the door. Victor was trying hard to keep up.

Suzette walked up beside Kevin. "Perfect match, huh?"

"How was I to know?"

Kevin felt a tap on his shoulder. He turned and ran smack into a well-placed right cross that knocked him back into Suzette and the two of them fell flat on the floor. April stood over them. "You son-of-a-bitch! Get out of my life and stay out!" She walked out to applause.

As Kevin was sitting on the floor, he caught a glimpse of Jean Pierre sneaking up the stairs following after April. "Jean Pierre! Come back here, you bastard!" He tried to get up, but was still dazed.

Jean Pierre watched April's taxi pull away. The time was right! He hailed a cab and used the words he loved to say, "Follow that cab!"

CHAPTER SEVENTEEN

Kevin, shook his head, and rubbed his jaw to make sure it wasn't broken. He was still a little wobbly. Suzette got up and stood in front of him, hands on hips, and laughed. "Perfect, huh?" she said.

"Did you see him?" Kevin asked her.

"Who?"

"Jean Pierre."

"No. Was he here?"

"I think I saw him."

"When?"

"Just now. Going out the door."

"That punch must've dimmed your eyesight. I didn't see him."

"Well, you were on the floor too."

"And your point?"

"Never mind." He glowered at her, then, slowly, a smile crept across his face. "Perhaps I made a slight error in judgment." They both laughed.

When they got back to the entrance to the Ritz Hotel, Jean Pierre was nowhere in sight. "Shit!" Kevin muttered.

April flung the door to her apartment open, stomped in, threw her wrap on the couch and headed for the bedroom. She was furious! She kicked her shoes off as she went into the bedroom and flicked on the lights.

Muttering to herself, she quickly undressed. Of all the unmitigated gall!" she said as she threw her dress on the bed. "That son-of-a-bitch!" she went on as she pulled off her panty hose and threw them toward the armoire. "How dare he!" she said unsnapping her bra and flinging it across the room. "And I fell for it! I can't believe I fell for it!". She stepped out of her panties and stomped into the bathroom and slammed the door.

As she turned on the shower, April remembered she'd left her front door open. She walked out of the bathroom and headed toward the living room. But, as she came through the bedroom doors, she stopped dead in her tracks. There, silhouetted in the doorway, was a man causally leaning against the jamb. The bright lights of the hallway in back of the man caused his face to be in shadow. As she stared at the man, she suddenly realized she was buck naked!

Quickly she ducked back behind one of the bedroom's double doors and peeked out. "Who's there?" she said in a tentative voice.

"You look ravishing, my dear," the deep bass voice responded.

"Who, who are you?"

The man's hand reached around the door and turned on the living room lights. It was Jean Pierre. "You really should close the door," he said smiling like a Cheshire cat.

"Jean Pierre! What are you doing here?"

"I took an earlier train. I finished my work sooner than I expected. As I was driving by, I saw the light on in your apartment, I thought I'd just drop in for a cup of coffee," he said, trying to sound sincere.

"Well, don't just stand there, come in and close the door. I'll be right out," April said closing the bedroom door.

Jean Pierre closed the door and walked past the bedroom to the couch. He was grinning from ear to ear.

A few moments later, April came out of the bedroom wearing a robe. "You nearly scared me to death!" She began pacing around the room.

"Sorry. I was just surprised to see your door open. I didn't want to come in uninvited."

"I just got home."

"You seem a bit upset."

"Oh no," she said snidely, "I just happened to have had the worse night of my life." She continued pacing.

"Do you want to talk about it?"

"No," she said too quickly. "I mean yes. I mean, I don't know." Tears began running down her face, and Jean Pierre fought the urge to laugh.

April collapsed in the chair next to the couch and put her face in her hands. "I have never been so embarrassed in my life. I'm so angry, and hurt."

Jean Pierre knelt down beside her and took her hands in his and let her sob. If ever a woman was vulnerable, it was now, he thought. Should I or shouldn't I take advantage of the situation? he debated with himself.

"Come now, it couldn't have been as bad as all that," he said in his most comforting tone of voice.

"You don't know. You weren't there," she said looking down into his eyes. The tears made her eyes glisten. It took all of his willpower to control his urge to say, "Ah, but I <u>was</u>," but he didn't. He reached up and gently wiped the tears from her cheeks.

"You are lovely when you cry."

"Thank you," she managed to say between sobs.

He took her hands and pulled her up and wrapped his arms around her. He could feel her trembling. "April, my dear, why don't you just tell me all about it."

April snuggled into his arms. He was strong, and she needed someone to hold her.

They stood there for a few moments saying nothing. He held her tightly, and she clung to him. Jean-Pierre decided to play along. After all, he said to himself, any drastic move could backfire.

Finally, April heaved a great sigh, straightened up and pulled away. She wiped her tears away and gathered herself together. "I'm sorry. I didn't mean to do that."

"I liked it," Jean Pierre said softly.

April took his face in her hands and kissed him lightly. "You're so sweet," she said.

"How about that cup of coffee? Then you can tell me all about it."

"I have a better idea," she said brightly. "How about a drink?"

Suzette sat cross-legged in her pajamas on the bed watching Kevin pace back and forth. "I swear I saw Jean Pierre," Kevin complained looking to Suzette for confirmation.

"I said I didn't see him."

"I did. He was following April out of the door at the Ritz Club. I know it was him."

"You're sure?"

"Positive," Kevin said and then mumbled, "I think."

"You think?"

"I'm sure. Almost."

"Well, one thing's for sure, April has a mean right cross," Suzette said.

Kevin instinctively rubbed his chin, "Yeah. She's mad as hell."

"I would be too."

"I didn't know Victor was gay."

"I did, but you didn't ask me. You were too busy with your grand plan."

"How did you know?"

"He told me."

"When?"

"Three years or so ago. You know, when the Goldman case was winding down. Victor was a suspect for a few days."

Kevin thought for a moment then lowered his chin. "Great. Now you tell me."

"I didn't recognize him at first, and then all hell started breaking loose. Besides, you didn't ask."

"You knew the plan," Kevin reminded her.

"I thought you knew."

"If I'd have known, I wouldn't have used Victor."

"I thought you were putting April on."

"I told you this thing with April is serious. I promised her publisher that I'd find her a man."

"So your little experiment didn't work," she said getting bored with the whole thing about April. "Forget it."

Suddenly, Kevin picked up his jacket and headed for the door.

"Where're you going?"

"I've got to talk to April."

"At three o'clock in the morning? She'll love that," Suzette said sarcastically.

Kevin hesitated. Suzette could see the wheels spinning in his head. Finally he nodded and opened the door. "I gotta do it," he said and slammed the door behind him. Suzette just shook her head in disgust. "Wrong again Kevin," she said.

April was nestled in Jean Pierre's arms curled up on the couch. She had finished telling him about her horrible night. She was very tired and feeling no pain. "And I don't know what got into me, but I just hauled off and socked him as hard as I could and left. I was so mortified!"

"Sounds like Kevin deserved it."

"He did. I hate him."

"As well you should."

April looked up at Jean Pierre. He was looking down at her with his best sympathetic face. He held her closer, and April felt comfortable - very comfortable. She yawned. Jean Pierre smiled. "Looks like I've got a weary lady on my hands."

"I am beat. I feel like I've just run a marathon."

"Time for bed," Jean Pierre suggested.

April sat up. She was pensive. She took a deep breath. "Jean Pierre. Why did he do that?"

"I don't know."

"I feel so, so used."

"May I remind you that Kevin is a strange fellow."

"That he is. Yet. Yet he seemed so normal when I first met him."

"Perhaps it takes time to get to know him."

April stood up. "Well, I know as much about him as I ever want to. Now, I just want him out of my life." As she said it, April felt a twinge of guilt. An ache. She didn't know why, but she felt as if she was trying to convince herself.

Jean Pierre got up and gathered up his coat from the back of the desk chair. He knew it was time to leave. He'd accomplished a lot and he didn't want to push his luck.

Just as he was about to give her a goodnight kiss, there was a loud knock at the door. They both turned toward it.

"Who can that be in the middle of the night?" April asked.

Jean Pierre shrugged. "Why don't you see?"

April went to the door and called out, "Who is it?"

"Kevin O'Connor, Miss Mason. May I speak with you for a minute?"

April turned to Jean Pierre who was still standing in the middle of the living room. He put his palms in the air and shrugged giving her a quizzical look.

"Go away!" April called.

"Please. Just a minute. I need to talk to you."

"I don't want to talk to you. Go away!"

Kevin banged on the door. "Look, I just want to apologize!"

April's anger began to rise. She had no intention of letting Kevin "The Traitor" O'Connor in. Especially after what he did to her at the nightclub.

"I have nothing to say to you," she yelled back at the door.

Kevin banged on the door harder. "Just give me a chance, dammit!"

April was torn. She didn't know why.

"Go away!" she said a little less convincing.

"I'm not leaving here until you let me in!" Kevin shouted.

"Stay there then. All night for all I care." April started to walk away from the door.

Kevin began banging even louder on the door. April's face turned bright red. Jean Pierre simply chuckled to himself.

"Stop that banging," April demanded. "You'll wake the neighbors."

"To hell with the neighbors," Kevin shouted and resumed banging on the door.

"April, I think you'd better let him in. The management might get very upset," Jean Pierre counseled.

"I don't want to let him in. I don't want to talk to him. I don't ever want to see him again," April said as she planted her feet firmly on the floor and pouted.

Kevin banged again.

"I am certain all of that is true, but it is very late," Jean Pierre said.

April looked at Jean Pierre, then back to the door. Her shoulders sagged, and she threw up her hands. "You're right," she admitted.

"I think it would be best if I were not in sight. I'll just go into the bedroom," Jean Pierre said turning and walking out of the room.

By now Kevin was banging incessantly on the door.

April watched Jean Pierre disappear then steeled herself and went to the door. She yanked the door open just as Kevin was pounding on the door. He tried to pull his punch, but it was too late. His fist caught April right on the forehead!

April reeled back. Kevin, horrified, raced through the doorway and caught her just before she fell down the two steps to the living room. "Oh, shit." was all he could say.

As he stood there with April in his arms, he looked down at her. Was she out? Then, April dazed, slowly regained her composure and shook the cobwebs out of her brain. Suddenly she realized where she was. In Kevin's arms! "Oh, God," she cried out as she pushed Kevin away.

Kevin tried to hold her from falling, but she pushed too hard and stumbled back and sat down on the floor. He went to her offering his hand.

"Get away!" she said as she struggled to get up, "I'm all right." But she wasn't, and she had to sit back down on the floor for a minute to clear her head.

"Hey, I'm sorry. I didn't mean to hit you."

"So you say," April said, the venom rising in her throat.

"I didn't."

"Really?"

"Yes. What kind of a guy do you think I am?"

April could think of a lot of things, but instead just stared daggers at him. She got up awkwardly and faced him. She was still a little unsteady on her feet but managed to stand reasonably still.

"Look, I just want to explain about this Victor thing," Kevin started his apology.

"There's nothing to explain," April insisted.

"Yes, there is!"

"I don't want to hear your so-called explanation. It's over and done."

Kevin was seething inside. She was the most unreasonable woman he'd ever met. He fought for control. "I am not leaving until I say what I came her to say," he said in a slow, measured, firm voice.

April put her hands on her hips and stood in front of him defiantly. "Kevin O'Connor you the most stubborn man I have ever had the misfortune to meet."

"Probably, but I have something to say, and by god I'm gonna say it."

All the time she faced him, her mind was racing. The whole situation was ridiculous! He looked like a little boy with his hand caught in the proverbial cookie jar. If she wasn't so mad, she would laugh. In fact, she felt like laughing. It was that weird side of her taking over. The more she thought about it, the more the laughter welled up inside her. She had to fight for self-control.

Carefully, trying to control her instincts, she spoke, "All right, say what you have to say and get out."

Jean Pierre, peering out of a crack between the double doors, sensed something he didn't like. He turned and began taking off his clothes.

"Okay. First, I didn't know Victor was - that way."

"So?"

"So I thought that fixing him up with you would help."

"Help? Help what?"

"You know."

"I do?"

"Yeah. This need of yours for a man."

April arched an eyebrow. The anger was coming back. "My need?"

"Call it what you like. We all know you need a man."

"And who is this 'we all" who know all?" Did she really say that she asked herself as an aside.

"Well, Julian, George and I for one."

"George?"

"Okay, not George. All right, so maybe I made a mistake. I knew you didn't know anyone in town, so I arranged it."

"Help the poor, helpless girl?"

"Yeah, something like that. You know Julian wanted me to sort of keep an eye out for you."

"So Julian put you up to this."

"No, Victor was my idea. I just thought you might be lonely."

"Well, you thought wrong. I am not 'lonely'."

"Yes you are."

"That's a lie."

"No it's not."

They both heard a loud cough. They turned toward the bedroom. "You seem to have the knack for making wrong assumptions, my friend," Jean Pierre said. "I don't believe April is lonely at all," as the double doors opened and Jean Pierre, clad only in a towel wrapped around his waist, emerged and strode over to April.

Kevin was dumbfounded.

April was ready to burst out laughing.

Jean Pierre was in his glory.

It took almost a minute for anyone to speak. They just stared at each other. Kevin stared at Jean Pierre. April stared at Jean Pierre. Jean Pierre smiled at April. April returned the smile. Jean Pierre put his arm around April's waist. April put her arm around Jean Pierre's waist and snuggled in a bit. They both had sly grins on their faces.

Kevin took it all in and felt like he'd just been hit in the pit of his stomach.

April broke the silence, "So you see, it was too a lie."

Kevin glared at her then at Jean Pierre. His worst fears were realized. He suddenly felt helpless - defeated. Finally, he spoke, "What the hell are you doing here?" he asked Jean Pierre.

"I think that's a bit personal, Kevin," Jean Pierre answered in a very matter-of-fact manner.

Kevin looked back at April. She was standing there in her robe with a defiant grin that made him sick.

"He's with me," April said as she pulled Jean Pierre closer and looked up at him with her best mock-adoring smile.

Kevin didn't buy it. Something was wrong. Deep inside he felt like April was putting on a show. He looked her in the eye, "He's wrong for you, April. He's a womanizer and a fake."

"I resent that," Jean Pierre said.

"Resent it all you want," Kevin said ignoring Jean Pierre and keeping his eyes fixed on April's. "Now look, this guy is..."

"My friend," April interrupted. "He's also a man I admire and respect." She realized she didn't say love anytime. "Now, you've had your say. Get out."

Kevin took a step toward April. Jean Pierre let go of her and stepped in between the two of them. "You heard the lady, Kevin. It's time to go."

Kevin wanted, with all his heart, to smash Jean Pierre's face in, but he knew that would only make things worse. He glanced over at April. She was enjoying this, he just knew she was. He rolled his hands into fists, then let go. Resigned, he nodded and headed toward the front door.

April was mixed up. She wanted him to go, yet, for some reason, she wanted him to stay. She started to follow Kevin to the door, but Jean Pierre grabbed her and held her.

When he opened the door, Kevin turned and looked at the two of them standing together, arm in arm. He'd never forget this scene. "April," he said quietly, "don't say I didn't warn you." He turned and went out the door, slamming it behind him.

As soon as the door closed, both April and Jean Pierre let out a whoop! They both began talking at once. "Did you see the look on his face when you came out of the bedroom?" "Did you see his face when you put your arm around me?" They burst out laughing. As Jean Pierre did so, his towel began to slip. April, in mid-laugh, grabbed it and wrapped it back around his waist. She had her arms around him, and Jean Pierre reached down, put his hand under her chin, and pulled her face to his and gave her a long, lingering kiss. April enjoyed it, but kept her hands on the towel.

Jean Pierre was getting in the mood for conquest, but April took his hands away. "You are right, you know. It is late. What time will you pick me up tomorrow?"

Jean Pierre knew better than to press the issue, tomorrow was another day. He took her hands, gave her a soft goodnight kiss and went to the door. "It's about a three to four hour drive to Giverny. I'll be here at - say ten?"

"I'll be ready," she said kissing him lightly on the cheek as she led him to the door. As she opened it she realized he was wearing only a towel. "Oops, sorry. Maybe you should dress first."

"I thought you'd never notice," Jean Pierre said and headed toward the bedroom.

After Jean Pierre left, April took the wine glasses into the kitchen and came back into the living room. She was wide awake. What a night, she thought. Poor Kevin, that look on his face when Jean Pierre came out of the bedroom was priceless, she mused. As she went to turn out the lights, she saw the old book lying open on the desk. "Well, maybe just a few sentences," she said out loud. She unwrapped her new dictionary, sat down at the desk and began reading <u>Recit de la Revolution</u>.

CHAPTER EIGHTEEN

The traffic noise coming from the open French doors woke April. She lifted her head off the desk and looked around. She was disoriented and squinted to see where she was. As she turned, her elbow hit the book and sent it sprawling onto the floor. She bent down and picked it up. "You're fascinating," she said to the book. Her body felt stiff and sore from being hunched over the desk during the night. She stretched her arms and turned to look at the clock on the mantle. It was nearly ten o'clock. "Oh, no, I'm late!" she yelled.

She jumped up out of her chair, and it fell over, tripping her as she headed for the bedroom. "Jean Pierre will be here any minute!" she said as she caught herself and raced into the bathroom.

She pulled off her robe and started the water running for a quick shower. She tugged the shower curtain around the ring and reached in to feel the water temperature. She jerked her hand back and shivered. She adjusted the tap and was about to hop in when the doorbell rang. She threw up her hands, "Not already!" she moaned.

April grabbed her robe and threw it over her shoulders as she headed for the front door. "Who is it?" she asked.

"Jean Pierre," the voice said.

April opened the door and Jean Pierre's eyes popped wide open. "Mon dieu!", he exclaimed looking April up and down. He was startled because her robe was half open.

"What?" she asked.

"Are you always in the habit of opening doors when you are undressed?" he smiled.

April looked down and turned red all over. She quickly closed her robe. "Ooops. Sorry. Come on in."

Jean Pierre came in and closed the door. April was already heading for the bedroom. "I overslept. I'll be ready in just a few minutes," she said closing the bedroom doors.

Jean Pierre chuckled to himself. What a woman, he thought. What a body, and she looks wonderful in the morning with no make up. Delicious! He wandered over to the French doors and closed them. He was about to go to the couch when he saw the chair by the desk overturned. He righted the chair, placed it by the desk and glanced down. He noticed the open book on her desk. He saw that the book was old, its pages were fragile. Carefully, he picked it up and glanced at the title on the cover. Ah, he thought, another book about the Revolution. He also saw a dictionary on the desk and noticed it was a special one for archaic French words and phrases. April was an unusual woman, he thought, to go to the trouble of reading such an old book. He laid the book back down on the desk, shrugged and went into the kitchen to make some coffee.

When it was ready, he knocked on the bedroom door. "Would you like some coffee?" he called through the door.

"Oh, that would be wonderful, Jean Pierre," April called back. She opened the door a crack and reached out. As he handed her the cup, he could see her reflection in the floor length mirror near the night stand. She was still nude. This is a wonderful omen, he thought with a devilish look in his eye.

April took the cup. "Be out in five minutes," she said as she closed the door.

April was just fastening her bra when her bedside phone rang. She answered it.

"Good morning, Miss Mason," Kevin said hesitantly.

April recognized his voice and immediately slammed down the phone.

In his cubicle, Kevin stared at the phone and slowly hung it up. He was torn between anger and frustration. He wanted to apologize for the Victor thing, but he also wanted to talk to April about seeing Jean Pierre. He knew Jean Pierre only meant trouble. His fingers danced on the phone as he thought about going over to see her, but the night before had proved a disaster. He decided to wait until evening when April'd have a chance to cool down. He had to explain his actions to her or neither she nor Julian would ever forgive him.

George tapped on the wall of Kevin's cubical. "Hey, wasn't that a lot of fun last night? We had a ball. And that April Mason is really something! She's not only a knockout, but she's smart as a whip."

"Yeah," Kevin said unenthusiastic.

"That Victor guy and her really hit it off."

"You can say that again. Hit being the operative word."

"Huh?"

"Never mind. I'm glad you had a good time."

"I can't wait to tell Julian how well things went."

"You do that. Just be sure," he was interrupted by the phone ringing. He answered, "Kevin O'Connor." He listened to the voice at the other end. If it were possible, smoke began pouring out of his ears. Finally the voice stopped. Kevin hesitated a moment, then, forcing himself to remain calm, he replied in measured, but very firm words, "No fucking way! I will not pay for your tux, I will not pay for the limo, and I sure as hell will not pay you! And a word of caution. Stay out of my way!" Kevin slammed down the phone.

"Wow! What was that all about?"

128

"George. Do you mind? I've got to get this article about the Ambassador's reception finished for this afternoon's edition."

"Well, sorry," George said and walked away in a huff.

Kevin went back to his computer.

Snooky stood next to the printing press and carefully inserted the plates into the press. She took a piece of paper, looked at it through the overhead light to insure that the watermark was right side up, and placed it on the printing plate. She pulled the handle and the rollers passed over the ink pad and then across the plates. Then the paper was forced between the plates then released. She carefully pulled the paper from the plate. She looked at it and smiled. It was a perfect replica of a sheet of four Algerian 1000 Dinar notes. Duer would be pleased.

She inserted another paper in the printer and again another perfect set of counterfeit notes were made. But the third time she inserted the paper, there was a loud clank and the press stopped.

"Merde," she cried. She expertly examined the press. After a few minutes, she discovered the problem. A broken roller hinge. She slammed her fist against the antique printer. Where was she going to get another hinge? She knew of only one place. In Lyon. She carefully wiped her hands and went upstairs to her office. She phoned Paul LeMieux and told him that there would be a delay in getting the shipment to him.

In Giverny, at the country home of Claude Monet, April and Jean Pierre stood by a small wooden bench beside the lily pond made so famous by the renowned painter. They were both tired after the long tour of Monet's home and the beautiful grounds around it.

April was completely awed by the afternoon's events. Jean Pierre, who'd done the tour many times, was surprised to feel a renewed sense of excitement as he listened to April go on and on about everything she'd seen. Finally, he got a word in edgewise, "I am so glad you had a good time."

"I can't thank you enough," she said looking at him with those big, brown eyes.

Jean Pierre could think of only one way she could thank him properly.

"Just think, he painted all those wonderful scenes right here. Right where we are now."

"Yes."

April put her arms around Jean Pierre and held him tightly. He responded by holding her and pulling her close to him. April felt his strong arms around her and relaxed. "I have never felt such peace and calm as I do right now," she said quietly.

Jean Pierre was becoming anxious. He had other things on his mind. He stood quietly with her for a moment longer, then said, "I know of a small, quaint country inn not too far from here. It's very peaceful there," he said. "Perhaps we should have dinner at the inn before we go back to Paris."

"That would be delightful," she said genuinely.

Jean Pierre pulled his BMW into the gravel parking lot in front of the inn. The inn, La Cour, was nestled in a small wooded area just off the main road. It was a long, one story inn of white-washed brick and siding. Multi-pane windows were evenly spaced all across the front except for two sets of French doors in the middle of the building. There were only a few cars in the lot. It was nearly sundown, and a red-edged cloud over the inn had rays of sunlight streaking through it, as it drifted across the pale blue sky. One of the sunbeams focused on the front doors of the inn. April pointed it out, and Jean Pierre took that phenomenon as a another very good omen.

They were seated in the dining room near the open-hearth fireplace. The waiter, complete with handlebar moustache and his hair parted in the middle, took their drink order. April looked around. There were twelve or so tables, but only three were occupied. One by a family of four laughing and having a good time, one with three older men who were having a very serious conversation, and the other with a couple who seemed very much in love as they gazed into each others eyes and held hands.

As the daylight dwindled, the room darkened and became very intimate. The waiter brought a candle to the table along with their drinks. Jean Pierre and April toasted Monet. "Thank you so much," she said softly to Jean Pierre.

They clinked glasses and drank slowly looking into each other's eyes. April sat back. She was relaxed. She felt warm and comfortable. She looked around the room again, then turned to Jean Pierre. She put her hand on his. She looked at him for a long moment and said, "I want to know all about you. Please?"

"I am certain," he began, "my past is not very interesting story compared to your life."

"I'm sure it is, and besides, my life hasn't been all that interesting."

"Meaning?"

"Oh, no," April chided playfully, "I asked you first."

Jean Pierre smiled. "Okay, but don't say I didn't warn you."

For the next thirty minutes, during dinner, Jean Pierre told April about growing up in a villa in the South of France near Nice. He was the only son of a politician who spent twenty years in the French Parliament. Jean Pierre's mother died when he was twelve, and he was actually raised by his father's valet who spent more time with Jean Pierre than his father ever did. Besides working on various Senate committees, his father had a very fascinating hobby - collecting mistresses.

"I truthfully admired my father's taste in women," Jean Pierre continued. "He never failed to surprise me with the next and the next. Each was different in many ways, their hair color, their figures, their senses of humor. It was as if he could

131

not make up his mind and simply went shopping every six or seven months."

April laughed.

"When I was at university, all my friends eagerly awaited my father's visits to see who he had on his arm. I remember for Christmas one year he brought a famous stage actress, or so he said she was. She was so beautiful, seemed so delicate, but she cursed like a sailor!"

April was enthralled by the way Jean Pierre talked. His French accent was not thick nor ostentatious, but unmistakably European aristocrat. His voice was low and soft, but very clear.

His eyes crinkled when he spoke of his father, and that she really liked. "As he got older, my father's mistresses got older, too. Finally he met a woman, Margarite, with whom he lived in a flat in Paris until he died suddenly at the age of 55. The rumor is that he died in bed with Margarite, and the mortician had a hard time wiping the smile off of his face."

April laughed and said that that was an old joke.

Jean Pierre assured her it was no joke, it was the truth.

"And do you follow in your father's footsteps?" April asked.

"No, they were far too big. So, I became a lobbyist as you Americans say, for the tourist board. When I got the job, my father laughed. 'Just like, you, he said, to find a better way to meet women than your father.'"

"And is it?"

"I'm not sure how to answer that," he said arching an eyebrow. "If I say yes, you'll think me frivolous, and if I say no, you'll think I am not telling the truth."

"Ah, you read me like a book."

"A best seller?"

"*Touche'*."

The waiter took away their plates and brought them café noir and Grand Marnier. Their two empty bottles of *Pouilly Fuisse* were upside down in the silver ice bucket.

"Now, please enough about me. Who is the real April Mason?"

"Truthfully?"

"As truthful as one can be when extolling one's own virtues"

April nodded. "How true. Well, I've had a lot to drink, and I may just let something slip. If I do, please be kind enough to forget it tomorrow."

"It would be the honorable thing to do, but it may be too juicy to forget."

April laughed. "I'll watch it. Well, here goes," she said as she and Jean Pierre clinked their brandy snifters in a toast.

"In the first place, I was not raised in a villa or anything close to that, but it was a nice, small house in Des Plaines, Illinois, a suburb of Chicago. My father bowled over my mother, literally, when he ran headlong into her as he was running away from a policeman."

"Why was he running from the police?" Jean Pierre interrupted.

"Well, to make a long story short, he stole a pair of bloomers off a clothes line as part of a fraternity prank. The bloomers belonged to the policeman's wife!"

They both laughed. April continued, "They met officially at the police station. When the cop saw my mother's look of consternation at my father being booked, he decided not to press charges. So, Dad was let go. They ended up having coffee at an all night diner. Ironically, six months later, to the day, my father proposed to her in that same diner."

"Tres romantic. I like him already. What business is he in?"

"He's an inventor."

"Inventor?"

"Yep. That was his avocation, but it turned into his vocation."

Jean Pierre looked at her quizzically.

"Well, see, he had a degree in finance, but hated working as a CPA, so one day he and a couple of friends started a small business making a part he invented for computers that makes them compatible with one another. The business grew and grew, and he just kept making things that worked, and that's what he does today."

"Fascinating. And your mother?"

"Well, while dad was getting started, my mother worked in the college library. When I was born, mom quit her job to raise me, but times were tough, and so when I started first grade, she went back to work at the library. I'm sure it was because she loved books so much that I became a writer. She'd always bring home a new book. By the time I was five, I could read almost anything."

"When I started middle school, we moved into a big house in Evanston, that's also a suburb of Chicago, so my mother could be near the university. Ironically, a few weeks later, dad's business became profitable, and she quit her job. Nowadays, she devotes herself to charity causes."

"What are they like, your father and mother?" Jean Pierre asked.

"I'm prejudice, but they're terrific. They're both caring, very much in love with each other, and have the greatest senses of humor. My father is droll, and my mother delights in pretending to be dumb. Which she is not. It's sort of a game they play with his business associates.

"When I was young, I'd crack up every time they'd have a dinner party. They'd go into this act with people. I'd watch the guests shaking their heads and talking behind my folks' back. Little did they know. Then I'd go up to my room and write stories about them."

"So you wrote even as a child?"

"Yes. I loved it. I still have all those awful stories I wrote about the dinner guests in my files."

"And when did you decide to become a professional writer?"

"I never did. It just happened. For example, when I was in the seventh grade, I wrote a short story about one of the dinner parties for my English class. Unbeknownst to me my teacher sent it off to a magazine. I was awe struck when it was published. Talk about encouragement. That did it. There is nothing like seeing your work in print. I wrote stories from then on."

"And you haven't stopped."

"I never thought of doing anything else. I suppose it's because I am so in love with books, stories, and really enjoy letting my imagination run wild. I love to daydream and just go walking and watching people and making up stories about them as they pass by. People are fascinating and fun."

"So writing is easy for you."

April hesitated. She did not want to get into the thing about having to be in love. Jean Pierre would think she was a nut! "I love to write. What else can I say?"

"Are you an only child?"

"Yep. I don't mind it a bit. In fact, I sort of like to be alone. And being a writer, you have to be alone to work, or at least I do."

"But why mysteries?"

"I guess it was because my mother was such a mystery fan. After I started grade school, when she went back to work for a while, she'd bring home the latest mystery.

We didn't have a lot of money then. My father was working on his inventions, but none of them had panned out yet, so when I came home from school, he'd be working in the basement, Mom would be working in the kitchen, so, I'd pick up one of her mysteries and read. That way, I got hooked on mysteries, Agatha Christie, Nero Wolfe, those kinds of books. The kids at school used to laugh at me when I told them about what I read."

"So you started writing mysteries."

"I didn't really start writing them until my summer job just before in my senior year in high school. I was working in a department store. One night they found a dead person in the elevator. It turned out he died of a heart attack, but I kept thinking "what if he was poisoned or strangled". So I started out to write a short story about it, and it turned into a novel. I showed it to my English teacher, Mrs. Welby. She was impressed with the story, and sent it to editor friend of hers. To my great surprise, he liked it and sent me to see Julian Maxwell in Chicago. He has been my publisher ever since. So, here I am, 15 years later, a professional writer. Ooops, I think I just gave away my age."

Jean Pierre sat back in his chair and laughed. "You are so old."

"Hey, fifty years ago, I'd been labeled a spinster."

"Spinster? I'm not familiar with that term."

"It means an unmarried older woman."

"Ah. That brings me to a very important question. Why have you never married?"

"That, sir, is a question that has plagued me since I graduated college."

"And your answer?"

"Truthfully?"

"As truthful as you like."

"The old cliche is that I haven't met the right man yet."

"But?"

"I think I have met him, two maybe three times."

"So you know him?"

"Each time I thought I did."

"Ah, so 'he' is several men."

"No, not quite that, what I meant was that I was ready to marry them, but they weren't ready to marry me. I do that a lot."

"Do what?"

"Drive men away."

"I see. Do you do this on purpose?"

"Not consciously. At least I don't think so. I mean I don't mean to drive men away, it's just that I do. Does that make sense?"

"Not a bit."

"I didn't think so," April said laughing and shaking her head.

Jean Pierre leaned forward, took April's hands and looked her right in the eyes. "I hope you'll pardon my intrusion into your life, but after listening to your story, it is my opinion that you do not understand the word 'love'."

April frowned and continued to look him in the eyes.

"Love is a gift we only have for a short time, sometimes minutes, sometimes days, and for those most fortunate - years. If we are fortunate to find love, with anyone, we must take it, and let it consume us. Love can be a very fleeting emotion, and when it is here, in our hearts, it is the most wonderful feeling in the world. But it is also fragile, and if anything gets in the way to distract us from it, it will vanish into thin air as quickly as it appeared. It sounds to me as if you have been in love many times, but that something or possibly someone has distracted you, and the feeling disappeared, as did your lover."

Jean Pierre kept hold of April's hands and sat back, pulling her toward him and never taking his eyes off hers.

April's mind raced back to each of her love affairs, and suddenly she understood. Then she smiled, "You, Jean Pierre, are very astute. Where did you get all this worldly philosophy?"

"By living, where else?" he said as he let go of her hands and sat back with a Cheshire smile. He knew he had her in the palm of his hand.

"There was one thing that was common to all of those times."

"A man?"

"No," she laughed, "A computer. My writing. I mean I always knew that I bugged them when I went off to write, but I guess I sort of closed my eyes and made believe that secretly they loved the fact that I was a writer. I never thought of it as a 'distraction'. Come to think of it, I'll bet that was what it was." She sighed, "There are none so blind as those who will not see."

"Now who's quoting philosophy?"

"Sorry," April reached across the table and took his hands. "Thank you," she said looking deeply into his eyes. "How can I ever thank you?"

Jean Pierre was smart enough not to say it out loud.

"Well," he said trying to put on his most gracious manner, "If I have been of some help, that is thanks enough. Besides, April Mason, I have grown very fond of you."

"And I you, Jean Pierre," she said sincerely. "You know, I never asked. Were you ever married?"

"No. Love has been very tragic for me," he said knowing this would come up sooner or later. "I nearly married five years ago, but on the night before we were to be married, Marie was killed in an automobile accident. Since then love has never been the same." Jean Pierre gave her his saddest look.

"Oh. You poor man," April said quietly.

"So you see why I feel the way I do about love."

"Yes. Yes, I understand. It must be very difficult for you."

"Oh, I'm not a martyr. I don't go around in sack cloth and ashes. Nor am I a monk. I have had other women, brief affairs, and one or two mistresses since, but no one I wish to spend the rest of my life with. But make no mistake about it, I do love women."

As he talked, April saw a new kind of man. Jean Pierre wasn't afraid to speak his mind. It wasn't what he was saying, it was how he was saying it. Openly. Honestly. Certainly not like the other men she had known, or was it that he was French?

April wasn't sure, but she was definitely pleasantly surprised.

"But enough about me," he said brightening up, "Let's celebrate your new insight. Waiter!" he called.

When the waiter was getting another Grand Marnier for them, Jean Pierre excused himself and went into the lobby. As he went out the doorway he looked back to make sure April wasn't facing the parking lot.

April gazed into the fire in the fireplace and thought about what Jean Pierre had said about love. And about not really knowing love. Was that it? Was that why men left her? She couldn't recognize it? Could be, she thought. She looked over at the young couple in the corner holding hands and occasionally kissing. They looked so happy. Then she glanced at an older couple who had just arrived. They were smiling at each other and chatting quietly. The inn seemed to be filled with love. She returned to her drink and waited.

Jean Pierre seemed to be gone for a long time, and when he appeared in the doorway, he looked very unhappy. He came over to the table, sat down and gulped down his after-dinner drink in one swallow without saying anything. Finally April's curiosity took over. "Is there something wrong?"

"I am afraid I have some bad news. I went to the car to get my cigarettes and discovered that I have not only one, but two flat tires. And to make things even more embarrassing, my spare tire is flat as well. I went to the innkeepers desk for some help, but he informed me that there were no garages nearby that were open. I will have to wait until tomorrow morning to get them fixed."

"Oh. But what...?"

"And, to make matters even worse," he interrupted, "They have only one room available. I took the liberty of booking it for you for tonight."

"But where will you sleep?"

"In my car, of course."

April thought for a moment before answering. If she didn't know better, this looked like a set up. On the other hand, it may just be the truth. Whatever the truth, she couldn't let this man who'd been so kind to her sleep in his car. "You will not sleep in your car," she said firmly. "We'll work something out."

"But I don't want you to think..."

139

"What? That you let the air out of your own tires?" she said laughing.

Even though Jean Pierre knew he had let the air out of his own tires, he wasn't about to confess. "No, I know you don't think that. I am just so very embarrassed about the situation."

They finished their drinks, and the innkeeper showed them to the room. It was charming, with French country furniture, a big bed with a down quilt covered with flowers. There was a tiny table and a rocking chair in one corner, and a small armoire near the foot of the bed. The bathroom was very small, and the tub was sitting on what looked like lion's feet. It was nestled in the corner. There was no shower and only a small washstand and commode.

A set of French doors led out to a small, courtyard with two chairs and a table. The courtyard was fenced off by a six foot high hedge which made the courtyard very private.

April was gazing at the round, full moon over the courtyard when a waiter from the restaurant brought a bottle of wine, and a small ice bucket with two glasses on a silver tray. April didn't see Jean Pierre order two more bottles to be delivered later. The waiter winked at Jean Pierre as he closed the door. Jean Pierre took the tray and went out into courtyard, "Shall we continue our little talk?"

April watched as he put the tray on the table and poured them each a glass. Everything was perfect, she thought, too perfect. The drinks before dinner, the wine with dinner, and the after-dinner drinks had left her feeling the buzz, but as he poured, April sobered up. She took the glass he offered, "What shall we drink to, Jean Pierre?"

"Ah, to love, of course," he said.

"Yes, to love," she said raising her glass.

Jean Pierre gave her his best, "and to bed" look.

April peered at him over the top of her glass. As she drank, she thought, okay, April, he's good looking, charming, sexy in his own way, and he's trying very hard to seduce you. So, why not go to bed with him?

As he sipped his wine, Jean Pierre thought, come on April, come on, this is costing me a fortune.

He held the chair for her, and as she was sitting, he brushed his lips across the back of her neck.

April felt it, and a chill ran down her back. It was kind of exciting, but there was something missing. Maybe she was just being too analytical about all of this, she thought. Perhaps she should let her emotions take over. But there wasn't any real emotion there.

Jean Pierre smiled to himself. He saw the hair on the back of her neck stand up. He was getting to her. He cautioned himself to take it slow.

For an hour they chatted about Paris, Monet, and their lives, and drank wine. However, every chance she got, April poured her wine into the potted plant behind her.

Finally, Jean Pierre told her about his mother dying when he was 12. That story always worked, he reminded himself. He had tears in his eyes when he said, "I raced home from prep school when my father called me. She'd passed away in her sleep. My father was sitting in his study crying when I arrived home. We held each other for a long time."

He hung his head and took a long, deep breath. April could not resist kneeling down in front of him and taking his hands. He didn't say anymore, he just peeked down at her with one eye, then heaved another big sigh and raised his head. "I am sorry. I hadn't thought of those days in a very long time," he said in a low, wistful tone. "Thank you for listening.".

April squeezed his hands and nodded. A smile washed across his face. "You are wonderful," he said and kissed her hands. Then he stood and pulled her up into his arms. "I want you," he said in a low, direct way that wasn't an order, but a statement of fact. He took her face in his hands and looked into April's eyes. She felt sorry for him and wanted to mother him, but mothering wasn't what he had in mind. He kissed her passionately.

April was tempted to let herself go. After all, it had been some time since she was with a man, but she had been in love with each one of them, or at least she thought she was. She definitely wasn't in love with Jean Pierre.

Jean Pierre didn't grab or struggle, he massaged, and rubbed her gently, and took his time. He ran his fingers skillfully over her body, finding the right spots to make her shudder with desire. He kissed her with soft, lingering kisses.

April returned his kisses, and she was beginning to feel the effects of his passion. It was catching. Suddenly, he picked her up and carried her into the room. He gently laid her down on the bed. As he did so, he let his hand wander between her legs. Unfortunately for him, this aroused April in the wrong way. She giggled. He stopped and looked down at her. She peered up at him trying to suppress another giggle. Her mood had changed, really changed. She could see his nose hairs, and she wanted to laugh, but instead, she pursed her lips so hard they turned white.

Jean Pierre did not know what to do.

"I'm sorry," April said trying to sound sincere, but she had the giggles, and when she had them, there was no stopping them.

Jean Pierre bent down to kiss her again. His lips gently brushed hers. April tried very hard to take this seriously, but on his second pass, his hair brushed her forehead and it tickled.

She quickly swiped at his hair, but instead hit Jean Pierre in the nose.

He flinched and pulled back.

"Sorry," April said again and tried to sit up in the soft bed. She couldn't. It was too soft! The more she struggled, the sillier she felt, and the sillier she felt, the funnier it was to her. Finally, she collapsed in a ball of uncontrollable laughter.

Jean Pierre did not think it funny at all. The woman was crazy. He slowly stood up and walked outside. He was furious.

Snooky was, to say the least, angry. She'd worked all night trying to get the new part on the antique printer to fit correctly. Twice it had seemed as if it was in the right position, and twice the spring had sprung and jumped out of place. Twice, she kicked the machine, and twice, it managed to hurt her toe.

Finally, three hours after she began, she sat down on the floor, and fumed. Minutes later, she slapped the floor, stood up, and nodded to the press. "All right, no more fooling around. She jammed the part where it belonged and checked it. She was ready to try once more. It worked! Snooky kicked the press once more. "That's for giving me a hard time!" she said and headed for the bathroom to clean up.

A few minutes later, Snooky carefully placed the paper on the printing plate and turned on the rollers, then pulled slowly but firmly on the lever. The ink pallet took the rollers and the paper was drawn up to the inked plate. This was the crucial moment. She pulled harder. It worked. When the cycle was complete, she looked at the paper - four perfect 1000 dinars. Snooky was back in business.

When the sun came up, Kevin yawned and sat up in his car. He was mad as hell. First he couldn't get April on the phone all evening, Duer didn't budge from his apartment all night, and to cap it all off, he spilled coffee on his crotch which was still damp. When his replacements arrived, he headed for his apartment. He was really frustrated with the whole Duer thing. He wanted to talk to Le Pluete, and he had to talk to April!

April awoke in the middle of the bed. She had a headache. She looked around. Jean Pierre was nowhere in sight.

Jean Pierre, on the other hand, felt fine. Anger had a way of sobering him up. He watched as the tow truck repairman finished putting on the last tire. He paid the man, kicked a tire on his car and headed back to get April. He vowed to keep from hitting her. They were on the road back to Paris by eight that morning.

CHAPTER NINETEEN

April and Jean Pierre arrived back at her apartment at noon from Giverny. April insisted on fixing them a light lunch. Although Jean Pierre was anxious to go, he relented, and as she went into the kitchen, he wandered around her apartment. He spied the old book again and picked it up. "<u>Recit de la Revolution,</u>" he muttered under his breath as he turned a few pages and saw that the book had been printed in 1797. He was impressed.

When April came out of the kitchen with a small plate of sandwiches and iced tea, he held up the book and asked her where she found it.

"It was purely by accident," she said and told him of being run into by a man being chased by the police and of the mix-up with the recipe book and the old book. She said she'd tried to return the book, but the bookseller was not there.

"And I see you have a dictionary of ancient terms. Do you need that to read it?

"Yes. It's very difficult."

"Why are you trying to read such an old book?"

"I don't really know, except that the forward in the book intrigued me so that I want to finish it. Besides, it's great practice for improving my French."

"It seems like a lot of work," Jean Pierre said with a shrug.

"Maybe, but I like things like that."

145

Jean Pierre put the book down, and they had lunch.

Kevin came out the Gazette office building, a copy of the paper under his arm, and into the late afternoon sun. He was depressed. He'd tried to call April all morning but there was no answer. He had given up trying at noon. He wanted to talk to her because he felt truly sorry about the evening with Victor. He didn't know why, but she was constantly on his mind. He decided to stop by her place that evening, but, first, he had an appointment to see Le Pluete. The case against Duer was going no where, and he wanted off it.

He looked at his watch. It was only four fifteen. His appointment was for five-thirty. He decided to get some coffee. He walked across the street to his favorite outdoor café, and sat down. He had only to nod to the waiter.

He opened his paper and began to read. Moments later the waiter brought his coffee. As he was about to go back to his paper, he saw Jean Pierre standing near the entrance. Then Paul LeMieux came in and the two greeted each other as old friends. He was surprised to see Paul LeMieux and Jean Pierre together. What the hell is Jean Pierre doing meeting him? He wondered. He ducked behind his newspaper and watched. Paul and Jean Pierre were seated at a table on the other side of the outdoor café. Kevin couldn't hear what they were saying, but from the body language, he guessed that they were friends. He was fascinated.

After they were seated, Jean Pierre and Paul LeMieux ordered coffee. When the waiter left, Jean Pierre asked, "So how is my sister?"

"My wife is excellent," Paul replied. "LeAnne sends you her regrets, but she could not get away this afternoon."

"Pity. I haven't seen her in nearly a month."

"Well, you know how it is. Besides, I have been very busy. I haven't been home for some time. My client is in town."

"Oh? The one from Algiers?"

"Yes. Duer," Paul said, then gave a shrug. "Hopefully, he'll be gone in a few days."

"He must be very important," Jean Pierre said as he spied the butt of a Beretta under Paul's coat. "I see you are carrying your gun again."

"A tool of the trade so to speak. Let's not talk about him."

"Why?"

"I just don't want to talk about him," Paul said forcefully.

"I don't like the sound of that, Paul. What's the matter?" Jean Pierre asked seeing the consternation on Paul's face.

"It's stupid. All over a book. And it wasn't my fault!" Paul said getting agitated. Just then the waiter brought their coffee. Jean Pierre waited until the waiter was gone, then asked calmly, "Fault?"

"It was a man Duer hired to get him something. A stupid man. He botched a very simple job, and now I'm the one in hot water."

Jean Pierre could see Paul's face getting redder and redder as he spoke.

"All Duvall had to do was get the book, which he did, but he wasn't careful and lost it. And now the police," Paul stopped in mid-sentence. "Look, Jean Pierre, I don't want to talk about this anymore. It upsets me every time I think about it."

"Sorry. I'm just curious. What kind of a book would make the police interested?"

"They're not interested in the book, it's the man they're after. The old book is what my client wants. He seems to think holds the secret to a treasure. He's insistent on getting it. Personally, I think he's crazy."

"A secret treasure? Like a pirate book?"

"No, nothing like that. It's about the Revolution and some crazy story about an aristocrat who made a map of a vault of some sort. That's all I know."

"The Revolution, you say." Jean Pierre said remembering the book on April's desk. His mind began racing. It was one chance in a million, but did April have the book Paul was looking for? He wanted to explore the subject further with Paul, but he didn't want to tip him off if April did have the right book. Maybe he could use it to get something from this Duer guy. He'd have to walk a fine line. "How did this man, Duvall, lose the book?"

"He dropped it when he was running along the Seine."

"And he couldn't pick it up."

"Jean Pierre, it is all very complicated. Can we talk about something else?"

"I don't understand, Paul, why is this Duer fellow angry at you?"

"Because he thinks I should have found the book by now."

"Are you in danger?"

"No, I don't think so, but with Duer you never know."

"I hope LeAnne is not in danger."

"Noooo. She's at our place in the country. I wouldn't put her in any danger. You know that."

"See that you don't," Jean Pierre said firmly. Paul got the message.

"So," Paul said, sitting back in his chair, "what are you up to these days? Still trying to make deals with the politicians for your tourist people?"

Jean Pierre decided not to pursue the book angle any longer. He smiled. "I am always trying to improve things for them. After all, tourism is a very big part of Paris' economy."

"And you are only a servant."

"Yes. A well-paid servant, I'll admit."

They both laughed. Then Jean Pierre sat back in his chair with a smug look on his face. Paul noticed the look immediately. Something is up," Paul said with an arched eyebrow.

"Nothing really. I've just had a rather good stroke of luck."

"A woman," Paul said as a statement of fact.

"Yes. A rich woman. An American. She is a novelist."

"Really? Will her next book be about you?"

"Perhaps," Jean Pierre said with a sly grin.

"Beautiful?"

"Attractive. Young. Very good in bed."

"Of course. As I remember, that is your sole criteria."

"A very important one."

"And how long will she be here?"

"I really don't know. She's on vacation, but she says she's also trying to cure her writer's block."

"Careful, she may not write again and lose all her money."

"I don't think there's any danger there. She's very bright."

"What is her name?"

"Not this time, Paul. She's very special."

"You never change," Paul said with a grin. "You know, Jean Pierre, one day a woman will be your downfall."

"As they say, 'what a way to go'."

Paul looked at his watch. He took a final sip of his coffee and stood. "I have to go."

Jean Pierre stood also, and put some money on the table.

"I'm worried about you, Paul. This assignment sounds very dangerous."

"No more than many I've had. Don't worry. I'll be fine."

"Tell LeAnne I hope to see her soon."

"I will," Paul said. They shook hands and Paul disappeared into the crowd of people walking along the street. Jean Pierre stared after him. This book, Jean Pierre mused, did by some freak of nature April end up with it? He decided to go see her that night.

Kevin watched the two men. When they parted, Kevin was more confused than before. They seemed like good friends. How could this be? Was Jean Pierre tied into Duer? Perhaps Le Pluete would know something about their relationship. He paid his bill and set out to see Le Pluete. Just as he got to the corner a sudden rain storm came up. He quickly hailed a taxi.

149

April poured herself a glass of wine and sat down cross-legged on the couch with the book and her new dictionary. The rain was coming down steadily. It was the perfect evening to curl up with a good book, she thought.

Duer was at his desk reading also. It was a report from one of his "business partners" about the Algerian economy. The dinar was rising in value. He thought of Snooky. When would she deliver?

There was a knock on the door. "Entre."

It was Paul LeMieux. He was drenched. "I'm sorry for the interruption, Monsieur Duer, but I think I may have some important news."

"Come in, Paul. You look a mess."

"I couldn't catch a taxi so I had to walk."

"Well, then," Duer said as he pulled his large frame up from the desk, "I think a brandy is in order."

"Thank you."

Duer went to a large Armoire and opened it. It was a full, mirror-lined, bar. He poured two brandies from a decanter and handed one to Paul. "Take off your coat and stand over by the fireplace. You're dripping on the carpet."

LeMieux did as he was told.

"Now, what is this news you've brought me?"

"It concerns the book."

"Oh?" Duer asked with mounting interest.

"A friend of mine told me he met an American woman. A writer."

"And that is unusual?"

"It is not unusual for him to meet an American woman, but it is unusual for him not to tell me her name."

"You know this friend very well."

"Yes. Very well. It is just a hunch, but I think a writer might be very interested in this rare book."

"Possibly."

"If I am any judge of character, my friend will lead me to her tonight. I'd like to take Duvall with me and find out who this woman is. Maybe, just maybe, she is the woman Duvall ran into when he lost the book. Duvall may be able to identify her."

"And she may have the book."

"A long shot I admit, but worth a try."

"Very well, Paul. Good hunting."

The young lieutenant put the dossier on Le Pluete's desk. Marcel opened it and scanned the file then looked up. "I'm somewhat surprised you didn't know this, Kevin," he said as he handed the dossier to him. "It seems that Paul LeMieux is married to Jean Pierre's sister."

Kevin frowned and read the file quickly. He nodded and put it back on Le Pluete's desk. "Well, at least that explains why they were meeting. There's nothing there to indicate that Jean Pierre is involved with Duer, though."

"Sometimes the absence of things does not necessarily tell the whole story," Le Pluete said.

"True, but I can't see Jean Pierre being involved with Duer. He's not the type."

"I see."

"Maybe they just got together to talk about family. I don't know. I wish I'd been a mouse under their table. They were in heavy conversation about something. Oh, well, forget it. It is probably nothing."

"On the other hand."

"Yeah, I'm suspicious, too." Kevin said with a nod.

They sat in silence for a few moments, each with his own thoughts.

"You could follow LeMieux," Le Pluete murmured.

"I could."

"Good. That's settled," Le Pluete said. "Now you wanted to talk about Duer."

"Yes. Suzette and my team have been watching him for several days now, and frankly, there's nothing to report. He stays in that damn apartment all day and all night except when he and LeMieux go out to dinner once in a while. He doesn't have any visitors, and he doesn't meet anyone when he's out to dinner. I'm not sure he's up to anything and neither is Suzette."

"Ah, but the wire taps turned up something interesting."

"Wire taps?"

"Yes we got a court order late last week. Did I forget to tell you?" Kevin nodded. "Well, he only made three calls from his phone. One to order a dinner brought in, one to Algiers about his holdings there, and one to the Bibliotheque Nationale about a rare book called Recit de la Revolution. The library does not have it. It seems their only copy was stolen years ago. Why this sudden interest in rare books? It doesn't fit his M.O.."

"Yes, that is odd."

"I know this book, Recit de la Revolution," Le Pluete said, nodding his head and smiling. "It's a very rare book. A collection of short stories about the Reign of Terror during the French Revolution. Written by Charles Du Pypes in 1797. There were only a few copies made, and they all seem to have disappeared. There are no records of the book any where. Why would Duer want this book?"

"I don't know, except that it might be very valuable."

"I am sure it is, but like you, Kevin, I don't see Duer interested in books, even rare books. I think I'll put my research department to work. See what else we can find out about this book. In the meantime, you concentrate on Paul LeMieux. Use Suzette, too, if you like. I'll put some others on the stakeout."

Kevin came out of the Palais de Justice into a driving rain. He didn't have his raincoat, so he decided to go to his apartment and get one. Then he'd see about Mr. Paul LeMieux.

"Oh, my God," April said out loud. "This story about the young aristocrat is fabulous!" She began pacing and reading out loud:

"I was being 'detained' in the Conciergerie, often referred to as "The Antechamber of Death," for writing an unfavorable article about the Committee of Public Safety and that villain, Robespierre. Alas, that is another story.

"It was in early June of 1794, and I was sharing accommodations with several men in a cell in one of the turrets of the immense prison. I'd been there seven days, and in that time, I had seen many men taken from this cell, never to return. Late one afternoon, a filthy, wretched-smelling young man was thrown into our cell. I could see he'd been beaten, there was a nasty cut over one eye and his expensive clothes were blood-spattered. His smell was so offensive that the other prisoners called to the guards to have him taken away. Instead, the guards brought a pail of water, some rags and a burlap robe.

"We insisted he clean himself up. He crawled to the bucket we had placed in the farthest corner. Facing the corner, he began to take his finely tailored clothes off. He washed himself, then surprised us by washing his clothes as well. He carefully laid out his clothes to dry, put on the robe and curled up in a ball in the corner. A guard was summoned and he took the foul-smelling bucket away.

"I woke in the middle of the night. In the moonlight that flooded the cell I could see his face. He, too, was fully awake. I could see the unmistakable fear in his eyes. He was trembling. I got up and went to him. "You look as if you need a friend," I said quietly.

"I have no friends," he said firmly.

"My name is Charles Du Pypes," I said as I sat down, uninvited, beside him. "Perhaps it might help if you shared your troubles with an old man."

"He didn't look at me for a long time, then his eyes searched mine. "Can you tell me anything about the women prisoners?"

"I told him they were kept in another part of the prison, and that I knew nothing about them. "Why?" I asked.

"My fiancé', Marie Gentimente, I think they have her." I could see tears running down his face.

153

"I offered to ask the guards, with whom I'd become too well acquainted. His face brightened. Then, as quickly as it had brightened, it turned dark again. "Do you think they'll take my head?" he asked.

"I thought it most likely, but I dared not say it.

"I have done nothing. Marie has done nothing. Why must we suffer?"

"I patted him on the shoulder. "My son, there are no answers to those questions in these terrible days."

"He looked into my eyes for a moment, then lowered his head, "My fate," he said flatly. He turned to the corner as if to dismiss me. I started to get up, and he turned around, "Thank you," he said, "my friend."

"The next day, we talked for a while, and he told me about himself and his fiancé, Marie. They were both aristocrats, his father was an army general, and her father was an advisor to the King. He seemed to want to talk, but whenever a guard opened the door, he crawled into the corner.

"The next afternoon, all of the other prisoners, except the young man, had been taken away. When the last one was dragged away, the young man motioned to me. I sat down beside him. "I've been thinking," the young man began, "that you have been the only one who has cared about me. And, I think that I am bound for the guillotine. I want you to promise me something."

"I assured him that I would if it were possible.

"I trust you for some reason, I'm not sure why, but I do," he said. His blue eyes stared straight into my eyes, and I could feel him searching my soul. He paused for a long time just looking at me, then he nodded, "I have a secret. In here," he said pointing between his legs. "It is a map of a buried treasure. Oh, I know it sounds far-fetched, but I assure you it is true."

"What I have to tell you must be kept a secret, at least until my death. Do you swear?"

"I could not resist a good story. After all, I am a writer. I swore. He told me this story:

"It seems that he and his fiancé, Marie Gentimente, were in bed at her parent's chateau in Montmartre making love as he said "in her *favorite position, on top". Marie was full of passion and they shared a bed as often as they could. It was early in the morning. Suddenly her maid, Collette, burst into the room and started shouting, "Get up! Get up! They're coming for you!"*

"I heard some Republican Soldiers talking about raiding the chateau and taking Marie into custody. They also said that her parents had already been arrested and that they were going to arrest her, too!

"Collette was running wildly through the room, shouting and pulling at their bed clothes. They were both naked. At last, the news sank in and they arose. He looked out of her bedroom window and saw a huge mob of people running across the lawn toward the chateau. He shouted to Marie to dress quickly.

"It only took him a couple of minutes to dress, but even with Collette helping Marie dress, she was much slower. They heard loud banging at the door to the chateau and then a crash. The front doors had been breeched.

"Marie ran to me and put her arms around me. They were so soft, so inviting."

"Go my love,' she said as she kissed me.

"I told her I would wait for her, but she wasn't even into her undergarments, and we could hear voices in the foyer below. "Go now," she said, "I will meet you tonight in the chapel at St. Pierre de Montmartre. Please go!"

"I didn't want to leave her! I didn't, but she insisted." He broke down and began to sob. A few minutes later he composed himself and continued.

"Collette pointed to the servants' stairs. They held each other a long time, then Marie pushed him away. "I ran, God forgive me, I ran," he said and sobbed softly. His body trembled. "I should have stayed," he said peering into my eyes with such pleading. I put my arms around him and tried to comfort him.

"What has happened to her?" he asked me.

"I told him I had asked the guards early in the day, and they knew nothing of a woman being taken in the past few days, only an old woman who died.

"Ferdinand sat quietly for a while. Finally he asked, "Could she be safe?" I said she could be, no one knows. He nodded. Then he took a dirty handkerchief out of his sleeve and blew his nose. He straightened up and began his story anew.

"He managed to get out of the chateau by way of the servants' entrance and ran to the woods. When he reached them, he looked back. All he could see was a mob of people wandering in and out of the house. Some took things from the house, others just smashed the windows or tore out the bushes. The whole place was in a shambles. Then he saw three soldiers running out of the servants' entrance with their long rifles. They looked around as if searching for someone, then they pointed to the woods, and he ran again. "I had no idea where I was going, but I wanted to get away from the soldiers. All day I ducked in and out of the trees and stayed away from the streets and shops. I was terrified that I would be caught and shot. Late that evening, I reached the Seine and rested. I couldn't think. My mind was on Marie and I feared the worse. I kept thinking that this was a nightmare, but I knew it wasn't so."

"He'd promised to meet Marie at the chapel at St. Pierre de Montmarte. He started off in that direction. When he arrived, he saw soldiers guarding the cathedral. He tried to sneak in, but it was too heavily guarded. He waited until dawn. No sign of Marie. He hid in the woods not far away that day. When it was dark again, he went back to St. Pierre's, but the soldiers were still there. It was no use. He wondered where he could go and be safe.

"Then he thought of Denise du Leon, his cousin who had an apartment in Les Halles.

"He made his way along the Seine, weaving through the Tuileries, darting in and out of the trees, until he came to the Pont Neuf. "When I looked across to Ile de la Cite, I shuddered, because in the moonlight I could make out the stark outlines of the Conciergerie, the Palace of Justice, inside of which I knew there was no justice."

"As he talked, I made notes on scraps of paper as he described his adventure.

"He made his way past the Pont Neuf to the Boulevard du Palais, he came to Rue St. Bon. He was only a short distance from his cousins'.

"Just as he was about to cross the street, he heard footsteps. He peered around the corner. Soldiers! He turned to go back the way he came when he saw soldiers at the other end of the street. He was trapped!

"Quickly he hid in a dark doorway and pressed himself as hard as he could against the door. The soldiers were laughing about a man they'd captured that day. Ferdinand shuddered. Then, the soldiers stopped. One called to the soldiers at the other end of the street. "Watch this street for us, we're going to get something to eat."

"The soldiers' voices faded as they walked away. Ferdinand didn't dare show his face. He stayed in the doorway. Suddenly a light came on in a house across the street. It lit up the doorway where he was hiding. He pressed against the corner of the doorway in what little shadow there was and waited. Then he saw it, no more than ten feet away. An iron cover that led to the sewer below. If only he could get down in the sewer. Just as suddenly as the light went on, it went out. He couldn't hear the soldiers at the other end of the street, so he peeked around the corner. They were facing away from him. He watched them and kept an eye on the sewer cover. He got down on his hands and knees and crawled to the sewer cover. As he tried to move it, it made a noise, and he looked up at the soldiers. They paid no attention to the sound.   "Slowly and as quietly as he could, he pulled the heavy iron cover back and climbed down a wooden ladder into the foul-smelling sewer. He pulled the cover back over the hole, climbed on down until he reached the bottom.

"He reached out and felt his way along the stone wall. It was slimy and the smell was overwhelming. He coughed. He waited. Did the soldiers hear him? He pulled his handkerchief from his sleeve and put it over his nose. That seemed to help. He was standing ankle-deep in something very gooey. He sloshed as he walked. The noise of his footsteps seemed very loud. It was pitch black in the sewer. He had no idea which way the sewer led. Yet, somehow, he felt safe.

"Ferdinand moved along the sewer as quietly as he could. He came to a bend and followed it.

"He was very tired. He stopped and leaned against the wall for a while to get his breath - such as it was - and then moved on. A few *minutes later, he came around a bend and could smell fresh air. Then he saw a ray of moonlight up ahead. He made his way to where the light was coming from and saw that it was a grate over the sewer. He could not see out, accept an outline of a building above him. The fresh air revived him somewhat, and he leaned against the wall to rest. He knew he had to move out of the light when daybreak came, lest anyone saw him, but for now, it was the best he'd felt in a long time. He fell asleep standing up.*

"The clatter of hooves on the street above woke him. Ferdinand quickly moved out of the light. He wanted to get his bearings, but didn't dare go above ground. By now he was filthy, smelly, and, of course, exhausted. He decided to move onto the next grate and see if he could determine where he was. It was a good thing he moved when he did because a woman dumped garbage and the night's droppings from her family down the grate only seconds after he moved away. Ferdinand moved slowly through the muck and mire to the next grate. He stopped short because a soldier was standing on it. He waited until the soldier moved then peered up trying to determine where he was. It was no use. He could see nothing but sky. He moved on. As he passed by other grates, he saw nothing familiar. By nightfall, he was very hungry and very tired.

"Ferdinand decided that when he could hear nothing above him, he would venture out through another manhole, if he could find one, and head for his cousin's house. He found a manhole late that night. He listened for several minutes and heard nothing. The wooden ladder leading up to the manhole cover was rickety. When he put his foot on the first step to test it, he heard a noise. It was coming from around a bend in the tunnel. He saw light from a candle casting a glow against the wall. Curious, Ferdinand went to the corner and looked down the long sewer tunnel. Perhaps a dozen meters away, he saw that the light was coming from a doorway in the wall of the tunnel. Then he saw a man, dressed in a dirty apron, come out of the door and go to the other side of the tunnel. The man began pulling stones from the wall. Soon there was a large pile of stones next to him. He picked up his candle and went inside the new hole. Ferdinand was puzzled. What was this man doing?

"Not long after, the man came out of the new hole. He'd left his candle in the new hole so that there was a glow coming from there, too. He went back inside the door.

"He wasn't gone a minute until he emerged with four golden candlesticks in his arms. He carried the candlesticks and put them into the new hole. Ferdinand heard him laughing and talking out loud to himself, "Fools, trading these for a few loaves of bread." He came out of the new hole and back inside the doorway. Then he came back out again, this time with a painting, and put that into the new hole as well.

"The man made three trips back and forth, each time carrying something of value, and each time staying in the new hole for longer and longer periods of time talking to himself.

"Then he went back inside the door and stayed for several minutes. Finally he came out again carrying a chest which made a metallic sound when he jiggled it. He carried it into the new hole.

"By now Ferdinand had a plan. He watched and listened to the man in the new hole. He seemed busy. While keeping an eye on the new opening, he quickly went to the door and looked inside. He was surprised to see a cellar, stacked with sacks of flour. He also saw a narrow set of steps. Trying not to make a sound, he went inside the cellar and up the steps. The stairway came up behind a long wooden counter. He knew right away that he was in a bakery. There were rows of fresh baked bread lying on a long counter. He grabbed the nearest loaf of bread and bit into it. It was like nectar from the gods! As he was eating the bread, he looked around the shoppe. Across the counter, to his left, in one corner was a large brick oven. Bread was baking. As he looked to his right, he could see the front of the shopped with a door and several tiny windows. In the corner near the door was a large barrel. There was also a chair and a small desk next to the barrel. The long, narrow shop was lit by a single candle near the oven. Light from a gas street lamp outside streamed in the dirty windows. Ferdinand could see rather well.

"Suddenly, he heard the man coming back into the cellar. He didn't come up the stairs, and then went back out to his "vault" across the sewer tunnel. Ferdinand carefully moved the loaves of bread so that the man would not miss one. He went around the

counter and peered through the dirty windows. Outside, he could see
that the shoppe was near an intersection. But what were the names of
the streets? he asked himself? Just then, he heard the baker coming
up the cellar stairs. He almost panicked, but managed to get behind
the barrel just in time as to not be seen.

"The baker was a large, stout man, and he walked very heavy
causing the floor to shake from his weight. He had a round face with
a large mustache. He wore a bill-less cap and the dirty apron. His
sleeves were rolled up revealing huge forearms. He went directly to
the oven, opened the iron door, and taking his long a wooden spatula,
he began to scoop out three loaves of bread at a time. He examined the
first, and satisfied it was done, placed it and the other loaves on the
counter. He didn't notice that one was missing. He took nine more
loaves from the oven, then went to the far end of the counter where
other loaves were rising prior to being baked. He stood only a few feet
from Ferdinand. He started putting the dough on the spatula when
he suddenly stopped and put them down. He began sniffing the air.
He turned toward the barrel, sniffing loudly like a dog. He walked
toward the barrel and stopped only a few feet away. He sniffed again,
then he looked down at his shoes, bent down and sniffed. "Whew!" he
said. Then, satisfied that the smell came from his shoes, he went back
to the counter and took the rising bread and three by three put the
new loaves into the oven.

"After he'd taken care of the baking, he went behind the counter
and pulled out two more gold candlesticks, a cane with a gold head,
several time pieces, an ornate clock, and a pistol. He filled his arms
with the loot and went back down the stairs.

"As soon as the baker was gone, Ferdinand tried to open the door,
but it was locked. As he started to go back to the stairs, he saw a piece
of paper on the desk. He held it up to the dim light and read. It was a
bill of sale for the bakery. The address of the bakery was on the bill.
He put the bill back on the counter and started to go back down the
stairs but he chanced to look under the counter. There was even more
loot! Obviously 'confiscated' from the rich. Earrings, jewelry of all
sorts, even a set of false teeth!

"The baker was rich! Or at least he would be when he sold the
goods. Ferdinand could hear the man in the vault, laughing and

talking to his bounty. If only he had some of this loot, Ferdinand surmised, he could get enough money to escape to England or Austria. He looked around. There were pen and ink on the desk, but no paper. He decided he would leave, and when the baker sealed up the wall to the cellar, he, Ferdinand, would open the vault and take what he wanted. He saw a leather apron hanging on a nail near the barrel. The underside of the apron was light colored.

"Ferdinand decided to draw a map of the location of the shoppe, its address, and where the 'vault' was. He had to wait, however, because the baker returned for more loot. When he had gone back down the stairs, Ferdinand drew the map on the leather apron. The apron was too big to hide in his clothes, so he took a knife from the counter and cut off the map and then wrapped it in a piece of oil cloth which covered the counter. It hung over sufficiently so a piece of it would not be missed. He decided he would throw the rest of the apron in the sewer. He took the map, wrapped in oilcloth, and put it inside his shirt, but it was too small and nearly fell out after he'd walked only a few paces. He had an idea. He put the map in the crotch of his pants. It didn't show much, and besides, he surmised, the ladies might think it appealing.

"The baker came back again for more loot, and Ferdinand waited a few minutes then, while the baker was playing with his treasures in the vault, Ferdinand slipped down the stairs, out of the cellar (with the map, a candle, and two loaves of bread) and back into the shadows of the tunnel. He planned to return the next night and get a share of the loot, enough for him and Marie to escape out of the country. He knew the sewer would be dark at night, and so he made two deep crosses in the wall of the tunnel near the bend so he could find the place.

"He made his way back to an open manhole, and resting on the ladder, ate the two loaves of bread and fell asleep.

"His sleep was too deep. For when he awoke, the manhole cover was being taken off. The sun was shining brightly in the tunnel, revealing Ferdinand. A man above him, probably a sewer worker, shouted for the soldiers.

"Ferdinand began to run as fast as he could. He heard the soldiers entering the tunnel through the manhole. Then one of them

shouted as Ferdinand ran under a grate, "There he is! Stop citizen!
Stop!" Ferdinand had no intention of stopping. He kept on running
as fast as his legs would carry him.

"Several times he came to deep pockets of sewage which slowed
him down. These pockets not only slowed him down, but wore him
down as well.

"Before long, Ferdinand could hardly stay erect. His feet felt as if
they weighed a ton! As he turned to see the soldiers gaining on him,
he fell. He tried to get up but it was too slippery and his feet gave out
from under him. When he looked up, all he saw was the butt of a gun
coming toward his face.

"The next thing he knew, he was being dragged through the halls
of the Conciergerie and thrown into the cell."

April stumbled to the couch and sank down onto it
exhausted. She was only halfway through the story, but she
just couldn't go on. What a story! she said to herself. She put
the book down on the couch. She was tired, her eyes were
burning, and her brain was reeling from all of the translation
she had to do to read the story. She rubbed her eyes, stood up,
walked to the French doors and opened them. It was still
pouring down rain, but the smell of the ozone-filled air was
refreshing.

She took a deep breath and let it out slowly. She knew
she'd sleep well.

As she stood there, her mind began racing. The author had
said the story was true. If it was, had the baker's vault ever
been found? What happened to Ferdinand? What happened
to the map? The more she stood there thinking, the more
refreshed she felt. Her insatiable curiosity was finally kicking
in after all those months of writer's block, and it was like being
born all over again. For the first time in a long time April was
happy!

She laughed out loud. There it was! The plot for her next
book. It would be all about a woman who discovered the

buried treasure! Sure, why not? She could actually feel the adrenalin begin to race through her veins.

She went into the bedroom and took off her robe, went to the armoire and got out 'old faithful', her white bikini! Her fingers were beginning to itch.

Just as she was fastening the bra to the bikini, the doorbell rang. "Damnit," she said. "Just when I was revving up!"

April called out, "Just a minute," and put her robe back on over the bikini.

She went to the door, "Who is it?" she asked.

"Jean Pierre," she heard the voice reply. "Are you all right?"

April wasn't. She wanted to get to work. Resigned, she shrugged and opened the door. "I'm fine," she said, "just a little tired. What time is it?"

Jean Pierre looked at his watch. "Just after eleven."

She had been reading for nearly six straight hours, she thought.

Jean Pierre stood in the doorway waiting. Finally, he said, "Are you sure you're all right?"

"Huh? Oh, yes, sorry," April said pulling her mind back to the present. She motioned for him to come in.

Jean Pierre took off his light brown trench coat, "This is a little wet," he said looking for a place to put his coat.

April took it from him and threw it on the nearest chair. Her mind was fighting her.

Jean Pierre looked at her with a questioning expression. "Perhaps I've come at a bad time," he said, not meaning it of course.

"Oh, no," April said. "I was about to go to bed, but let's have some coffee. I need to clear my mind anyway. Sit down. I'll make some." April went off to the kitchen. Jean Pierre crossed to the French doors and closed them. He saw the book on the couch. Ah, ha, he thought, I'll bet that is the book Paul was talking about.

Just as he was about to pick it up, April poked her head out of the kitchen door. "I forgot to ask, would you rather have a drink or something?"

"No, I was just in the neighborhood. I had to have dinner with a couple of clients. I just decided to see if you were up."

"Oh, okay," April said, closing the door.

Jean Pierre picked up the book and took it to the desk. He wrote down the name of the book, the author's name, and the date it was published. He would follow up in the morning with a couple of historians at the Sorbonne. He had to know what this was all about.

He had just put the book back down on the couch when April came in from the kitchen with a tray and two coffee mugs. "I hope this is all right. I just can't get my coffee to taste the same as the bistros around here," she said as she put the tray on the coffee table in front of the couch. She picked up the book and put it on the coffee table. She flopped down on the couch.

"I must confess," Jean Pierre said as he sat down next to her, "I did have an ulterior motive for coming."

"Oh?"

"I couldn't get you out of my mind. You are so wonderful. I hesitate to say this, but I think I'm falling in love with you."

April was in mid-sip of her coffee, and when he said he was falling in love with her, it triggered a thousand thoughts. None of them romantic. He's in love. I got a new idea for a book. It's the same old story, except reversed. I'm not in love with him. Yet, I want to write, she thought. She was staring out into space as her mind went on without her.

"April? April did I say something wrong?"

April heard Jean Pierre say something somewhere in the distance. "Oh, sorry," she said refocusing on him. "I got the stares. I get them sometimes. You were saying?"

"I was saying that I was falling in love with you."

"Yes, I know."

"You know. But you don't care?"

"Oh, yes, I care, Jean Pierre. I care very much. It's just that it's, it's," she searched for the right answer, instead she came up with a cliche that when she said it she winced inside, "it's just too soon."

Jean Pierre did his best to look disappointed, "Oh, I didn't mean to rush you," he said in his best hurt tone.

"I'm sure you didn't," April said, kissing him on the cheek, "I just am kinda funny that way. I need time to sort out my feelings," she said. She said it because she didn't know what else to say.

"I am sorry that I was pressuring you."

"Oh, that's not it, Jean Pierre. Really. You were a perfect gentleman." Ouch, she thought, another cliche. She turned to face him. "Look, I don't know what I feel right now. I had a great time yesterday and last night, and it was terrific, but sometimes I jump into things and regret them later. I don't want to do this to you or frankly to me. Jean Pierre," she said taking his hands, "please bear with me a little while. I'm not trying to hurt you, or to say I don't love you because I don't know whether I do or not, I don't know what I feel," she was talking fast, and she was on a roll. She got up from the couch and began pacing as she talked. "You see I have a history of jumping into things, affairs, ideas, everything without really thinking them out, and then, later, I'm sorry I did, and yet I keep doing it. I want to break that habit, but I don't know how unless I just put my foot down on myself and stop. You're a wonderful man. You're charming, sexy and very good looking, and that's part of the problem because I'm always drawn to your type, and when I get drawn to you, I let my emotions overrun my brain, and then I get into a lot of trouble. You see what I mean?"

Jean Pierre watched as she paced. She's a psycho, he thought as she prattled on. "It's too soon?" he asked as a joke.

April stopped and pointed at him. "You understand! Great! So you see, I can't tell you what my feelings for you are because I don't know. I will, soon, I think, but right now," she stopped in front of him, looked down and held her hands out to him. "I don't know."

Jean Pierre did not want to blow this relationship, at least until he had found out all he needed to know about the book. He got up, reached out and took April's hands. "Darling, forgive me. I've been such a bore. I had no intention of upsetting you. I just wanted to be honest about my feelings for you. I understand that it will take time for our relationship to grow."

April breathed a deep sigh of relief inside, and smiled at him. "You are so thoughtful. Thank you," she said, and she meant it.

Jean Pierre decided that retreat was the better part of valor, and took her in his arms. "April, I want you to know that I understand, and I respect you for being so honest with me. I will give you however much time you will need. I would appreciate your calling me when you've thought it all over. Until then, ma cherie, au revoir."

With that, he picked up his coat, opened the door, blew her a kiss and closed the door quietly.

April heaved a great sigh of relief. And as she stood there, her fingers began to itch. It was time for the ol' bikini to get back to work!

CHAPTER TWENTY

Kevin and Suzette followed LeMieux in Kevin's Citron as LeMieux's car wove in and out of the cluttered Paris traffic. Suddenly, LeMieux pulled into the familiar courtyard in front of the apartment house where April was staying. To their further surprise, Pepe Duvall got out of the car with LeMieux.

"Who's the other man?" Suzette asked.

"Unless I miss my guess, he's Pepe Duvall."

"Isn't that the guy they want to question about that killing St. Tropez?"

"Yeah, that's the one."

"So he's connected to Duer," Kevin mused. "The plot thickens."

Kevin told Suzette that the apartment house was the one where April was staying. Suzette arched an eyebrow and gave a low whistle. "Do you think she's involved with Duer?"

"No, of course not," Kevin said too quickly.

"Really? You don't seem all that sure."

"Suzette, April Mason is just a tourist, and you know damn well that's all there is to it."

"Well," she said sitting back in her seat, "if you say so."

Kevin gave her his best mock grin then shook his head. "Wait a minute. You don't suppose that Jean Pierre's sister lives there."

"And LeMieux is just visiting his wife? I don't think so."

After leaving her apartment, Jean Pierre stood outside April's door for a moment trying to collect his thoughts. He took the notes he'd made about the book out of his pocket and looked at them again. A smirk crept over his face. He put them back into his pocket and started down the long hallway to the elevator. This was going to be very interesting, he thought.

Just as he approached the elevator Paul LeMieux and Duvall stepped out of an alcove and confronted him. Jean Pierre was shocked. "Paul. What are you doing here?"

"We want to talk to you, Jean Pierre, about your American friend."

Jean Pierre began to sweat. "Why?"

"You said that she was a writer, I believe," Paul said.

"Yes."

"What does she look like?" Duvall interrupted.

Jean Pierre didn't like the looks of Duvall - especially his beady eyes that blinked constantly. "Is this your 'assistant', Paul?" Jean Pierre asked, not bothering to answer Duvall.

"Yes."

"I see." Jean Pierre said looking Duvall in the eyes. He wasn't about to betray Paul's confidence and ask if this was the man who lost the book, but he was certain it was.

Duvall moved a step closer. "You didn't answer my question. What does the lady look like?"

Jean Pierre glanced at Paul who nodded. "She's about five foot six, brown eyes, brown hair and a body that would be the envy of many women."

Duvall rolled his eyes and thought back to the book stall. "Yeah, that could be the one," he said to Paul.

"What is this all about, Paul?"

"The book, Jean Pierre."

"What book?"

"The one I spoke to you about this afternoon."

"Ah, yes. The one that was lost," Jean Pierre said with a quick look at Duvall.

"Does she have such a book?" Duvall interrupted.

Jean Pierre fingered the notes in his pocket. If he told them yes, his chance to make money from the sale of the book was gone. If he said no, and they found the notes on him, his life could be in danger.

"Jean Pierre. Does she have the book?" Paul repeated with a strong edge to his voice.

They don't even know if April is the right woman, Jean Pierre thought. He decided to take a chance. "Frankly, I don't know which book you're talking about. She has a lot of books in her apartment."

"You would know this one," Paul said. "It is small, very old and to us very valuable."

Jean Pierre was sweating a lot by now, and the perspiration began running down his forehead and onto his nose. This was not lost on either Paul or Duvall. He couldn't think.

"Let me persuade him," Duvall said stepping closer to Jean Pierre. Jean Pierre backed away.

Paul reached out and pulled Duvall back. "I don't think that will be necessary. You do know, don't you Jean Pierre?"

Jean Pierre looked first at Paul then to Duvall. They both looked as if they could kill him at any moment. Especially, Duvall. It was decision time. He drew a deep breath, then said, "She does have an old book which she is reading. I saw it on her desk."

"Good," Duvall said. "And what's the name of the book?"

"I really don't know. She didn't tell me, and I never saw the cover."

"Well, let's go see," Duvall said moving toward the hallway.

Paul stopped him. "Wait. I don't want any trouble tonight. Jean Pierre, what is her name?"

"April Mason."

"I think we have all we need tonight," Paul said and nodded to Duvall. He was reluctant but finally moved toward the elevator. "Let's get some fresh air, shall we Jean Pierre?"

Jean Pierre was relieved. He knew he wasn't completely out of the woods, but at least they didn't attack him. He followed Paul and Duvall to the elevator.

The three men came out of the apartment house and stopped beside LeMieux's car.

"Well, look over there!" Suzette exclaimed.

"What the hell is Jean Pierre doing with them?"

Suzette took her camera with the long lens out of her handbag and clicked off several pictures of the three men standing under the lights by the entrance. "I'll get these printed up first thing in the morning."

"Good," Kevin said. "I hope you took the lens cap off this time."

Suzette winced, "You'll never let me forget that will you?"

Kevin chuckled, "Never."

Paul motioned for Duvall to get in. As he did, Jean Pierre started to walk away, but Paul grabbed his sleeve. "Jean Pierre. This is very serious business. Something you should stay out of. Duvall wouldn't hesitate to kill you or the woman. My advice is to stay away from her for a while. If she isn't the one, I'll let you know and you can continue your fun, but for now, don't even think of seeing her."

Jean Pierre was sweating profusely now. He could see the danger in Paul's eyes, and he knew he had to do as Paul said.

"All right, Paul. Whatever you say. I don't want to cause trouble."

"Trouble is a very mild way of putting it, Jean Pierre. Remember that." With that, he let go of Jean Pierre's coat and got into his car.

Kevin and Suzette watched the exchange. They couldn't hear what the two men were saying, but from their body language, they both knew something was up. When LeMieux started the car, Suzette asked, "What do we do now? Follow them and risk breaking our cover? After all I'm sure Jean Pierre will recognize your car."

"Let's sit tight. Maybe Jean Pierre will leave right away."

Sure enough, Jean Pierre went immediately to his car, started it, and sped out of the parking lot.

"They turned left, Jean Pierre turned right," Suzette said anxiously.

"Got it," Kevin said starting his car and pulling out of the enclosed courtyard parking lot. He immediately turned left.

He saw LeMieux's car three blocks ahead. "Got 'em," he said.

LeMieux went directly to Duer's apartment. Kevin and Suzette parked a block down the street right behind the new stakeout crew.

A few minutes later, Duer rocked back in his desk chair in the library. He was pondering what the two men seated on the other side of his desk told him. Finally he got up and walked to the fireplace. "So you are not sure this is the right woman nor whether or not she has the book, but from what you've told me it seems very possible she is the woman at the book stall."

"Why don't I just go there and see, and if she is the one, I'll get the book," Duvall said.

"Yes, I'm sure you'd get the book, Duvall. But if she is not the right woman, I'm also certain you'd cause trouble. I don't want to risk that at this time. On the other hand, you are the only one who can recognize her. Paul. Are you positive your brother-in-law won't warn her?"

"Jean Pierre is no fool. He understood every word," Paul said confidently.

"All right. First we must make certain she is the right woman. Duvall, I want you to work with Paul and come up with a suitable disguise. We know the police are looking for you. Tomorrow morning I want you to stake out that apartment. If she is the one, I want you to do nothing, do you understand, nothing," Duer commanded. "Once you are certain she is or is not the right woman, I want you to come back here and report to me. Do you understand?"

Duvall nodded.

"Good. And Paul, be very careful leaving and returning here. I do not want the police connecting Duvall to me. Do you understand?"

"Yes, Monsieur Duer. I will be very careful." Paul said.

Suzette and Kevin were filling in Le Pluete on the night's activities when a man came in the office and dropped a manila envelope on Le Pluete's desk. He turned and left immediately. Le Pluete opened the envelope and took out several 8 X 10 pictures. "Very nice, Suzette," he said, handing her the photographs.

"Thank you," she said quickly scanning them before handing them to Kevin.

"You were right, Suzette, the man in question is Pepe Duvall. And you say the other man is Jean Pierre Demain, Paul LeMieux's brother-in-law?"

"Yeah. I can't figure out why he's with those two. He may be a rotter, as they say, but he's no criminal. My only guess is he ran into them at the apartment house. He's seeing a woman who lives there."

"Why don't you tell the Inspector about the 'woman', Kevin?"

Kevin gave her a look that could kill, but Suzette just laughed.

"Do you know this woman, Kevin?"

"Yes. It's a long story."

"Enlighten me," Le Pluete said as he sat back in his chair.

April put down her cup of coffee and curled up on the couch. She picked up the book and began to read:

"*Ferdinand came close to me and whispered, 'I have the map with me,' he said pointing to his trousers' crotch. I was surprised. 'I want you to have it. You are my last friend.' He began to reach into his trousers when we heard the clanking of the keys of the guards approaching. We separated immediately. The guards unlocked the door, and I was summoned. I was subsequently released after making my apologies to the Committee for Public Safety. Robspierre was feeling generous that day.*

"*I did not see Ferdinand until three days later in the Place de Revolution. I had been informed that Ferdinand was among the several aristocrats who were to be guillotined that morning. Curiosity got the best of me.*

"*The crowd was tremendous. Several thousand people jammed the huge square to witness the spectacle. I was pushed and tousled as the mob strained to see. I made my way to the small pathway created by the soldiers for the tumbrils which held the prisoners. The carts were lined up as far as the eye could see. I wanted to see if this was Ferdinand's day. It was. I saw him. He was standing alone in an old tumbril about fifty feet from my position. His hands were tied in front of him. He stood there, very erect, proud, almost like a statue. As the cart moved forward one more position toward the platform, he balanced himself so as not to fall, and when it stopped, he again resumed his stance. It was impossible to hear or be heard above the noise and cheering of the crowd.*

"*The rest of this story I must attribute to Collette, Marie's maid servant, whom I sought out later. She told me that when the mob invaded her chateau, Marie managed to dress in servants' clothing. When they tore down the door to her bedroom, she and Collette simply stood there and pointed to the servant's door and said that their mistress had escaped out that way. They showed the mob the door, and they raced through it. However, one of the men in a tri-cornered hat with the red, white and blue culotte, stayed behind. Both women froze as he walked over to them. He was a tall, powerful-looking, shabbily-dressed man. He had a glint in his eye as he approached them. He first grabbed Collette and pulled her to him.*

Now Collette is a small woman, with a pleasant, but not pretty face. He pulled off her cap and then took hold of her hands and examined them. Then he shoved her aside and grabbed Marie.

"She tried to fight him off, but he was far too strong. He pulled off her cap and her long, flowing blond hair came tumbling down. He grunted and looked at her hands. Then he laughed. "You're far too pretty to be a servant," he said. Marie shuddered. "But, if you do as I say, perhaps you can be spared."

"Marie tried to pull away again, and he slapped her hard across the face. She would have fallen back, but he still had hold of her hand. 'One more move like that pretty one, and you'll lose your head.' With that, he ordered her to put her cap back on to hide her hair. Marie, by now, was in shock and did as she was told. Then he picked her up and threw her over his shoulder. Collette tried to come to her aid, but the man flicked her away. 'If you want your mistress to live, woman, you'll do nothing. And, if you like, you can come along. But I warn you, if you try to do anything to help her, I will turn her over to the authorities, and kill you.'

"Collette followed the two of them down the stairs and out onto the lawn. Everywhere, people were throwing furniture and paintings out onto the lawn. A fire had already been started in the upstairs of the house, yet the mob continued to ransack the house and the grounds.

"As they passed through the mob, Collette heard one of the women shout, 'There goes Jacques with his booty!' Everyone within earshot laughed. "Jacques took Marie and Collette to the cellar of a tavern. It was his place. There he tied Collette up and tore the clothes off Marie. He tied her to the filthy bed and repeatedly raped Marie as Collette was forced to watch. He drank heavily in-between his bouts with Marie. When he tired of having his way with Marie, he'd beat Collette. She passed out in a stupor. This went on for two days. By this time, Marie was completely spent. Finally, when she passed out three times during one of his escapades, he hit her, but could not wake her. Collette was hanging by her ropes now, her body bloody and beaten. Through a haze she could see him coming toward her and braced for another beating, but he cut her ropes and she fell to the

floor. Jacques shouted for her to attend to her mistress, kicked her and left, locking the door behind him.

"*Collette managed to crawl to Marie and untie her. She found a bucket of water and some bread. She ate to regain her strength, then went to Marie and began to wash her. Within a few hours, Marie was sitting up and eating. The two women were completely broken in spirit as well as body.*

"*Jacques did not return that day. Each time they heard a noise, the two women huddled together in fear.*

"*It was not until the morning of the fourth day that Jacques returned. He was sober, but still as mean as he could be. Marie and Collette were sitting on the bed shaking from fear. He looked down at them and laughed. 'You were good for while, woman,' Jacques said to Marie, 'but you're not worth my trouble any more. Get out!'*

"*Both were stunned. Jacques then raised his hand as if to strike them, but seeing them cower, he merely laughed and walked out of the room.*

"*Marie and Collette, now dressed in rags, fit in with the crowd in the tavern above the cellar. Because their faces were swollen and bruised, no one paid attention to them. Arm in arm they shuffled out of the tavern and into the street.*

"*As they made their way, not knowing where to go, they saw a soldier nailing a list upon a tree. It was the list of people to be guillotined that day. Marie pulled Collette over to the tree and read the list. There was Ferdinand's name! She implored Collette to take her to the Place de Revolution.*

"*They arrived in time to see Ferdinand, his hands tied, standing in a tumbril. Marie shouted, but he did not hear her. She summoned up all her strength and pushed and shoved her way toward the cart, shouting Ferdinand's name. Tears streamed down her cheeks as she fought to get to the cart. Each time the cart moved, she had to change direction and fight her way through more people. Collette did her best to help Marie, pushing people aside and kicking men in the shins to get them out of the way. Marie finally reached the soldiers lining the makeshift roadway for the carts. She screamed Ferdinand's name time and time again, but it wasn't until his cart pulled up only a few feet away that he finally heard her. He strained to see her, but the* crowd was so huge he shook his head in frustration. *Collette managed to wriggle her way beside Marie, and they both shouted and waved. Then he saw her. Tears ran down his face as he tried to move toward her, but the soldier guarding the tumbril hit him with the butt of his long rifle.*

"Marie was straining between two soldiers who were pushing her away. Her hands reached out for Ferdinand. He tried to reach out, too, but he was too far away. She was screaming, 'I love you, Ferdie!'

"I love you, Marie," Ferdinand shouted repeatedly.

"The soldiers in the line were becoming annoyed and turned to push her away, but just as they turned, Collette kicked them both as hard as she could. Marie burst between them, ran to the cart and threw her arms around Ferdinand's feet. The soldier guarding the cart began to pull her away. "Take me with you," Marie pleaded.

"No!" Ferdinand shouted.

"You must. I have nothing to live for but you!" she replied.

By now the soldier was pulling her arms loose from around Ferdinand's legs. Marie hung on for dear life. Then Collette was beside Marie pushing the soldier away. The crowd loved the fight. They roared with glee. As they struggled, an officer on horseback arrived on the scene, pulled his sword from its scabbard and was about to strike Collette, when Marie let go and raised her hand to the officer, 'Stop. It is I you want,' she said pushing Collette aside. 'I am Marie Antoinette Gentimente, daughter of the Minister of Finance for the City of Paris and a good friend of King Louis.'

"The officer sat back on his horse and roared with laughter. He put his hands on his hips and said, 'I had the honor of putting your father to death!' Marie grabbed for his foot, but the horse moved, and she fell on the cobblestones in a heap. The soldier bent down to pick her up, but the officer commanded him to get back to the cart. "You, too," the officer shouted, "should have your head cut off."

"Marie picked herself up and stood in front of the officer, 'That is precisely what I want,' she said. 'I want to die with my fiancé,' she said, pointing to Ferdinand.

"Nooo!" Ferdinand screamed.

"The officer looked at her. There was a hush in the crowd nearby as everyone waited for his answer. His lip curled, and he looked at

her for a long time, then motioned to the soldier in the cart, 'Put this bitch in the cart. She shall have her wish!' The crowd roared with approval.

"Marie curtseyed to the officer, went around and climbed up on the cart, and stood beside Ferdinand. She put her arms around him and gave him a kiss. The crowd roared again!

"The officer looked at Collette, 'Do you want to get on the cart, too?'

"No," Collette said shaking her head, and she ran to the line of soldiers who let her back into the crowd. This gave the people even more reason to laugh and cheer.

"From my vantage point I could see everything that happened, but I could not hear what was said.

"Marie untied Ferdinand's hands, and they embraced as the tumbril moved closer to the platform.

"When it was their turn, Marie asked to go first. Ferdinand, standing on the platform with her, watched as the blade did its work. The cheering was extremely loud. Then Ferdinand bowed his head, crossed himself, and let the executioners do their job.

"I made my way over to where Collette was standing. Her tears were dried on her face when reached her side. I introduced myself to her, and we went to find the bodies.

"I left Collette as she walked beside the cart carrying several bodies including Marie and Ferdinand. She promised to come and see me, and so she did. And that is how I knew Marie's story.

"As she left that cold evening in September, she left me with a point to ponder. She said that she had made sure that they received a proper burial with a priest, and that they would be together for eternity. When I asked her what that meant, she said that no one would ever find their bodies. Thus, the secret of the baker's vault will never be revealed."

April closed the book slowly. She had been crying for a long time. She was exhausted. She heaved a great sigh, got up and walked out onto her terrace. "Where are you, Marie?" she asked softly.

177

CHAPTER TWENTY-ONE

April reread the story of Ferdinand and the baker's vault story several times the next day. The only clue she could find to the whereabouts of the grave was that the couple was given a Catholic funeral. But where? She decided to call the office of the Catholic Diocese of Paris to see if there were still records from back then, and if so, how she might access them.

Paul LeMieux and Duvall had been waiting in the hallway outside April's apartment for several hours. Both were tired, impatient and getting nervous each time one of the other residents walked by them. "That is the third time that woman has seen us," Paul said as an older woman walked past them and entered the apartment across from April's. "I don't like the way she looks at us."

"Would she call the police?"

"I don't know," Paul said, rubbing his chin. He paced back and forth for a few seconds then made a decision. "We have to get out of here for a while. Monsieur Duer said we should avoid trouble, and unless I miss my guess, that woman is on the phone to the manager right now. Come on." Paul turned and walked toward the elevator. When he turned back, he saw Duvall knocking on April's door. "What are you doing?" he whispered loudly.

"What we came here to do," Duvall said knocking again.

April was making notes when she heard the knock on the door. She got up and went to the door. There was another, more insistent knock. She pulled the door open. There stood a rather short man wearing an obviously fake beard and a raincoat. "Yes?"

Duvall stared at April. He wasn't sure. She wasn't wearing her coat and hat. He was confused.

"May I help you?" April said looking at him expectantly. There was something sinister about with the way he looked at her, but she couldn't make out what it was.

LeMieux walked up behind Duvall and looked at April. The two men were just staring at her. April felt very uncomfortable. Then LeMieux said, "Well?"

Duvall said, "I'm not sure."

"Sure about what?" April asked.

LeMieux put his hand on Duvall's shoulder. "I'm sorry," he said to April as he pulled Duvall away, "I believe we have the wrong apartment. Please excuse us."

April frowned. Something was wrong here, she thought.

Duvall resisted LeMieux's attempt to pull him away at first, but after giving April the once over again, he shook his head, turned and the two men headed down the hall to the elevator.

April didn't say anything. She just watched as they got on the elevator and the doors closed. Then a chill ran down her spine. She shuddered, shook her head and went back inside her apartment. After she shut the door, she leaned against it and tried to figure out what that was all about. Finally she shrugged her shoulders. It was a mystery to her. She went back to her desk.

Outside, in the parking lot, LeMieux shoved Duvall against the car. "What the hell were you doing?"

"I had to see her."

"And?"

"I'm not sure it was the woman I bumped into on the Quay. She looks somewhat like her, but without her coat and hat I cannot be certain."

Paul rolled his eyes. "All right, let's get out of here." They got into the car and drove away - closely followed by two Interpol detectives.

Kevin was in his cubical writing an article when the phone rang. It was Inspector Le Pluete. "Kevin. Our people following LeMieux tell me he went back to that same apartment house this morning. They seem to have waited on the third floor for nearly two hours. Three of the residents reported seeing them just standing outside the elevator pretending to be looking up an address or something. A lady down the hall reported the men to the manager who called the police who called us. The lady said that they knocked on the apartment across from door to hers and briefly spoke with the woman there. Then they left."

"Do we have a name for the woman they spoke with?"

"Yes. Miss April Mason."

Kevin almost fell off his chair. Oh god, he thought, how in the hell did she get mixed up with that bunch?

"Kevin, are you still there?" Le Pluete said into the phone.

Kevin nodded his head and answered, "Yes, I'm still here."

"We are going to investigate this woman. She may be the key to what Duer's up to."

"Don't bother, Inspector," Kevin said. "I know all about her."

"You do?" Le Pluete said.

Kevin heard the surprise in Le Pluete's voice. "I'm on my way over. I'll explain then."

Kevin put down the phone and grabbed his coat off the back his chair. As he was walking out, George approached.

"Kevin, when am I going to get that copy on the Ritz bar?"

"Later," Kevin said as he brushed past George. George stared after Kevin. He's not doing his best work, he said to himself. I don't want to fire him, but he has to learn respect.

Jean Pierre fingered the notes in his hand as he sat at his desk in the tourism building. He was stymied. He didn't dare go see April, but if he didn't, he couldn't get his hands on the book. His calls to rare book sellers had all been encouraging, but without the book he had nothing to sell. As much as he hated to admit it, he had to go see her and take his chances with LeMieux.

Snooky, in her white smock, carefully removed another sheet of Algerian dinars and put them on the rack near the printing press to dry thoroughly. Piled in one corner of the room were six, very neatly stacked piles of the bills. She estimated the street value of this money was about six million American dollars.

As she placed the next clean sheet onto the press, she noted that she had only enough of the specially watermarked paper to print fifty more sheets. It was time to call Paul LeMieux.

"You aren't sure?" Duer asked incredulously.

"She wore a hat and coat, Monsieur Duer. It all happened so fast."

Francois looked first at Paul then at Duvall, then shook his head. He threw up his hands and pulled his enormous bulk out of his desk chair, walked around the desk and stood squarely in front of Duvall. "Duvall, if you had said yes, this was the woman, I would have been happy. Had you said no, it was not the woman, I would have been disappointed but accepting, but," he stood on his toes and looked down at Duvall and shouted right in his face, "But, when you say you don't know, it makes me crazy, and I can't stand to be crazy!" He looked at LeMieux. Paul was avoiding his eyes.

Francois rocked back on heels and tried to compose himself. He walked to the fireplace and rubbed his face with both hands. Both men stood watching him. They were afraid of what he was going to say or do next.

Finally, after about a minute of silence, Duer took a deep breath and looked at them over the top of his eyes. "Tell me again everything that happened."

Duvall went over every minute of the morning. But when he began telling of going to the apartment and knocking, Duer stopped him. "Wait a minute. Tell me again why you went to that specific apartment?"

"Because of Jean Pierre," Duvall started, but LeMieux interrupted.

"That was the apartment that Jean Pierre had come out of the other night. He told me he was seeing an American, so I put two and two together. I knew this had to be an American woman. So I wanted Duvall to see her."

"All right," Duer said holding up his hands. "I remember now. And you are right, Paul, she is the only lead we have." He began to pace. He was thinking hard. Finally, after a couple of minutes, Duer stopped and rubbed his chin. "I think it is worth the risk. I want you two to search her apartment, but only when you are certain she is not at home. We need some sort of ruse to get her out of the apartment this evening."

A few minutes later, LeMieux put down the phone. "I called the apartment manager. Her name is April Mason. We could call her and ask her to go somewhere," Paul suggested.

"Yes," Duer nodded. "Think of something, Paul. Do it tonight, if possible."

"I'll make up something plausible."

"Good. If she has the book, take it. But, don't get caught."

"I'll see what I can find out and call you," Suzette said putting down the phone. She was confused. It didn't make sense, she said to herself, April Mason is from Chicago. It's her first time in Paris. Why her? Why is she so important? Well, she'd just have to pump Kevin for more information.

April hung up the phone. She had a meeting with a Monsignor Ignatius at seven that evening. She picked up the book and began leafing through it. Hand written on the inside of the back cover were the letters C.m. The letters appeared to be written fairly recently. She wondered what they meant. Were they a clue of some sort? Just then the phone rang. "Hello?"

The voice at the other end was deep and muffled. "Miss April Mason?"

"Yes."

"My name is Gorges Saint Clearly. I am with the Literary Foundation. I know this is very short notice, but we would like to invite you to a small gathering of our literary club this evening at the Hotel Deville," Paul LeMieux said, holding his handkerchief over the phone.

"Oh?"

"Yes. It is to celebrate the birthday of Jean Paul Sartre. It's informal, but many of our members would love to meet you."

April didn't like the sound of the man's voice. It was too muffled, as if he had a handkerchief over the phone. And who knew she was in Paris? She decided to play along for a while. "Well, that sounds delightful. Tell me, how did you know I was in town?"

"We read a small article about you in the Paris Gazette last week."

April didn't know about any article. Strange? Then it occurred to her that maybe Kevin O'Connor had put something in the paper. But he would have told her wouldn't he?

"Are you still there Miss Mason?"

"What? Oh, yes," she said as her thoughts were interrupted by the man on the phone.

"We are meeting at seven in the Tuscany Salon."

"Oh. Well, I'm very sorry, but I have a previous engagement tonight."

"Ah. Well, we are disappointed, of course, but perhaps another time."

"Yes. Perhaps," she said frowning now.

"Have a good evening, Miss Mason," the man said and hung up immediately.

April slowly hung up the phone and stared at it. She didn't like it. The man sounded phoney, and then the abrupt hang up. Something was wrong, but she didn't have a clue as to what it was. Why would he hang up like that? As she was pondering that, the phone rang again. I must be very popular, she said to herself as she picked up the phone. "Hello?"

"Ah, I caught you at home," Jean Pierre said. "I was afraid you might be out."

"Nope, just staying home today. I had a lot of notes to work out on my story."

"How is it coming, ma cherie?"

"Actually very well."

"And how are you doing with your reading of that old book?"

"I finished the story I told you about. It was intriguing."

"Really? You must tell me all about it. Perhaps we could have dinner tonight. I could bring something over."

"I'd love it, but I have an appointment this evening."

"Oh?" Jean Pierre said. His curiosity was peaking.

"Just a visit with someone. But I'd love to have dinner afterward. Say about eight?"

Jean Pierre was pleased. He could get his hands on the book that very night. "Wonderful. How about Les Champs Bistro at eight?"

"Eight thirty would be better. I'm not sure how long I'm going to be."

"Until eight thirty, my love," Jean Pierre said as he hung up the phone.

"So that's what I know about her," Kevin said as he leaned back in his chair across from Le Pluete. "I can't see any way April Mason is tied to Duer."

"Then why are his men watching her?"

"You got me. It doesn't make sense."

"I think you should talk with her. She may be in danger. These are very bad people - especially Duvall. We have just gotten confirmation from St. Tropez that Duvall was seen at the Du Pypes villa several times before the murder of Andre Du Pypes. And, we know that Duvall is capable of murder. He was implicated in three murders in Algeria and one in Athens although he was never caught."

"So you think there is some connection between this murder in St. Tropez and Duer?"

"We know Duvall boarded a train from St. Tropez to Paris the night of the murder. We also know that he was seen, at least on one occasion, with Duer in St. Tropez. I think it is time we arrested him."

"On what charge? The murder of this guy in St. Tropez?"

"Well, frankly we have no proof of that, although the circumstances point to him. I was thinking of having the French police charge him with stalking Miss Mason. It will at least get him off the streets for a while - until Miss Mason leaves Paris."

"But arresting him would only alert Duer that we're watching him."

"True," Le Pluete said with a sigh of resignation.

"Look. We've got a tail on him now," Kevin said as he began to pace the room. "I think we should wait and see if we can pull Duvall and LeMieux in with Duer. I'm sure he's behind all of this. You know, when we first started this case, I didn't think there was anything to it. Now I'm sure there is. But the trouble is, I haven't got a clue what the hell he's up to."

"We've waited this long for Duer to make his move, I agree we should wait a little longer," Le Pluete said. "In the meantime, Suzette and the stakeout teams will continue the surveillance of Duer, LeMieux and Duvall. Kevin, you can concentrate on this Jean Pierre Demain."

Le Pluete rubbed his face, sat back and made a tent with his fingers. "It is this thing with Miss Mason that troubles me most. If she is, as you say, innocent of any involvement with Duer, what do we do about her?"

"Well, I'm going to talk to her as you suggested. She's a bright lady," he said slowly. "I don't think she's involved, but I've been wrong before. At the very least, she'll be warned that she is being watched."

Le Pluete pondered this for a moment, sighed, and sat back in his chair. "All right, Kevin. Your instincts have been very good in the past. I am inclined to go along, but if Duvall, LeMieux or Duer make a move on Miss Mason, she will be your responsibility."

Kevin didn't like that idea, but he knew Le Pluete had a point. It was a risk he had to take. "Okay, but make sure your men watch Duer and company closely. I'll go see her tonight."

CHAPTER TWENTY-TWO

It was nearly seven in the evening when Kevin and Suzette returned to his apartment. "I'm gonna call April right now," he said, walking to the desk.

"Oh, and she's going to tell you all about what she's doing with Duer," she said sarcastically.

"I don't think she's involved with him. I'm going to warn her to be careful," he said as he picked up the phone and dialed.

There was no answer.

It was drizzling rain when April got out of the cab and went in the side entrance of St. Severin cathedral on the Rue St. Jacques. She shook her umbrella and closed it as she walked up the stairs to the second floor where an older nun was waiting outside the door to Monsignor Ignatius' office.

"Mademoiselle Mason?" the nun asked.

"Yes."

"The monsignor is waiting. May I take your coat?" she asked in French.

April took off her coat, handed the umbrella and her coat to the nun, fluffed her hair, and straightened her conservative black dress. "Do I look all right?" April asked also in French.

"Yes. Very appropriate," the nun said approvingly.

April followed the nun into the office. It was very large and exquisitely furnished with antique furniture. There was a fireplace on the right side of the room with two wingback chairs facing each other. The large desk was highly polished and had only two things on it - a small gold clock and a white pad of paper. Behind the desk sat Monsignor Ignatius, a grey-haired, patrician man she guessed was in his late sixties. He was dressed in his black robes with the red piping and red sash. What impressed April was the look of peace and contentment on his ruddy face. He rose when she entered.

"Miss Mason," he said holding out his hand. April didn't know what to do, whether she should kiss his hand or what since she wasn't Catholic. She'd been a Methodist all her life. She hesitated, and he understood. He nodded toward her hand, and she shook his.

"Thank you very much, Monsignor," April said in her best French, somewhat relieved she'd done the right thing, "for agreeing to meet with me."

"Not at all," he said in English. His voice was calm and confident. "Please," he said indicating one of the chairs in front of the fire in the fireplace.

April tucked the skirt of her dress under her as she sat down.

He sat across from her in the other chair. His smile was so open that April felt comfortable right away. "Now," he said, "I understand that you are looking for information about the French Revolution. Something to do with the guillotine I believe." His English was very good.

April decided to speak English. "Yes. I asked my French professor to recommend someone who might help with my problem and he suggested I talk with you."

"Ah, yes. You are referring to Professor Montrer, I believe."

April nodded.

"A very dear friend. We were school boys together at St. Marions in Toulon during the war."

188

"Yes, he told me. I beg your pardon, Monsignor," she interrupted, "but you speak English very well."

"Well, I should. I was raised in Buffalo, New York."

April frowned.

"You see, my parents were killed during the war, and an American Army Chaplin, a Catholic Chaplin, found me one night and took me in. After the war was over, he took me to America as a refugee. I lived with a very nice French couple who were also refugees. When I was 18, I wanted to go back to France. They had enough money and sent me to Paris to study at the university."

"Professor Montrer said that you began as a professor of history."

"Yes. We met at the university after all those years. We shared the same rooms. When we graduated, I began teaching French history - that is, until I felt the hand of God," he said quietly. "But one does not lose one's education. Our revolution has always fascinated me, and I still read extensively all the new works. Shall we discuss your problem?"

April sat up in her chair. She steeled herself. "I know this is going to sound very strange, but I've recently come across a book about those times, and it raised a question that, frankly, I can't get out of my mind."

"Is this a recent book?"

"No. A very old one. I brought it with me." She reached into her purse and pulled out the book. It was loosely wrapped in the same brown paper. She got up and handed it to Monsignor Ignatius then sat back down and watched him.

He carefully unwrapped the book. He turned up the light next to his chair. He studied it, turning a few pages very gently. After a few moments, he carefully wrapped the book back in the paper and put it in his lap. He looked at April. He was frowning. He seemed to sit there, thinking for a long time. April wondered why. Then, he spoke. "May I enquire how you acquired this book?"

April told him the story of her shopping and being knocked down and ending up with the book. How she tried to return it but couldn't, and that she had read all of the stories.

The Monsignor listened quietly. His hands were folded in his lap over the book, and his eyes never left hers. When she finished, he got up and carefully placed the book in her lap. He stood there looking down at her for a while then walked to the fireplace and looked at the fire. Finally, he turned. "What do you know about this book?" he asked.

"Well, there are four stories," April began.

He held up his hand to stop her. "No, what I mean is, what do you know about the history of this book?"

April shrugged. "Nothing really."

"I thought not." He went back to his chair and sat down. He seemed to have become very serious, April thought. "Miss Mason," he said as he leaned forward toward April, "What you have there is an extremely rare book. It is very valuable, and it is also reputed to be a very dangerous book to own." He leaned back now almost in a state of repose. "Years ago, I read this book, or another copy of it. There were only six copies published in 1797. One was in the Bibliotique Nationale until it was stolen in the seventies. One, it is assumed, remained with the Du Pypes family, and the other copies seem to have been destroyed. This has been documented. Several men and one woman have been killed that we know of over this book. All this is because of the story of the baker's vault. It is said to hold the key to a tremendous treasure. I assume that is the story that intrigues you."

April nodded. "I had no idea," she said, letting all of this information flood her mind.

"I think it's important you understand the ramifications of having such a book. There are people who would kill for it."

"I see," she said softly. She didn't know how to feel. She was thrilled to know about the book and it's history, and at the same time, she was uncertain what to do. She wanted to pursue her ideas. While she wasn't a treasure hunter, and had no intention of being one, she also felt as if she could solve the mystery and find the treasure.

"I know you are thinking that you could find this baker's vault, but you should know a few things first. For example, many people have searched for it over the past 200 years. There are more than a hundred reports of attempts to find the treasure. While they didn't have the map that is supposed to be on the body of the young aristocrat named Ferdinand, who by the way, was a real person, these people scoured the sewers for years. They destroyed many of the sewer walls the area of any bake shop that was remotely near. As to the grave, no one knows where it could be. The grave of his fiancé, or at least the grave of whom many others believe is his fiancé, has been dug up - several times - but no one has ever found his grave.

"In the mid-1860's, the main part of Paris was completely redone. Streets were changed, addresses were changed, buildings were built over entire areas. Whole neighborhoods were torn down and replaced with parks, apartments, and so on. The sewer system itself has been changed. Even with the map, I doubt very seriously if anyone could pinpoint the exact location today.

"And finally, suppose by some miracle you found his grave, what shape would the map be in? Probably simply dust just as the rest of his remains. I am sorry to be so negative about this, but I want to be completely honest with you."

April was devastated. Her bubble had been completely burst. She had been a fool. She looked down at the floor almost ashamed to look at him. She should have known she wasn't the first to try and solve this puzzle. What was she doing here? She pulled herself up by her stomach muscles and stood. "Thank you, Monsignor," she said quietly.

Monsignor Ignatius stood when she rose. "I can see you are taking this news very hard, my dear. I assure you I had no other intention than that of telling you the truth."

"I know," she said. "I appreciate that. I suppose I was carried away a bit when I read the story," April said and then brightened. "It is a terrific story, and I love it. And," she said with a smile, "it did do one thing for me."

"Oh?"

"It cured my writer's block. I can't wait to get home and write a book using the baker's vault as a background or something."

"Well," the Monsignor said as he put his hands on her shoulders, "I am glad the book served a useful purpose for once."

April smiled and held out her hand. They shook. "Thank you for your time, and the information, Monsignor. It has been a great pleasure meeting you." She turned toward the door then back to the priest. "Oh, one other thing. Is there a map of the city in 1794?"

He smiled and thought to himself, she won't give up. "Yes. Several in fact. I believe you can get a copy at the hall of records."

"Thank you again," April said.

"It was my pleasure, Miss Mason."

He walked her to the door and opened it. The nun stood at the outer door with her coat and umbrella. April smiled at him once again and took her coat. Then she remembered another thing she wanted to ask about the story. She turned, "Monsignor, I know this sounds silly, but I do have one more question. Where is his fiancé buried?"

The priest smiled. "I thought you'd ask. Actually, the clue is written on the back cover of the book. The initials CdM?"

April nodded.

"They stand for the Cimitiere de Montmartre, the cemetery in Montmartre. I forget the exact location, but the grave registration says 'Charwoman'."

"Charwoman. Thank you, again," April said, taking her umbrella and walking briskly away down the hall.

The Monsignor shook his head. Would this madness never end?

They had been inside April's apartment for nearly thirty minutes. No sign of the book, just a dictionary on her desk. Paul looked at Duvall, "Are you sure you put everything back in its place?"

"I'm sure," Duvall grumbled. He was disappointed and mad at himself again. This was not the woman. Francois would be displeased.

Paul went to the door and listened. When he heard nothing, he opened it a crack. There was no one in the hallway. He motioned to Duvall who followed him out into the hall. Paul closed the door and the two went to the elevator.

The door across the hall from April's opened. An Interpol agent looked out the door toward the elevator. He watched them get on and the door close. Satisfied they were gone, he put his fingers to his lips and motioned toward the old woman who was standing behind him. In French he said, "Remember, this will be our secret."

She nodded. He headed toward the stairs.

The parabolic microphone atop the car was pointed directly at the entrance to April's apartment building. When Duvall and LeMieux came out the door, the Interpol agent sitting in his car pressed the record button on the listening device.

"What are we going to tell Duer?" Duvall asked as the two men walked toward their car.

"What else can we tell him? This Mason woman is not the one."

"I know we didn't find anything, yet something tells me I am not wrong. She is the one."

"Don't say that to Duer. He will take your head off," LeMieux cautioned. They got into the car and drove off.

The agent stopped the recording.

April arrived at the restaurant a few minutes early. Jean Pierre wasn't there yet. She was depressed. She couldn't stop thinking about the story and especially the grave. Something was bugging her, but she wasn't sure what. The waiter seated her at a table by the wall. She was alone with her thoughts. She had been silly. Too many years had gone by, and everything the Monsignor said was probably right. The map was probably nothing but dust. Yet, she still wondered. She took the book from her purse and unwrapped it. She turned to the last page of the story and reread it.

As she was reading, Jean Pierre came up to the table. He leaned down and kissed her on the neck - eying the book in front of her. April was startled and turned quickly. As she did, the book fell on the floor. Jean Pierre reached down before she could, retrieved the book and placed it back on the table.

"Jean Pierre."

"April, my dearest," he said as he sat down next to her. "I'm sorry I'm late."

"You weren't, I was early," she said patting his hand.

Indicating the book, Jean Pierre said, "You must be very fascinated with that old book."

"I am," she said enthusiastically. "It's changed my life."

It is about to change mine, Jean Pierre thought.

"I've got that old feeling again. I want to write. I even have a lead character in my head. Oh, Jean Pierre, it feels so good, and I owe it all to this book. For once in my life, it isn't a man."

"Oh," he said trying to look dejected.

April looked at him. "Oh, I'm sorry Jean Pierre. I didn't mean that you weren't a help, you were, but, well, I don't feel the same. What I mean is I like you, I like you very much, but."

"You aren't 'in love with me'." His voice was low as he interrupted April. She could see the disappointment on his face when he spoke.

"Please, don't feel that way. I do care for you."

"Well, I'll accept that for the time being. Perhaps later I can change your mind."

"I'm sure you will," she said knowing in her heart it wasn't going to happen.

"Now," Jean Pierre said brightly, "Let's have a look at the menu."

"Great, and I'll tell you all about my visit with Monsignor Ignatius."

Kevin sat in his car and watched LeMieux's car pull into the garage under Duer's apartment house. He could see Duvall in the front seat with Paul. "Now where have you two been?" he said aloud. "And what the hell are you guys doing?" As if on cue, his radio crackled. He tuned it in and listened. He turned it off and said, "So you don't think she has this book either. Good."

Jean Pierre racked his brain as he got into his car after letting April off at her apartment. She wouldn't even let him walk her to the door she was so anxious to write. He had to get that book, but she seemed to be guarding it with her life. It would take an army to get it away from her. He had to come up with something and fast before she decided to leave Paris.

Paul and Duvall stood in front of the desk. Duer was sitting back in his chair. His hands were cupped to his chin as he listened to their report. They'd searched the apartment thoroughly. There was no book, and no raincoat. She wasn't the woman. Francois was grinning as they completed their report.

"I see," he said.

Both men were confused. Duer wasn't mad? He wasn't yelling. They waited.

"I believe she does, in fact, have the book," he said, looking at them with a smile in his eyes. "Paul, correct me if I'm wrong but didn't you say that your brother-in-law was connected in some way with the Mason woman?"

"Jean Pierre?"

"Yes."

"I thought so. You see, this evening I received a phone call from an 'acquaintance', Gilbert Lucase, whom I talked with when I first learned of the book. He is a dealer in rare books. I won't go into the details, but it seems that your Jean Pierre called on him this morning. He claims to be able to get the book and wants to sell it to Gilbert. He was asking what it was worth. I don't know how he could do so unless he knew where it was and who had it. By deduction, I, therefore, believe that Miss Mason has the book. Can you think of any other way Jean Pierre could get it?"

Paul shook his head. He didn't like this at all. It meant that Jean Pierre was in danger.

Duvall grinned, "I knew I was right! She has the book."

"Or he has by now." Duer went on, "I believe you should pay a call on Jean Pierre tomorrow and arrange to get the book either from him or her. I don't care how," the menace in his voice was unmistakable. "Is that clear?"

"Yes, Monsieur Duer," Paul said quietly.

"See to it."

April was up bright and early. Her mind had been full of too many things to write last night, and so, all night long she tossed and turned thinking and rethinking about what the Monsignor had said. At dawn, she decided to pursue the story, at least she would go to the cemetery.

Just as she was walking out the door, the phone rang. She went to the desk and answered it. "Hello?"

"Miss Mason, please don't hang up the phone. What I have to say is very important - a matter of life and death."

April recognized Kevin's voice and was tempted to hang up, but something told her not to. "Isn't that a bit dramatic, Kevin?" she said with sarcasm oozing out.

"April, I'm not kidding. Please listen. Somehow or other you seem to have gotten mixed up with a real bad character."

"Come on, Kevin, Jean Pierre isn't," but she was interrupted.

"It's not Jean Pierre. The man's name is Francois Duer. Do you recognize the name?"

"Francois what?"

"Duer."

"I have no idea who you're talking about."

"Good," Kevin said letting out a sigh. "Look, April, this guy Duer is a real bad character. If anyone talks to you about him, let me know."

"How do you know about him?"

"I'll tell you all about it sometime, anyway, stay away from him. He's very dangerous."

April didn't know what to think. Kevin had lied before, but she didn't think he was this time. But, on the other hand, she had no idea what he was talking about. "Are you sure about this guy?"

"Positive. We don't believe he will do anything, but just for safety sake, be sure to lock your doors and take cabs instead of walking around for a couple of days."

April heard the pejorative "we" and wanted to say something, but she was too intrigued. What was Kevin up to?

"Above all else, stay alert. If you want my help," but this time he was interrupted.

"I don't need your help. I still remember the last time."

"That was different."

"So you say. All right, Kevin, I'll be a good girl and watch my step. Now, I'm late. Thank you for the warning." She hung up. Kevin was getting really weird!

Kevin hung up. He called Le Pluete and told him of the conversation with April.

Suzette was standing in his cubicle at the paper. "She doesn't know Duer, right?"

"Right. Never heard of him."

"And you believe her."

"Yes."

Suzette shook her head. "Sometimes you can be so naive."

197

April walked through the huge iron gates of the Cimitiere de Montmartre and along the tree-lined street to the caretaker's building. It was a long, two story stone building with windows only on the second floor. There were statues of angels carved into the stone walls of the building. She knocked at the large, wooden door. No answer. She opened the door and a musty odor crawled out. It was one room, dimly lit with a single bare bulb. "Anyone here?" she called out in her best French.

Out of the shadows a small, bent-over old man in a long green apron shuffled to the door. He had bad teeth and only a few strands of grey hair left on his shiny head. His eyes were almost completely covered with wrinkles. His voice was thin and whiny, "May I help you?"

April had practiced this conversation with Professor Montrer that morning to be sure she could ask the questions she wanted in perfect French. "Are you the caretaker?"

"Yes. Whom have you come to see?"

April began explaining about the book and the grave. She had only gotten a few words into her explanation when the old man cackled. "Another one," he said. "It's been a long time."

April was thrown. She forgot where she was in the explanation.

"I think you should talk with my son, Richard. My eyesight isn't so good any more." He shuffled off up a small flight of stairs.

April looked around. The first floor was filled with file cabinets and book shelves. There was a small wooden desk near the door piled high with papers. Organization wasn't their best suit, she thought. The place was eerie. She shivered.

Moments later, the old man returned with a tall, handsome man in his forties. He had a head full of curly black hair and his eyebrows were dark and very bushy. His face was long and angular with a perfect nose. "My father says you've come about the grave of the aristocrat's fiancé," he said.

"You know about it?" she asked.

"Yes. It's a very old story around here. I am Richard Covey. You met my father. Our family has been taking care of this cemetery for over two hundred and fifty years." The old man smiled and ambled away down a long aisle toward some file cabinets.

"I'm very impressed, Richard," April said as she looked up at him. He must have been six foot five and very broad shouldered. "I am referring to,"

"<u>Recit de la Revolution</u>, I know," Richard said. "You are not French," he said.

"No. American."

"Then," he said in English, "let's speak American. I'm sure you would be more comfortable, and I need the practice. I'm going to America this year."

"Really?"

"Yes. I've always wanted to go there."

"I think you'll be impressed."

"I hope so. Now, I suppose you want to see the grave."

"Well, yes and no," she said. "Are there any records I could look at?"

"They are very old and fragile."

"I'm sure. But you see, I'm a writer, and,"

"A writer? I'm a writer!" he said. A wide grin spread across his face. "Ah, now I see. You are doing research."

"Yes. Exactly."

"But of course. No one bothers to read the records any more now that they know which grave to dig up. But, a writer must be thorough."

"Yes."

"All right. We will look at the records. Follow me."

He led her down the long aisle pausing along the way to turn on bare light bulbs every ten feet or so. There were several aisles crammed full of boxes. Each box had a date on it. The air was dry and stale smelling.

"We must keep the records in a controlled environment because many of them date back to the sixteenth century. This is one of the oldest cemeteries in Paris. This way."

He led her to an aisle near the back of the large room. He stopped to examine the boxes and finally pulled one from the top shelf and carried it to a table. He turned on another bare light bulb and opened the box. He removed a large leather-bound record book that was shrink-wrapped in plastic. "We have to be very careful with these," he said as he pulled a pocketknife from his pants and carefully slit the plastic. April walked up beside him to get a good look. He opened the front cover, and she could barely see it was a handwritten ledger. The date inside the cover was 1792-95.

"I wanted to make sure this was the right volume," he said, closing the book. "The light down here is very poor. We will go upstairs to my office." He turned off the light, picked up the book and motioned for her to follow him.

They went upstairs to an office that was very neat and clean. The room had two windows which let the sunlight in and a large brass lamp on the desk. He put the book on a small table in one corner of the room and turned on a florescent light that had a magnifying glass attached. "I think you will be able to see everything clearly, but feel free to use the magnifying glass."

Richard opened the book to a well-worn page about half way through. "I think this is what you are looking for," he said as he ran his finger down the list of names. "Ah, yes. The charwoman," he held his finger on the entry. "The woman was identified in 1803 by the first people who raided the grave as Marie Gentimente but the name in the register was never changed."

"So you are certain it is Ferdinand's fiancé?"

"Yes." He turned the page and a separate piece of paper was inserted. He took it and handed it to April. "We kept this record of each time the grave was opened. As you can see, it was opened twenty-two times over the years. The last time was in 1951."

April read down the dates on the page and handed it back to him. "Where is the body of Ferdinand?"

"No one knows," he said with a shrug.

April went back to the register and read - Charwoman, Guillotined, June 23, 1794, C-4. "This is the date she was interred?"

"Yes. That is also the date she was guillotined according to the public record on file in the Hall of Records."

"May I look over the rest of the entries?"

"But of course. I must do a few chores. I'll leave you here for a while." Richard left, and April began looking at all the entries on that page. There were six people buried on June 23, 1794, a baby, a husband and wife, two other women, and Marie. There were no clues to Ferdinand's grave. She read on. The next day only two people were buried, both women. None were buried the next day or the next, but a Jacques Le Blanc was beheaded and buried the next day. And none the next day. There seemed to be no clues as to Ferdinand's grave.

When Richard returned, he asked if she wanted a cup of coffee. April nodded, and he returned in a few minutes with the coffee. He handed her a cup and took his cup to his small desk.

"It is a mystery, no?" he said.

"Yes. Do you have any idea what happened to his body?"

"No. I have given it a great deal of thought. In the book, the author said that they were given a Catholic burial, but if that were true, the bodies should have been taken to a church as was the custom in those days. And, I believe that the bodies had to be consecrated. That process alone should have taken at least a day or two. There is something wrong here. What I cannot, nor could many others, figure out is where the body of the man is. It makes no sense."

"Is it possible that she was not buried on the day that is in the record?"

"It is possible, but my ancestors say no. As you can imagine, this grave has been the subject of many, many conversations in my family over the years. I think that what is in the record is correct." He sat back. "Collette, her servant, brought the bodies here."

April nodded.

"According to my family, she stayed in the area working for a family. It is said that she visited the grave every Sunday until she died in 1826."

"She visited that grave?"

"Yes. This very one. She was somewhat of a celebrity. Many people came to talk to her of that day. She talked of the day's events when Marie climbed on the tumbril with Ferdinand. But when she was asked what happened to Ferdinand, she would only say that his body was stolen before it could be buried."

"So his body is probably not here at all."

"Well, the story the driver of the tumbril told was different. He said Ferdinand's body was not stolen. He said he left two bodies here with Collette and took the other bodies away."

"If she lied, why? She didn't know about the map did she?"

"I don't know if she did. If she read the book, then perhaps she did. But, her behavior would suggest she didn't read the book. If the author is correct, only he and Ferdinand knew about the map."

"So this could be just a farce. Something the author made up."

"Yes. But the legend, and that is what it has become, is more powerful than what I suspect is the truth."

"And the truth is?"

"That Ferdinand is probably buried elsewhere in one of the mass graves to the north of the city." "In spite of what Collette told Du Pypes?"

"Yes."

April didn't want to believe Richard, but he had a point. If no one could find his grave in more than two hundred years, he wasn't buried in this cemetery. It looked hopeless. April thanked him for his time.

"Would you like to see the charwoman's grave site?"

April decided it wouldn't hurt and followed him out of the building. They only took about ten steps until he stopped at the head of a grave. It was very close to the caretaker's building.

Richard saw April shake her head, and he laughed. "We built our offices next to the grave on purpose several years ago. There has always been so much curiosity we decided it would be simpler to be near the grave."

April walked around and saw that the headstone was old and simply said "Charwoman - 1794". Richard saw her frown and said, "The coffin has been dug up and searched so many times that the bones are in disarray. I was here in 1951, the last time it was disinterred, and saw for myself. The coffin was replaced because it had been smashed by whoever dug the grave up. At least her bones are resting more comfortably."

April thanked him again and left, more discouraged than ever.

CHAPTER TWENTY-THREE

D uer frowned. "You say we are being followed by Interpol?" he asked into the phone. He listened carefully as the caller told him about Duvall and LeMieux being followed to April's apartment house. "I see," he said as he picked up a pencil and began to make notes on a pad in front of him.

The caller asked if he knew the whereabouts of the book. "Actually, I believe I do know where the book is, and who has it. I got a call from Gilbert, you remember him I believe? He told me he had an inquiry about buying the book. So, I will have it soon. Thank you for the information on Interpol, my dear. We must have dinner when this is all over." He hung up the phone and pressed a buzzer under his desk.

Moments later Paul entered. He saw Duer grinning. "Something good has happened?"

"Yes," he said hesitantly, "it's in the category of 'forewarned is forearmed'. One of my best sources called to say we have had company for some time. It seems that Interpol has been following us since I came to Paris."

The hair on the back of Paul's neck stood up. He didn't say anything, but he was very worried.

"I'm told they are playing a waiting game hoping to catch us doing something illegal, but, now that we know they're there, we can act accordingly. I even have the makes and models of the cars they are using to follow us," he said, handing the pad to Paul.

Paul had to fight to keep his hands from shaking. "Your source is inside?"

"Quite. An old friend."

"Do I know him?"

"No. It is, shall we say, a private contact. So, I think it's time to lead them on some merry chases. However, before we do that, we must address two immediate problems. First, Snooky is going to have to wait to deliver the packages. Call her and let her know that there will be a delay."

"And the second?"

"Your brother-in-law, Jean Pierre Demain."

Paul was waiting for this. "I was planning to go to his office today as you asked."

"No, with the watchdogs outside, I would rather you handle this delicately. I think a call to him from a public phone would be more appropriate. Tell him we know he has the book and that we will pick it up when it is convenient for us. We don't want him selling it right out from under our noses."

"Right away," Paul said starting toward the door.

"Paul," Duer said in a very commanding voice. Paul stopped.

"I hope we can get this matter settled without violence, but if it is necessary."

"It won't be, Monsieur Duer. I will convince him of the importance of this matter."

"Do that, Paul."

There was no doubt in LeMieux's mind what 'that' meant. He left the room in a hurry. It was, of course, a matter of life and death. Possibly his own.

He went to a pay phone down the street from the apartment and called Jean Pierre's office. His secretary told Paul that Jean Pierre was out of the office at a meeting for the day. She wasn't sure where, but she said Jean Pierre told her he would be at the meeting all day. "Merde," Paul said after he hung up the phone.

April was in the middle of washing her hair when it hit her. The clue to Ferdinand's grave was in the story somewhere. She felt it, knew it. She was going to go over the story until she found it.

Fifteen minutes later, April was at her desk reading each sentence of the story over and over looking for the clue. She was so certain she was right, she trembled. Her fingers moved slowly over each word.

At seven that evening, Jean Pierre was locking the door to his apartment when he heard the phone ring inside. He paused for a moment, decided it wasn't important, and continued on his mission - to get the book.

Paul LeMieux hung up the phone. Where the hell was Jean Pierre? he asked himself. Then he answered his own question. "He's at the woman's apartment." He had to handle this carefully. First, elude the Interpol tail, then find Jean Pierre, get the book without hurting his brother-in-law, give the book to Duer and find a new job. This one was driving him crazy!

It wasn't LeMieux's car, she didn't know whose it was, but it was certainly Paul LeMieux and Pepe Duvall in the front seat. Suzette cursed, started her car and slowly pulled out in traffic. She kept a reasonable distance and let LeMieux lead the way.

April stopped reading, got the dictionary and looked up a word. She was right. She sat back. Her mind was racing. Could that be the key to the puzzle? She got up and walked out onto the terrace and looked at the Eiffel Tower all lit up in the night sky. Did Collette know? Was that why she buried them that way? Of course, she thought. Marie and Collette must have shared their secrets. She was Marie's personal servant. They were about the same age. Girl talk. She nodded. "I'll bet I'm right," she said out loud. She felt an adrenalin rush. "I know I'm right," she shouted to the sky!

Paul LeMieux recognized the car behind him as one on Duer's list. It was five cars back. "Damn, they're on our tail," he said to Duvall.

Duvall looked back. "Which car?"

"The black Peugeot with the woman."

Duvall spotted Suzette's car. "She's very pretty," he said.

"Stop staring at her, she'll know we know."

Duvall turned back. "We must lose her before we go to the woman's apartment."

"I know, but the traffic is too heavy. Let's take Duer's suggestion and lead her on a merry chase."

Jean Pierre still wasn't sure just how he was going to get the book from April when he arrived at her door. If he just took it, April would know it was him, and that was bad. He needed some ruse to get it. He had thought of asking to simply borrow the book, but that seemed to be silly. Why would he want the book? To practice his French? Silly. He could tell her he wanted it for a friend. Too lame. He decided to see what fate would offer.

April reread the passage, "*Marie was on top, her favorite position.*" "Yes!" she shouted. "That's it!" April threw her arms in the air. She got up and began dancing around the room chanting, "She's the top, he's the bottom!" She stopped in mid-celebration. It dawned on her. How was she going to prove it? She couldn't just go and dig up the grave alone. How was she going to do it? Her thoughts were interrupted by a knock at the door.

April opened the door. It was Jean Pierre. One look at her and Jean Pierre knew something was up. She stood there grinning from ear to ear. "Jean Pierre, my hero. You've come just at the right time," April said, taking him by the hand and leading him into the living room.

To say Jean Pierre was surprised is a great understatement. He didn't know what she was talking about. He stood there as she took off his coat and threw it toward a chair in the corner. Then she led him to the couch, pushed him down, flopped down beside him, gave him a big kiss, and said, "Have I got a story for you!"

Jean Pierre couldn't help but laugh. He hadn't seen her like this. She was like a whirling dervish. He let her fluff up one of the pillows and put it behind his head. "Comfy?" she asked.

"Very. What is this all about?"

"Funny you should ask," April said teasingly. "I'm about to tell you a story, and you're going to be a big part of it."

He frowned. What the hell was she talking about? What did she mean he was going to be a part of whatever it was?

April kissed him again, jumped up and went to her desk. She grabbed the book and settled down beside Jean Pierre again. "This book is the key to a fabulous treasure," she said, handing him the book. "Be careful with this. It's very old. Now where was I? Oh yes." She was talking very fast, and she was very excited. "For two hundred years people have hunted for this treasure, and I know where it is! Well, I think I do. At least I think I know where the treasure map is. So, Jean Pierre Demain, I am going to let you in on my secret, and in return you are going to do me a big favor."

Jean Pierre just stared at her in awe. She was speaking in riddles. She didn't make a bit of sense.

"So," she said fluffing up the pillow again. "Sit back, relax and listen to the tale of the baker's vault!" April got up and began pacing and talking with her hands. "The time, 1794, the place Paris, France." She began.

They had been driving for an hour. Suzette was still on their tail, and both Paul and Duvall were, to say the least, frustrated.

"I'm hungry," Duvall said. "Let's stop and eat something. Maybe she'll go away."

"We've tried everything else," Paul said. He pointed to a bistro on the corner. There was a parking place right next to it. They pulled over.

Suzette saw them park and looked for a parking place, but there were none to be had. The traffic was backing up behind her already. She slammed her fists on the steering wheel in anger. She turned the corner and double parked for a moment. She watched the two men go inside the restaurant.

LeMieux watched Suzette wait for a few seconds, double parked, then because of several cars honking at her, she drove off around the corner. Duvall was just sitting down when Paul grabbed him. "We've got to move," he said urgently and began pulling Pepe back toward the car.

"But I'm hungry!"

"We only have a minute," Paul said dragging Duvall to the car and opening the door. "I know this neighborhood. She'll have to make several turns to get back here. Get in."

Duvall did as Paul said, and Paul jumped into the driver's side, revved the engine, and sped off. Suzette's car was nowhere in sight.

"And so, when Ferdinand was guillotined, Collette followed the tumbril," April was saying enthusiastically. "Somehow she persuaded the men who were going to bury all of the bodies in a mass grave, to give her both Marie and Ferdinand's bodies. She took them to the Abby at Montmartre and made sure they received the last rights. Then she and someone buried the bodies at the cemetery. And, now here's the kicker, she had them buried in their favorite position."

Jean Pierre had listened intently to April as she told the story. His mind was whirling. It was all there - all the things that Paul had alluded to when they met for lunch. So this was why the book was so valuable. It contained the clue to the whereabouts of a vault with a huge treasure. The clue was the map, and that's why Duer wanted the book. I'll make a killing! he thought, when I get the book. Those estimates the rare book dealers were offering were peanuts compared to what he could make if he had the book - and the map!

Jean Pierre frowned. "Their favorite position?"

April gave him a sly grin. "Sex. It's always the answer. Either sex or money. And in this case, I think sex leads to money."

Jean Pierre didn't have the slightest clue what she was talking about. "I'm sorry, my dear," he said interrupting April's wild ravings. "What are you talking about?"

"The charwoman's grave. I want you to help me dig it up."

Jean Pierre looked at her incredulously. "Are you serious?" he asked.

"Very."

There was a long pause as Jean Pierre tried to fathom this turn of events. She was asking him to dig up a grave. A grave! All on a hunch. A hunch that had no facts to back it up. It was just a guess. He got up from the couch and walked out onto the terrace. April watched his every move. She didn't want to spook him. She needed him.

Jean Pierre rubbed his chin. This was certainly the craziest thing he'd ever heard of - let alone be involved with. He had to laugh, he told himself. Yet, he reminded himself, if she was right, and they did find Ferdinand's body and the map, they would have the key to a fortune. It was all tres bizarre.

April stood in front of him and pleaded, "Jean Pierre, I know this is crazy. I know the odds are against it, but my intuition tells me I'm right."

Jean Pierre was instantly reminded of a piece of advice his father had given him years ago, "Jean Pierre, I want you to always remember that women have a sixth sense. They call it women's intuition. Never bet against it, and never fight it."

April's insides were shaking. Would he do it?

Jean Pierre put his face close to hers and whispered, "I think I am losing my mind, but I can't help it. Besides, I've never dug up a grave before." He kissed her.

April's insides began turning flips. She was going to see for herself! She returned the kiss with so much fervor that she ended up nearly pushing them both over the railing. She caught them just in time.

"We almost didn't live to see the grave," Jean Pierre said.

"You are a very persuasive young woman, April Mason."

"Let's celebrate! I've got a bottle of champagne in the refrigerator," she said as she headed for the kitchen.

Jean Pierre stood on the terrace gazing down on the courtyard. Then his eyes steeled. They were fixed on two men getting out of a car. He knew them both, and it sent an ice cold chill racing down his back. Paul and Duvall! They were heading toward the entrance!

CHAPTER TWENTY-FOUR

Jean Pierre panicked! He could see both Duvall and LeMieux clearly as they walked toward the entrance to April's apartment house. Suddenly, both looked up. They saw him on April's terrace. Duvall pointed toward him. Jean Pierre had to act fast. He had to head them off. He did not want to put April in danger.

April came out of the kitchen with the bottle of champagne, two glasses and a big smile just as Jean Pierre ran past her and picked up his coat. "Okay, it's time to seal the deal," she said.

"I'm sorry, my dear, but I just remembered I have a meeting tonight with the head of the Spanish Tourist Bureau. It's very important," he said as he ran to the door and flung it open.

"But what about our treasure?"

"Yes, well, we'll find it. I'm sure. I'm sorry, but I really must go."

April started to say something, but Jean Pierre was already out the door and slammed it shut.

"Your meeting is more important than the treasure? You're nuts!" she said to the closed door. April frowned. Something was rotten here, and she didn't like it.

Jean Pierre reached the elevator just as the doors were opening. There stood Paul and Duvall.

"Why Paul, what a surprise!" Jean Pierre said.

"Step in," Duvall commanded.

Jean Pierre didn't move. He did not like the look on Duvall's face nor the fact he had his hand in his coat pocket. There was a definite bulge there. He looked mean. His hand moved.

"Of course," Jean Pierre said looking at LeMieux with a frown and nodding toward Duvall.

"Do as he says, Jean Pierre," Paul said stepping back.

"What is this all about?" Jean Pierre asked.

"Step in," Duvall repeated and then slowly drew out a pistol out of his coat pocket.

Sweat beaded up on Jean Pierre's forehead. He was scared and looked toward LeMieux. Paul motioned with his head. Jean Pierre got on the elevator.

"I don't know what you want with me."

"The book," Duvall replied hastily.

"What book?"

"The one you tried to sell to Lucase, the rare book dealer." Duvall said as the elevator doors closed and it started down.

Jean Pierre's mind began to whirl. How did they know he had called Lucase? What was going on? And why the gun?

Paul pulled Jean Pierre to him almost as an act of protection for Jean Pierre. "Jean Pierre, we know all about your trying to sell the book," he said in a loud whisper. "We want the book."

"We?"

"My boss."

"And we want it now," Duvall said in a low, even, and menacing tone.

"I. I don't have it. I was just doing a friend a favor."

Paul put his hand on Jean Pierre's shoulder. "Please don't make things worse for yourself. I don't want you hurt."

The elevator stopped at the ground floor and the doors opened. Before Jean Pierre could move, Duvall shoved the gun into his ribs and said, "We'll talk in the car."

Paul led the way followed by Jean Pierre and then Duvall, his gun ramming Jean Pierre in the back. They went across the lobby and out into the courtyard to their car. "Get in the back," Duvall ordered. Jean Pierre got in the back seat and Duvall was right beside him. Paul got in the driver's seat and turned to face Jean Pierre. "I told you when we met last week that my boss was very well connected. He has a way of knowing a lot of things. People tell him things. Lucase told him about your trying to find out how much the book was worth, so please don't lie to us anymore. Just hand over the book, and I promise you won't get hurt."

Jean Pierre felt the nose of the gun in his ribs. He didn't want April to get hurt, yet if he didn't tell them she had it, he was sure Duvall would kill him. He decided to stall. After all, they weren't going to hurt him before they got the book, and maybe he could figure out some way to get them the book without endangering April. "I don't have it," he said trying to sound cool and collected. "I think I know where it is, but I'm not sure. At any rate, I can't get it tonight. Maybe I could bring it to you tomorrow."

Duvall rammed the gun into Jean Pierre's ribs, and he winced in pain. "Wrong answer," Duvall said. "We want the book now!"

Jean Pierre wanted to lash out and hit the man, but that was, to say the least, impractical. "I don't have it," he said.

"I think you might find it if I blow off your kneecap," Duvall said.

"Stop it, Duvall. That won't get us anywhere. Jean Pierre, I can only hold Duvall back for a short while. This is very serious, and I don't want you hurt, but you must cooperate."

"Paul, I swear I don't have the book."

"The woman must have it," Duvall said. "Let's go get it," he said reaching for the door handle.

"No," Jean Pierre blurted out, grabbing Duvall's arm. "She doesn't have it. It's, it's in a safety deposit box," he said trying to buy time.

Paul sighed deeply. He shook his head in frustration.
"Then you leave us no alternative. I think we need to consult
with the boss." Paul started the car. "Duvall. The hood," he
said. Duvall reached under the front seat and pulled out a
black hood and placed it over Jean Pierre's head.

"Sit back, Jean Pierre," Paul said as he drove out of the
courtyard.

Fifteen minutes later, Paul turned the car into an
underground garage about a half a block from the garage to
Duer's apartment. He could see the Interpol car up ahead.
They had no idea they, too, were being watched. He smiled to
himself.

LeMieux parked the car in a reserved spot, and Duvall
pulled Jean Pierre out of the car. Duvall led the hooded Jean
Pierre through a doorway and up a flight of stairs to another
door marked "Authorized Personnel Only."

Paul took out his keys and unlocked the door. The three
walked down a long corridor, through three more doors until
they were by the elevator which led to Duer's apartment.

Suzette threw her purse on the bed and screamed in anger.
Kevin came flying out of the bathroom in mid-shave. "What
the hell?"

"I lost them," Suzette said. "I fell for one of the oldest tricks
in the trade!"

"Lost who?"

"LeMieux and his side kick," she said pacing furiously. "I
saw them pull out of an underground garage, nearly a block
away from Duer's apartment. I recognized LeMieux and
followed them. They weren't in Duer's car. And it was as if
they knew I was following them."

"Well, tailing people in a car isn't your best asset."

"Oh yeah, well, I'll have you know this is the first time I've
been had."

"Are you speaking figuratively?"

"Mind out of the gutter, O'Connor," she chided. "I can't believe I let them do this to me!"

"Okay, so you lost them. It happens. Cool down."

"Oh, sure."

"Look, Suzette, you said you thought they knew you were following them. Why?"

"Because they, they just drove around. No real destination. It was like they were leading me nowhere."

"Maybe it was a diversion."

"Possible. I called in back up to watch Duer's apartment. He reported no action whatsoever."

"Did the backup see them come back?"

"He hadn't as of fifteen minutes ago. He promised to call if he saw them return."

"Okay, so you've got it covered. Nothing else to do but wait."

Suzette sat down at his desk and ran her hands through her hair. "Kevin," she said peering up at him, "Did you ever find out why they were at that apartment house April Mason lives in?"

"No. We got a list of the residents and talked to them, but no one recognized them or met with them or even talked to them."

"I think you were right in the first place. There is nothing to this. We are just wasting our time."

Duvall marched Jean Pierre into Duer's library. Jean Pierre was sweating, and he had a hard time breathing in the heavy black hood. His knees were weak and his stomach was turning flip-flops. He was quite simply scared out of his wits. It didn't help matters that he had no idea where he was.

Duer frowned when he saw Jean Pierre. "How dare you bring this man here," he said firmly.

Paul LeMieux walked around Jean Pierre and stood in front of the desk. "I take responsibility, sir," he said. "He is my brother-in-law, and I don't want him hurt."

Duer got up from his desk and pulled the window drapes shut. He returned to his desk, turned on the desk lamp and aimed it at Jean Pierre's face. He motioned to Duvall to turn off the other lights in the room. Duer was surprised that LeMieux was so bold, but hid his concern.

For his own part, Paul was frightened, too, but he was determined to protect Jean Pierre as long as he could.

"All right, Paul," Duer said in a condescending tone. "I, too, dislike violence. How do you propose to save him?"

"Frankly, I don't know just yet, but there must be a way."

Duer nodded. "Perhaps." As he sat down, he motioned to Duvall to take the hood off of Jean Pierre's head.

Jean Pierre squinted at the light. He was disoriented and looked around. Paul stood beside him. Duvall was behind him.

Jean Pierre could see the outline of a man behind the desk, but could not make out his features because of the bright desk lamp pointed toward him.

Duer looked at Jean Pierre standing in front of him. He quickly assessed the man and decided that he was very frightened, as he should be, Duer thought. He could see the beads of sweat on Jean Pierre's forehead and noticed that he was rocking slightly on the balls of his feet. He looked at Duvall. There was no doubt in his mind that Duvall would kill Jean Pierre on the spot, if necessary. He glanced at Paul LeMieux. Paul was unusually up tight. He was acting strangely forceful. Duer attributed this to Paul's relationship to Jean Pierre, and possibly Paul was thinking of his wife, whom Duer knew Paul loved very much.

He sat back in his chair and folded his hands on his lap. There were many possibilities that this situation offered, he thought. The primary reason for this man being here was the book, and that was of paramount importance. He decided to get the book first and then let Duvall have his way. "Please, Monsieur Demain, have a seat," he said, as he gestured toward a nearby chair.

Duvall pulled the chair directly in front of the desk and motioned for Jean Pierre to sit.

Jean Pierre looked at Paul. Paul nodded. Jean Pierre sat down.

"Now, then," Duer began, "Where is the book?"

"He says he doesn't have it," Paul answered.

"And you believe him?"

"Yes."

"Is it true you do not have it?"

"Yes," Jean Pierre said his voice cracking.

"I see. Do you know where it is?"

Jean Pierre hesitated. Duer smiled inwardly. So, Jean Pierre did know where it was.

"I might," Jean Pierre said.

Just then, Duvall, who was standing right behind Jean Pierre cracked Jean Pierre across the neck with a sharp snap of his knuckles. Jean Pierre lurched forward. The blow was not very hard, but it surprised him.

Paul started to move toward Duvall, but Duer held up his hand, "Please stay where you are, Paul," he commanded.

Paul stopped. He didn't like what was going on, but Duer was the boss.

"Duvall. While I appreciate your - enthusiasm - I shall tell you when to act, if necessary. My apologies, Monsieur Demain," Duer said, "but as you can understand, this matter of the book is quite serious. And if you have any doubts, let me assure you, I mean that in the most forceful way."

Jean Pierre swallowed hard. The look in Duer's eyes was unnerving. He wanted to look over at Paul but didn't dare.

"Would you care to answer my question again?"

Jean Pierre didn't like the tone of the man's voice. He didn't like getting slapped, and he was afraid that wasn't the end of the pain unless he was careful. He was in a box and there was no way out. He breathed deeply to try and regain his composure. "I. I do know where it is."

"Very good, Monsieur," Duer said lightly, calmly. "It is very wise of you to understand your position. Now why don't you tell us where it is?"

Jean Pierre's mind was spinning. He hesitated again.

Duvall raised his fist, but Paul cried out, "Stop."

Duvall looked at Duer. Duer nodded.

"Let me talk to him," Paul asked.

"Of course," Duer said.

"Jean Pierre," Paul began as he walked in front of his brother-in-law and stood between him and the desk, "you must tell the truth. I cannot help you if you do not. Please, for your sake, for our sake, just tell the truth."

Jean Pierre looked up at Paul. He nodded and Paul stepped away.

"The book," Jean Pierre said, clearing his throat, "is at April Masons's apartment."

"You said it was in a safety deposit box," Duvall said quickly. "You lied!" He raised his fist.

"No! Yes, I lied, but, " Jean Pierre shouted. "you have to listen to me, now."

"Go on, Monsieur," Duer said waving Duvall back away from Jean Pierre.

"April, that is, Miss Mason, has read the book. She told me all about it. She also said that the mystery of the location of the treasure map has not been solved in more than two hundred years."

"Yes, that is true."

"She thinks she knows where it is buried."

Duer sat up in his chair and leaned forward. "And where is that?"

"I don't know. I mean, I know it's in a graveyard, but I don't know which one. But, she asked me tonight to help her dig up a grave."

"She wanted you to help her dig up a grave?"

"Yes."

"And just why does she think she's solved this puzzle that has eluded men for all this time?"

"I don't know. Really I don't. She said it had something to do with a passage in the book."

"What passage?"

"I don't know that either. She was about to tell me when your men came for me."

Duer sat back in his chair and pondered this for a long time. The silence in the room was deafening. Finally, he spoke, "So perhaps we should go ask her."

"I don't think she'll tell you," Jean Pierre said.

"She'll tell me," Duvall said.

"Sir, with all Duer respect, I think that if she's threatened, she'll be hard as hell to break. I've seen her in action. She's one very strong-willed woman," Jean Pierre said to Duer.

"But she'll tell you?" Duer said.

"Yes, she was about to."

"Still, Duvall does have a way about him," Duer commented.

Jean Pierre wiped his mouth with his hands. They just didn't understand April. They'd have to kill her. He didn't want that. "There must be some other way without hurting her," Jean Pierre blurted out.

"Oh. I see. You have an 'attachment' to Miss Mason."

"It's just that I don't want her to be hurt." Jean Pierre was pleading but not getting anywhere. He put his hands in his face and bowed his head. He was sorry he'd ever mentioned her.

Duer studied Jean Pierre for a moment. There was something very sweet, foolish, but sweet, about men who tried to save women. It was, he had to admit to himself, his soft spot. He loved women. He sat forward and put his elbows on his desk and studied Jean Pierre again. He knew Jean Pierre was protecting her, but he had also said that she was very bright. Perhaps bright enough to solve a problem no one had solved before. If she cooperated, she could be useful, but if she did not, maybe Jean Pierre was right, maybe she'd take her secret to the grave. That would be foolish. Ah, but women are often foolish. There had to be a way of using her without her knowing. Suddenly, he had it. It was simple, easy to control, and, if Miss Mason did actually solve the whereabouts of the map, very rewarding. A solution without any downside. Just his kind of operation. He sat back and again folded his hands in his lap. He was satisfied he had made the right decision. "Monsieur Demain," he said slowly, "I have a proposition for you. I will give you your life in exchange for the map."

"But I don't have the map."

"Ah, but you do believe Miss Mason knows where it is."

"I don't know. I mean I think she thinks she knows."

"Do you trust her instincts?"

Jean Pierre was shivering from the cold sweat sliding down his back. What was this leading to?

"Let me put it another way. Are you willing to stake your life on her belief she knows where the map is buried? If not, of course, I can send Duvall to get her."

"I don't understand." Jean Pierre was confused now.

"I am just trying to assess your judgment. I want an answer."

"She's very intelligent, I know that, and it's possible she knows what she's talking about. I guess I'd bet on her."

"Ah, but will you bet on yourself?"

Jean Pierre sat up. All he could really think of was that he was a good judge of women. He had been for a long time. He was sure April would put up a hell of a fight if they tried to interrogate her. Yes. He did know her. "If you're asking me to bet on her, I would. Yes, I would."

"Good. Then I think the wager is on. It will be up to you to see that neither Miss Mason, nor you, meet with an unfortunate accident. I want you to stay in her confidence, report everything she says and does to Paul, and if you are correct, and more importantly, if she is correct, and the map is found, you both will live. Otherwise, I am sad to say that Duvall will have his way. Are you willing to 'cooperate'?"

Jean Pierre sat back. He didn't really have a choice, but either way he was putting April in mortal danger. Come to think of it, he reasoned, she was already there. He shrugged. "You want me to find out what she knows and report back."

"Not quite. I want you to help her find the map."

"But she wants me to dig up a grave."

"And so you shall."

"But I don't know how to dig up a grave."

"With a shovel, I presume," Duer said with a chuckle.

"I mean, it's illegal."

"Yes. Very." Duer heaved a great sigh, "I can see you'll need help. Paul and Duvall will help when the time is right. You may go."

Jean Pierre sat there. He was stunned.

"Yes, you may go. But, Monsieur Demain, do not try to cross us. Duvall can be very unpleasant. Don't call the police or try anything. Do your job and live."

Paul walked over to Jean Pierre. "Let's go," he said.

Duvall flipped the hood back over Jean Pierre's head then pulled him out of the chair, and led him out of the room.

"Paul," Duer called out.

LeMieux stopped at the door. Duvall pushed Jean Pierre out of the room.

"You are a very loyal aide, Paul. I don't want to lose you. See that I don't."

LeMieux nodded and closed the door softly.

CHAPTER TWENTY-FIVE

"Keep moist," April said repeating the instructions from the person on the other end of the phone. "Okay, I got it." She wrote the instructions on her pad as she sat at her desk in her white bikini early in the morning. She listened again, "Seal it in a plastic bag as air tight as possible. Okay."

She finished writing and put down her pen. "Now, Robert, from what I've told you what are the chances we'll get anything?" She listened and frowned. "That bad, huh?" she said sitting back in her chair. "Well, I've got to try. I hope to be there tomorrow or the next day at the latest. Thank you again for all your help."

She hung up the phone and sighed. She sipped coffee from a mug and looked down at the pad in front of her. It was a "To Do" list. She crossed off "Laboratory" and looked at the next item, "Shovels." She passed that item and went on to the third, "Call Kevin re: City Hall."

She rubbed her eyes and got up from the desk. It was too early to reach Kevin at the paper. She decided to take a shower and dress.

Snooky was getting anxious. She hated having her 'work' in her office. It was too dangerous. She knew she had a reputation, and it was always possible the police would do a spot check on her even though she was no longer on parole. She'd called Paul the night before, but he wasn't in. She had to reach him and get him to take the 'work'. She dialed his number. Again, there was no answer.

Kevin and Le Pluete had coffee and Danish at the café across the street from Kevin's office.

Le Pluete was in a good mood. "Suzette, told me she lost LeMieux's car last night, which of course bothers me, but she also said it did not come out of the garage at Duer's apartment. It just drove by her while she was on the stakeout. How did it get out of the garage?" Le Pluete wondered out loud.

"You think it's possible they're wise to us?" Kevin asked.

"I suppose anything is possible."

"Maybe they simply have a car somewhere else."

"Perhaps."

"Why don't I take a look around the neighborhood? See what I can dig up," Kevin offered.

"Why not?"

"Also, we seem to park in the same place all the time. Maybe we should change our location as well."

"Yes. It is possible that they have seen us or are very cautious. Work out a plan with my assistant after you've had your little stroll."

"Okay." Kevin looked at Le Pluete and squinted his eyes. He couldn't quite figure out what it was, but the Inspector was behaving out of his norm. "You know, Marcel, for a case that hasn't one single clue, you still seem very determined."

"Yes, I suppose you all think I'm being silly, but between you and me, Kevin, this is very personal. I want Duer."

"Personal?"

"Yes. He and I go back a long way. I was still with the Surete in those days, and there was a drug smuggling case which we all believed Duer masterminded. We were very close to implicating him. I had a young assistant, a very attractive young woman. Her code name was Coco. We had

224

become very close, too close in fact. She went undercover to prove the Duer connection. It was my mistake. She wasn't trained well enough. One night she called me to say that she had found a way into Duer's confidence. Whatever that way was, cost her her life. We found her body several days later."

"I'm sorry," Kevin said. "I didn't know."

Le Pluete nodded and bowed his head. "I should never have let her do it."

"It wasn't your fault."

"Ah, but you're wrong. It was my fault, and I have been haunted by it all these years."

Kevin felt bad for his friend. He, too, had lost friends on other cases, in the States, Saudi Arabia, and France. It was dangerous work, and they all knew it, but the reality of death always stayed with you, you just never expect it to strike you or your friends. He knew how Marcel felt. He patted him on the back softly. Marcel slowly raised his head and looked at Kevin. Both men understood each other without saying another thing. "We'll get him Marcel."

"Yes," Le Pluete said firmly.

Jean Pierre awoke from a restless sleep. He'd been awakened during the night several times by nightmares of being shot, stabbed and hanged. Each time he woke up, he was sweating so much he had to change his pajamas. He felt miserable.

He sat up on the edge of the bed and put his head in his hands. He could still see "the boss" telling him that if he wanted to live he had to do as he was told. He wasn't sure that if he did as they asked he'd still live, but he knew if he didn't he'd surely die. And all of it over a book. A damned book! Then he thought of April. He wasn't a hero, but he didn't want her hurt. He'd have to do this very carefully, so she didn't become suspicious and get them both killed.

When he got to his office, Kevin found a message to call April. He immediately picked up the phone and dialed.

April was just coming out of the kitchen when the phone rang. She hurried to her desk and picked it up on the third ring.

"April. Are you all right?," Kevin asked anxiously.

"I'm fine," she said with a frown.

"Good. Good," Kevin said. April felt the relief in his voice.

"Oh, you thought something was wrong. No. I'd almost forgotten about your advice. No, really, I'm fine. I just wanted to talk to you," April said brightly. "First of all, I want you to know you accomplished at least some of your assignment."

"I don't understand."

"I talked at length with Julian last night."

"You told him about Victor," Kevin said wincing.

"No. Victor never came up in the conversation. Why would I mention him?"

"No reason, I guess," I love you, Kevin thought.

"So, anyway, Julian confirmed your assignment to find a man for me to get me back to writing. I simply called to tell you I have begun writing again."

"Who is he?" he asked cautiously.

"Actually, it wasn't a man who started me back writing."

"Really?"

"Yes. Really. What I'm calling for is I need some help for my research."

"Sure. What can I do?"

"I was wondering if you had any contacts at city hall."

"City hall?"

"I need to find some old maps of the city, and frankly I'm not sure where to look. Back home I'd go to the hall of records, but here I haven't the slightest clue."

"What kind of old maps?" Kevin said. He had no idea what she was talking about.

"Maps of Paris during the French Revolution."

"Is your book about history?"

"Not really, you see I read this old book called <u>Recit De La Revolution</u>."

When he heard the title of the book, Kevin's mind perked up. The book Duer was interested in!

"And one of the stories gave me an idea. And I just need to do some research."

Kevin needed time to think. "I'm not really sure how to find what you're looking for, but I have a few contacts. Let me see what I can dig up."

April chuckled to herself when he said 'dig up'. "Thanks. Oh, Kevin, I am in kind of a hurry."

"I'll get back to you today."

"I'll wait for your call. Oh, by the way, how's Suzette?"

"She's fine."

"Good," she said, but somehow she didn't mean it.

Kevin hung up the phone. That was strange, he thought. Why does she have the rare book that Duer is looking for? Is there a connection? And what is this thing about a city hall? And why didn't she ask Jean Pierre for help? He's one of the best sources for questions about the city. He shook his head. Weird, he thought, and worth talking to Le Pluete about.

April had just hung up when the phone rang. "Hello?"

"April, my love," Jean Pierre said. "I was hoping to catch you."

"And I wanted to talk to you. You were on my list."

"List?"

"When I start writing, I start making lists. It's the only way I can keep things straight. Anyway, have you thought of a way?"

"A way?"

"You know, the grave."

"Ah, yes. The grave. I think I have found a solution."

"Great."

"But I still don't know where."

April snapped her fingers, "Right. I forgot to tell you the location. Look, I know this sounds silly, but I'd rather not tell you over the phone. Do you think I'm paranoid?"

"No. I'll come over, if that's all right."

"Perfect," she said. "This afternoon?"

"I think I can get away about four."

"Wonderful. I'll expect you. Oh, and bring a couple of umbrellas, it going to rain tonight."

"Tonight? You want to do this tonight?"

"Why not? No one would expect us to do it on a rainy night."

That, he thought, was a great understatement. "I'm not sure I can arrange things that fast."

"Well, if you can't, you can't, but I'd sure like to get it done as soon as possible."

"Until this afternoon," Jean Pierre said and hung up the phone. He immediately placed another call.

"She's right," Francois said to Paul when he told him about Jean Pierre's call, and what April had said, "No one would expect us to dig up a grave on a rainy night."

"This Miss Mason is very bright, Paul. We will do it tonight, after, of course, he finds out the location of the grave. Have Jean Pierre call you the minute she tells him where," Duer instructed.

"There are actually three good places to check out," George said to Kevin, handing him a list.

"Thanks," Kevin said.

"Anything else?"

"Nope, that'll do it. I'd better start checking this out," he said as he got up and turned off his computer.

George stopped him. "Kevin, you're up to something."

Kevin looked back at George. "Not yet," he said taking George's hand off his arm. "I have to go."

Suddenly his phone rang. Kevin walked over to the coat rack where his raincoat was hanging. "Get that for me will you?" he asked George.

Reluctantly, George answered the phone. He listened, then pointed the receiver at Kevin. "It's some guy named Marcel about a party."

Kevin was torn, but took the phone from George. "Hello, Marcel, what can I do for you?" he said in his most businesslike tone. He listened as Marcel told him that they had the latest phone records for both Duer and LeMieux, and he wanted Kevin to come to his office as soon as possible. Kevin nodded as he spoke, "I see. I'll be there soon. Thanks for calling." Kevin hung up.

"Who's Marcel?" George asked.

"Just a contact. Hey, I've gotta run. Be back later," he said as he grabbed his coat and headed out the door.

"I'm seeing her this afternoon at four," Jean Pierre said over the phone from his flat.

"Good," LeMieux replied. "Jean Pierre, I cannot stress how much danger you are in if you fail."

"Paul, I want you to promise me something."

"If I can."

"Promise that you will not harm Miss Mason."

"That depends on her, Jean Pierre. On her cooperation. And, of course, upon you."

Jean Pierre did not like LeMieux's answer. His brother-in-law had become a different man. He was hard now, and scared of his boss. Very frightened. Jean Pierre was more upset than ever. He now understood the danger.

Kevin arrived at Le Pluete's office dripping wet. It was pouring down rain again. Suzette was already there looking as if she'd just stepped off the runway at a fashion show. "We've got to stop meeting like this," she said to Kevin. "How's my favorite husband?"

Kevin rolled his eyes. She was in that "cute" mood she used in front of Le Pluete. It was to say that she and Kevin were getting along very well. Actually, they were. The excitement of her arrival had worn off, and their schedules didn't mesh any longer so they didn't see each other much. When they did, they had fun, and, when time permitted, sex.

Kevin watched her batting her eyes for Le Pluete's benefit and decided to play along. She did that to him. He held out his arms and went to her and planted a big wet kiss on her surprised lips. "Hi, gorgeous," he said as he sat down in the chair next to hers.

"Well, if you two are through," said Marcel, shaking his head and laughing. They both looked at each other and nodded to him. "Good," he said as he sat down in his chair behind the old desk. "We have a lot to talk about. We just received the latest phone records, and my men have gone through them. They highlighted what they felt were unusual calls. Both Duer and LeMieux had some very interesting phone calls."

"Such as," Kevin said.

"Let's start with Duer," Marcel said, indicating a thick pile of papers in front of him. He took a single page off the top of the pile and scanned it, then handed it to Kevin. Suzette pulled her chair close to Kevin's so she could look over his shoulder.

Kevin looked down the short list noting restaurants, a tailor, two calls to Algeria with a notation Chad Ben Al Chim was a banker, and one call to a Gilbert Lucase with a notation 'book dealer', and six calls to Paul LeMieux.

"What do we know about this Ben Chim person other than he is a banker?" Suzette asked.

"We are checking this out with our people in Oran. Should have something late tonight."

"And Gilbert Lucase?" Kevin asked.

"Quite a lot, actually. Lucase is a dealer in rare books."

Kevin's head popped up. "Rare books?"

"Precisely. It seems we were wrong. He does have an interest. And from what I am told, collecting rare books is a very expensive hobby to have."

"Is that so unusual?" Suzette asked. "I mean the man is a world traveler. Maybe this is his hobby."

"Perhaps," Marcel said skeptically. "But it doesn't seem likely. On the other hand, we were wrong once before. Nevertheless, I think you, Suzette, should talk to Lucase."

"Me?" Suzette said.

"Women, especially in Paris, are more likely to get information from a man than a man. And, we shouldn't act officially now. We have nothing specific to go on."

"Perhaps you could bat your eyes at him?" Kevin teased. "Or another body part."

"Will you men never stop!"

"Not until the day I die," Kevin interjected.

Suzette heaved a big sigh. "So what do you want to find out?"

"Whether Duer is a regular customer, and, of course, if he is trying to buy this specific book." Marcel handed her the name of the book on a scrap piece of paper.

"Recit de la Revolution? Oh, sure, he's going to tell me that," she said sarcasm dripping from her lips.

"If not, we'll make an official inquiry. However, I think you can do this, Suzette. It's not much different from your task in Geneva with that banker."

"You want me to screw him?"

"Oh, no. He is an old man. The banker was young, and as I remember, very handsome. And, I believe, the sexual encounter was your idea."

Suzette stared daggers at Le Pluete then burst out laughing. "You're right, he was very handsome, and very good in bed," she said, looking out the corner of her eye at Kevin and grinning.

"Can we get back to business?" Kevin said flatly.

"Jealous, O'Connor?" she quipped.

"Nope."

Suzette looked at Marcel. He looked at her. They both smiled, then both said at the same time, "He's jealous."

Kevin started to say something, but Marcel cut him off. "So much for what we have on Duer's calls. I just hope he doesn't get wise to the phone taps as well."

"What do you mean, 'as well'?" Suzette asked.

"We now believe Duer knows he's under surveillance. As you know, LeMieux has stopped using the garage at Duer's apartment house. It's no wonder we haven't seen any action around there. But, thanks to you, Suzette, we think we've found where they are hiding their cars. If you hadn't seen them coming down the street in back of you yesterday, we might never have suspected anything. Good work, Suzette. " Le Pluete said with a smile.

"Thank you," she said coyly.

Marcel looked at his watch. "Suzette, I am very interested in this rare book angle. Would you mind going to see this Lucase this afternoon?"

"Not at all, if that's what you want, you got it."

"It's very puzzling and the sooner we know something about it, the better."

"I'll go right after the meeting."

"He closes at four, could you go now?"

"What about the phone calls from LeMieux?"

"I'll fill you in at the apartment," Kevin said.

Suzette grabbed her raincoat and went to the door. "Oh, it might be nice to know the address," she said.

Le Pluete scribbled the address on another piece of paper and handed it to her. Her eyebrows raised. "Oh, Saint Honore, la-di-da!" She closed the door as she left.

"Now to Paul LeMieux," Marcel said, taking another paper off the stack on his desk and handing it to Kevin. "As you will note, this list is much longer and has a couple of surprises as well."

Kevin's eyes ran down the list of phone calls. Several were to Duer's apartment, a few to Jean Pierre's, and some to his home. In addition, there were six calls to an antique store and two to a woman in Montmartre.

"An antique store?" Kevin asked, seeing the notation beside the number.

Marcel shrugged, "A small establishment in the Latin Quarter that seems to be doing very little business."

"And the woman?"

"She, it seems, is the proprietor of the antique's store."

"LeMieux's got woman on the side?"

"Possibly," Le Pluete said, "but if so, it would be strange."

"She's married?"

"No, she is not married. At least we don't think so. Her neighbors see her very little. She appears to go to the store early in the morning, seven days a week, and doesn't come home until around midnight. She is never with anyone. Aside from that we know very little about her."

"What's her name?"

"The license for the store is under the name of Michelle Montedeiu. Kevin, I'd like you to check this place out."

"Will do," Kevin said.

"There is one other thing. Each time, less than a minute after LeMieux talked with the antique store, he called Duer. We think there's a connection."

"I'd say the odds are on our side," Kevin said.

Jean Pierre arrived at April's apartment right on time. He was anxious. He wanted to get the information as quickly as possible and call LeMieux.

April took his umbrella and raincoat. She offered him coffee, and he nodded. She noticed he didn't seem himself. He was pacing when she came out of the kitchen. "Are you all right?" she asked.

"I'm fine," he said just a little too quickly.

"Look, Jean Pierre, if you don't want to help...."

"No, no I'll be all right, it's just that I don't usually go around digging up graves."

"That makes two of us," April said.

"Are you certain you want to do this?"

"I know this sounds silly, but I've got to try. All day long I've been haunted by the notion that I'm right - that I have the solution."

"Then shall we begin? I need to know so much," he said, sitting down on the couch.

"Right," she said as she went to the desk and picked up the book and brought it over to the couch and sat beside him. "Here goes. I told you the story about the aristocrat finding the baker's vault and how he made a map of the location."

"Yes, yes I remember."

"He wrapped the map in part of a leather apron, covered that with oil cloth and hid it in his crotch. He was arrested, and if the author, Du Pypes, is right, he still had it when he was sent to the guillotine. Collette and a couple of her friends took his body and Marie's and buried them after making sure they had the proper last rites."

"Yes. And you found the grave where?"

"Oh, that's right, I didn't get to tell you. I went to the cemetery."

"How did you know which one?"

"There was a note in the book. The initials CdM were handwritten in the book. See, the story didn't mention the name of the cemetery, it only said that Collette had taken the bodies to a small Abby in Montmartre to be given the last rites. But when I asked Monsignor Ignatius, he told me the initials stand for Cimitiere de Montmartre."

"You went to see a priest? You are very good at research."

"Thanks. Anyway, I went to the cemetery and talked with the caretaker. He showed me the grave, which is only marked 'Charwoman', and told me that the grave had been dug up several times over the past two hundred years. Are you with me so far?"

"And that is in the story?"

"Some of it. Anyway, Collette met with the author, a Charles Du Pypes, after she buried the bodies and told him her side of the story."

"You said many had dug up the grave."

"True, but now here is where my instincts come in. Collette was very close to her mistress, Marie."

"As many servants are."

"Right. Anyway, Du Pypes mentions that Collette had a great sense of humor. Ferdinand told Du Pypes that their favorite position for making love was with her on top. So, I guessed that Marie had told Collette the same. Collette played a big joke on everyone. She buried them both together but - where is Ferdinand?"

"On the bottom?" Jean Pierre said, not sure he had any idea he was right.

"Precisely!"

"And that's why you think his coffin was buried under Marie's."

"Right again!"

"So when you told me that the secret was sex, it was!" Jean Pierre said, now very proud of himself. "And you want to dig that grave up again?" he said incredulously.

"Yep. Because my instincts tell me that's where we'll find the body of Ferdinand, and the map to the vault."

April paused, looking at Jean Pierre. She was looking for some sign that he believed her. There was none.

Jean Pierre's mind was on keeping Duer happy.

April grabbed Jean Pierre by the shoulders and pointed him toward her. "You don't have to say it. I can see it on your face. I'm out of my mind. But that's what I thought, too! I tried every rational way of getting this idea out of my mind, but it wouldn't go. Then, the longer I thought about it, the longer I dissected it, the more plausible it became. Now, I know I'm right. You believe me, don't you?"

Jean Pierre let out a long, slow breath. "I believe you."
Then he shrugged and held up his hands, palms up, and
nodded. "I also believe you have a wonderful imagination."

"But, Jean Pierre."

He stopped her by putting his hand over her mouth. "I'm
not finished, ma cherie." He got up from the couch and
walked to the French doors and opened them. It was getting
dark, and it was still raining heavily. He took a deep breath.

April watched Jean Pierre. She wanted him to believe her,
but he looked like he'd just been hit by a truck. Old stone face,
she said to herself. "Jean Pierre."

He held up his hand to stop her. "Please, April, give me
some time to think."

She nodded and sat back. She could see he was having a
difficult time. His right eye twitched and he played with his
hands which were clasped behind his back. He rocked back
and forth on the balls of his feet.

Jean Pierre was thinking all right. He ran down what he
knew. He knew the whereabouts of the grave. He knew that
April believed that Ferdinand's coffin was beneath Marie's.
And, he had to admit to himself, that she might be right. After
all, he thought, the grave had been dug up several times over
two hundred years, and they found only one coffin. There was
a chance no one had thought of digging deeper. What he
didn't know was the exact location of the grave in the
cemetery. He turned and looked at her. She was staring at him
with those big, brown eyes. They seemed to be pleading with
him. He turned back and closed his eyes. Now, what was he
going to do? He had to find a way to spare April. The only
way he could do that was if she wasn't there. Then it dawned
on him. There was a way, but he had to know the exact
location of the grave. He turned and walked back to the couch
and stood over her. "Just suppose, my dear, that you are
right."

"I know I am."

"Yes. And you know where this grave is in the cemetery?"

April leapt up from the couch. "I know exactly where the grave is. I made a map," she said enthusiastically as she went to the desk and pulled a piece of paper out from under a pile of other papers and handed it to him. "It's right there," she said pointing to an 'X' on the map.

Jean Pierre studied the map. It wasn't very clear. There were no points of reference that he needed to find the grave. He frowned.

"Okay, so I'm a terrible map maker," April said as if she were reading his mind, which, of course, she was.

Jean Pierre rubbed his hand across his mouth several times. He was deep in thought.

"I know," April said, her eyes brightening. "Let's go and I'll show you."

"That is a very good idea, but we cannot dig up the grave tonight."

Disappointed April asked, "Why not?"

"We need to get the proper equipment. If, as you say, Ferdinand's coffin is beneath Marie's, we need to have some way to haul it up. We couldn't lift it ourselves."

April had to admit that was probably true. "Block and tackle."

"Something like that, yes. You see there is much more to this than a few shovels full of dirt."

April was happy that Jean Pierre sounded enthusiastic about digging up the grave. She was anxious to get to it, but he was probably right, they did need to plan better. "Let's go there now so we can see what we'll need."

"All right," he paused and put his hands on her shoulders. "April, my dear, I know you want to do this soon, and I promise you we will do it as quickly as possible, but for now, let's find out just what equipment we will need."

April nodded and picked up her raincoat from off the coat rack. Jean Pierre put his on and they left, arm in arm.

It was nearly five when Kevin got back to his apartment. Suzette was waiting.

"How'd the meeting go with Lucase?"

"Nothing. He was home, ill."

"Let's have dinner somewhere nice for once. We don't have stake out tonight."

"Okay," he said, "but first I want to stop by April Mason's apartment."

"Why?"

"Well, she called me and wanted to know where to find some old maps of Paris."

"Old maps?"

"Yeah, it's some sort of research thing. Oh, did I tell you? She's writing again."

"How very novel of a novelist."

"You know what I mean."

"You mean that was part of that crazy job you took on with that publisher just to get your next book, if there is a next one, published."

"Well, it doesn't hurt. So, I picked up the maps on my way back here. We'll drop them off at her place on our way."

"Let's do it fast. I'm famished."

April and Jean Pierre arrived at Cimitiere de Montmartre. She led him to the grave site. It was still raining. He made a mental note of everything to be sure he could find his way back to the grave site. Now it was time for phase II of his plan.

CHAPTER TWENTY-SIX

"In a way, I'm sort of glad she wasn't there," Suzette said as she picked up her menu.

"I wanted to talk to her."

"So, you left the maps under the door. I'm sure April will find them."

Kevin nodded. He didn't know why, but he felt uneasy about April. Why did she have a rare book? Then he suddenly slapped himself on the forehead. "The treasure," he said out loud.

Suzette looked up. "What?"

"That's it. The treasure. April's going to try to find the treasure they wrote about in the book!"

"What book?"

"The one Le Pluete mentioned. The book April's been reading. Recit de la Revolution. How the hell did she get it? That book's so rare they don't even have a copy in the library."

"Like I know," Suzette said, curling her lip.

"I know you don't know. I don't know."

"Who cares? She got it."

"Right. Now I'll bet she's after the treasure. I know it."

"But I thought Marcel said people have been looking for that treasure for hundreds of years."

"He did. And now, unless I miss my guess, April's going to try for the treasure, too."

"So let her try."

"Something's very fishy about this whole thing."

"Kevin, you're being very melodramatic. I'm sure there's a simple explanation," Suzette said trying to calm him down. "Besides, what does it matter whether she has a rare book or not? It's not like she's in danger or anything."

Kevin had to admit Suzette was right. Having a rare book wasn't dangerous. "Okay. Okay. Maybe I am going off the deep end about this, but I know I'm missing something."

"If it will make you feel better, call her in the morning and ask her how she got the book."

Kevin nodded and pinched his lips tightly. "Right. I'll call her in the morning."

"Come on, let's eat," Suzette pleaded.

Kevin looked at her and picked up his menu.

Suzette could see the muscles in his face relax. "What are you going to have?" they said in unison.

It was nearly nine o'clock when April and Jean Pierre got back to her apartment. April was drenched and went into her bedroom to change.

Jean Pierre was as nervous as a cobra at a mongoose convention. He wanted to call LeMieux and tell him the location of the grave and April's hunch that there was a second coffin, but he couldn't do it in front of her. He suddenly grabbed his coat and called to April, "My dear, I just remembered that I have some important paperwork I must do tonight."

April cocked her head. That was strange, she thought. And that's the second time Jean Pierre "suddenly remembered" something. She pulled on her robe and walked out into the living room. Jean Pierre was already at the door with his coat on. "Must you go? I was hoping we'd have a chance to decide what we need to dig up the grave," April said with a pout.

Jean Pierre came to her and put his arms around her and held her tightly. She could feel him trembling. "April, my love, there is nothing I'd rather do, but, uh, I have to give a speech tomorrow morning, and I must make notes."

"Oh, I thought you had everything in your head."

Jean Pierre looked down at her and smiled, "I do. I have you in my head."

"And your speech."

"Yes, well, it is a very important speech to the representatives of Japan, and to me I just realized. I need to make some more notes."

"Oh?" she asked.

He stepped back, and she could tell he was anxious to go. Too anxious, she thought. What was he up to?

"Yes. As soon as I finish my speech, I will make all the necessary arrangements to dig up the grave. It will take some planning."

April fixed her eyes on Jean Pierre. "Yes. I know."

"Good," he said going to the door.

April followed him and opened the door. "Well, if you must go."

Jean Pierre gave her a quick peck on the lips and stepped out into the hall. "Au revoir, my love."

"Give a great speech tomorrow, Jean Pierre," she said warily.

He turned and started toward the elevator at the end of the hall.

April started to close the door, then peeked out again. Jean Pierre was running toward the elevator. "Oh, oh," she said as her warning senses kicked in. She watched as he got on the elevator and the doors closed. She slowly shut her door and leaned back against it. What was Jean Pierre up to?

Kevin was quiet all during dinner. He was thinking about April. What was she up to?

Jean Pierre burst into his flat. He had to act fast. He had a plan, and it had to be done that night. He went into his

241

bedroom and reached into the drawer of his bedside table. He took out a small, semiautomatic pistol and laid it on the bed. From his closet, he pulled out a brand new black rain suit, rubber boots and a cap and started dressing quickly.

Minutes later, fully dressed, he made two phone calls. The first to Lizette. "I will pick you up in fifteen minutes. You understand what to do."

"But it's cold and raining out there. I'll catch a cold."

"It will be worth it. Trust me. Fifteen minutes." He quickly hung up the phone and dialed Paul LeMieux.

When Paul answered, Jean Pierre said, "I have the location."

Paul was pleasantly surprised. "Very good."

"There is one thing."

"What?"

"I want your promise that April Mason will not be involved and that if there is no map, she won't be blamed."

"I've told you over and over, I'll see what I can do. That's all I can promise."

Jean Pierre didn't like Paul's answer, but he now had no choice. "All right. Meet me in one hour at the intersection of Rue des Dames and Avenue de Clichy."

Paul repeated the instructions as he wrote them down. "Got it."

"I hope you have all the necessary tools and plenty of rope. If Miss Mason is right, we'll need a lot of rope."

"I will make sure we have everything."

"Good. One hour." Jean Pierre put down the phone. He was sweating heavily under the rubberized rain suit. He put the pistol in his rain coat pocket, took a deep breath, and headed for the door.

As they were leaving the restaurant, Suzette excused herself to go to the powder room. Kevin paced back and forth in the foyer. He couldn't get April off his mind. She was just bullheaded enough, he thought, to try and find that treasure.

He had to talk to her if only to confirm his suspicions. He vowed to call April first thing in the morning.

Paul and Duvall came into Duer's library and were startled to see him dressed in heavy rain gear. "I've decided to go with you," Duer said.

Both men looked at each other and shrugged. "I have some unfortunate news, however, and we must solve this first. It seems that Interpol now knows where our alternative garage is and are watching it. We must find another way out of this complex."

Paul smiled. "I have a back up plan."

"Really, Paul. I am very impressed," Duer said. "And that is?"

"A decoy."

"And who is this decoy?"

"I have a friend."

"Call him."

"Her," Paul said with a grin. "And I already have. We will trade automobiles, and she'll drive ours out of the garage first. We can then see if our watchmen follow her. If they do, we go next, if not, I will call her on her cell phone, she will return and we'll try again. Personally, I think it will work the first time."

"Then, lead on."

"You can stay dry with this black tarp over your head," Jean Pierre said as he positioned Lizette, dressed in a long rain coat and scarf, behind a large monument not far from the grave site. The rain was still coming down hard and the ground was soaked.

"But my feet are all muddy," Lizette complained.

"Tuck them under the cover and take off your wet shoes. You will be warm enough."

Lizette pouted, "I don't like this."

"Would you rather I pay someone else? I can get Monique."

"No!" Lizette said. "That bitch has enough."

"All right then, stay here and watch over there," he said pointing to the grave site. "And what is the signal?"

"You say 'this is perfect'."

"Right. Now, I have to leave, but I will return shortly with the others. Don't move from this spot."

Lizette looked at him over the top of her eyes. "I want half now."

"Merde!" Jean Pierre said angrily. He reached into his pocket and pulled out a money clip. He peeled off a few bills and handed them to her. "I have no idea where you're going to keep the money."

"I have just the place," she said with an evil grin.

"Now are you ready?"

"Yes."

"Good. Stay here." Jean Pierre pulled the tarp over Lizette's head and positioned her carefully so that she could not be seen from the grave site. "Comfortable?"

"How long will you be?"

"I don't know," he said evenly and in a dead monotone. "Stay here." He walked away toward his parked car.

April paced back and forth. She was getting agitated with herself. Something was nagging at her. She started back to the kitchen to get another glass of wine when she saw an envelope by the edge of the steps leading to the front door. She frowned. How did that get there? she wondered. She picked it up and tore open the envelope. It contained the three maps. There was a handwritten note from Kevin. "I hope these are what you need. If you ever need any help, please call. Kevin."

She took the note to her desk and put it down slowly. "Kevin," she said out loud. She reached for the phone then stopped herself. No. She didn't want to involve Kevin. Like any secret, she remembered, if one person knows it's a secret, if two know it's a still a secret, but if three know it's a disaster.

She sat down at her desk and looked at her list. She had done everything. She crossed off the last item - maps. She stared at the list for a long time. Then, slowly, she began shaking her head. "No. No. No," she said softly. "I made a mistake. I just feel it." She got up and began to pace. She was thinking about Jean Pierre. Once he got the information, he split, she thought. Why? Why is it I don't trust him? She remembered. Kevin didn't trust him. Is that why she didn't trust Jean Pierre?

She had to admit that she didn't trust Kevin either, but there was something about Kevin she did trust. It was his instincts. He'd warned her about Jean Pierre. The more she thought about Jean Pierre, the more nervous she felt. What if Jean Pierre was going to dig up the grave and get the map himself? How could he do that alone? Impossible. But, what if Jean Pierre had help? She clamped her lips together and let out an audible "ugh!" She stamped her foot and turned and headed for the bedroom. She was going to the cemetery!

Duer congratulated Paul. The ploy of having the woman drive his car worked. The stakeout car followed her. They had gotten away cleanly. Just to make sure, they had driven down a few side streets and parked. No one was following them. They drove to the rendezvous. Jean Pierre was parked on the corner on Rue des Dames facing the cemetery. Paul pulled up beside him. Jean Pierre told him to park up ahead of him.

The three men got out of their car. Each was dressed in heavy boots, long rain coats and slouched hats. It was still raining, although it had let up some. It was more like a heavy mist.

"The grave is not far from here," Jean Pierre said when he walked up to them. "We will have to walk. There is a pedestrian gate beside the main gate, and I have taken care of the lock. I hope you have all of the necessary equipment."

"It's in the boot," Paul said as they walked to the rear of the black Mercedes. He opened the trunk, and they took out shovels, a pickaxe, and rope.

"The caretaker lives in the upstairs apartment of the main building. We must be quiet," Jean Pierre said, then motioned for them to follow him.

The four men arrived at the grave. They talked in whispers. Duer motioned for Paul and Duvall to begin digging. Even though it was raining hard, they took off their coats and began.

April, dressed in black slacks, a black turtleneck sweater, and boots, fastened a "fanny pack" around her waist, pulled on her black rain coat, and walked out her front door.

She managed to get a taxi about a block from her apartment. She got in and said, "Cimitiere de Montmartre, s'il vous plait."

The cab driver turned around in his seat and stared at her.

"Le Cimitiere de Montmartre?"

"Oui."

"Maintenant?"

April was getting frustrated. "Oui," she said loudly. "And I'm in a hurry."

"Ah," the driver said raising his hands then slapping the steering wheel. "An American. I should have guessed."

"Good. You speak English," April said with a smile.

"Yes. I speak English," he said haughtily. "Do you know you asked me to go to the cemetery in Montmartre?"

"Yes."

"But it is closed. It is nighttime, and it is raining," the driver said as he turned to April and gestured to the window.

"Yes, I know. Now can we go?" April asked.

"I don't think this is a good idea."

"I do," She said holding money in front of his nose.

He turned back around, put his hands on the wheel and shook his head. He pulled down the handle on the taxi meter and they drove off into the night.

"I'd better not find you there Jean Pierre," April said.

CHAPTER TWENTY-SEVEN

Duer, standing comfortably under his large black umbrella, watched as the two men dug. It was going slowly because the dirt was quickly turning to mud. "We need another man. Jean Pierre, please," Paul said. He gestured toward the grave.

Jean Pierre didn't like the idea at all. He was opposed to manual labor of any kind. "You are doing all right," he said.

Duer pulled a pistol out of his raincoat pocket. "Please?"

Jean Pierre shrugged, shed his rain coat, picked up a shovel, and got down into the hole with the other two. He was furious. Not only was he digging, but his pistol was in his raincoat pocket. He began digging.

As April's cab was coming up the Rue des Dames, they crossed a large intersection. She saw it. "Slow down, please," she said rolling down the window. "Damn it! It is his car! That son of a bitch!" she said. The driver stopped.

"What madam?"

"Nothing, drive on."

When they came to the entrance to the cemetery, he stopped again. She could see that the pedestrian gate was open. "Wait here," she said.

"Oh, I cannot do that. It is raining. There are many fares to be had."

April reached into her fanny pack and took a hundred-dollar bill. She showed it to him, and he smiled eagerly. She started to hand it to him, then at the last minute pulled it back, tore it in half, and gave him one of the halves. "You'll get the other half when I get back. I won't be long."

With that, she got out of the taxi and walked into the cemetery.

"Tie the ropes around it carefully," Jean Pierre said as he climbed out of the grave. Paul and Duvall struggled with the coffin. It was wooden and looked relatively new, but it was also getting soaked in the rain and had become slippery.

Duer rubbed his hands in glee. "So now we get the map," he said looking down at the coffin.

"No," Jean Pierre said as he put on his raincoat. "There's no map inside that coffin. It has been opened many times."

"So why did we dig this one up?" Duvall asked.

"First," Jean Pierre said, holding up his hand. "I must remind you that this is all a hunch. It is Miss Mason's guess. She has a theory but no proof. So, I want your assurance that Miss Mason will not be harmed if she is wrong."

"This theory of hers," Duer said. "How did she develop it?"

"It's a long explanation, but I can sum it up in one word. Sex."

"Sex?" all three men said in unison.

"Yes. And that is all I will say unless you, monsieur," he said pointing to Duer, "will give me your assurance Miss Mason will not be harmed."

Duer knew he was about to lie, so he did. "All right, no harm will come to this woman. Now what is this theory?"

Jean Pierre turned to Duvall. "You asked why we dug this coffin up? The answer is simple. To get to the other one."

"I don't see another one," Paul said shining his flashlight around the grave.

"She believes there is another coffin buried beneath this one, and that that coffin contains the map."

"Oh, so she knew about this one being dug up?" Duer asked.

"Yes. Many people have dug this one up."

"And, again, why does she think there is another coffin?" Duer wanted to know.

"As I said before - a hunch. A hunch based upon what she read in between the lines of the story in the book. An interpretation that I think only a woman would devise. The map, if April Mason is correct, is in another coffin buried on purpose beneath this one."

"It is an interesting theory, Monsieur Demain. Let us hope she is correct." Duer said. "Let's pull that one up and then resume digging," he commanded as he shined his flashlight down into the grave.

It was pitch dark and pouring down rain again as April carefully made her way through the gates and into the Cimitiere de Montmartre. She walked quickly up the Avenue Principale (each of the roads of the cemetery are named) and on to the Avenue Dubisson then left on Avenue Hector-Berlioz toward the caretaker's building. April used her flashlight sparingly. She didn't want Jean Pierre to know she was there. Suddenly she stopped. She heard muffled voices in the distance.

She stepped off the road and onto the grass to mute her footsteps. She proceeded slowly, cautiously toward the voices. A few steps later she saw the light from a flashlight just ahead of her. It cast a faint, eerie glow, but it was enough light to allow her to see the outline of the caretaker's building to her left.

April tiptoed over the road and headed for the corner of the building. She had to cross an open space between where the men were and the building. She watched the men for a moment. None of the men were looking in her direction. She scampered across the open space and hugged the building. She had not been seen. With her back to the wall, April crept toward the corner.

She peeked around the corner. She saw two men. One was Jean Pierre! The other was a heavy set man holding an umbrella. He was talking to two men who were digging. Even though she was only about twenty feet from the grave, she could barely make out what they were saying. What little April could hear surprised her. They had just found the first coffin.

She knew she had some time to wait until, with her fingers crossed, they found Ferdinand's coffin. With her back to the wall, she walked back a few steps, and slid to the ground. She would wait to make her move. Right now she wanted them to do the digging. She pulled her rain coat tightly around her.

A few minutes later she heard them straining as they pulled the first coffin out of the grave and put it onto the growing pile of mud.

Jean Pierre climbed back down in the grave, grabbed his shovel and poked it into the ground several times where the first coffin had rested. Nothing. Duvall and LeMieux did the same. Nothing.

Jean Pierre put his boot onto the shovel and pressed down. All he came up with was dirt. He threw his shovel down.

"I don't think one shovelful will suffice," Duer commented.

"Can't we take a rest?" Duvall asked. "This is hard work."

"Yes, it seems to be, but we do not have much time. Every minute is precious. Now dig!"

Twenty minutes went by. The three, by now, were near exhaustion and caked with mud. Duer was pacing back and forth like a nervous father.

Jean Pierre had had enough. He was convinced there was no coffin down there. He viciously stabbed his shovel into the ground. It was met by a dull thud.

All three men stopped. Jean Pierre stabbed again, and again came the dull thud. Duer came to the edge of the grave and shined his light down into the now nearly eight foot deep hole. "Do that again," he commanded.

Jean Pierre did and there was another thud. All four men smiled. The three in the grave began to dig furiously.

April heard the thud and wanted to scream "Yes!", but bit her tongue and waited.

Ten minutes later, Duer threw the ropes down into the pit and the men wrapped them around the other coffin. "Gently now gentlemen, the wood is very old," he warned.

After securing ropes around each end, the three mud-caked men climbed out of the grave. They had had to build a small series of steps to climb out it was so deep. They were all very excited.

"April was right," Jean Pierre said as he brushed mud from his clothes. "She is magnificent!"

I told you so, you bastard, April mused.

"Yes. It appears so. If, the map is in there," reminded Duer. "Now pull it up."

"I am afraid, you must help, too, Monsieur Duer," Paul LeMieux said. "It is so deep it will take all four of us to raise the coffin."

'Duer', April said to herself. He must be the leader of the gang. Where have I heard that name? Kevin? Yes. Kevin used it. Hummm.

Duer reluctantly put down his umbrella, slid his gun into his pocket and took one end of the rope. Each man grabbed one of the four rope ends. Mud was everywhere around the grave. It was piled high on one side of the grave, but it was all around it. "Careful now," Duer said. "We don't want it to hit the side of the hole. It is probably very fragile."

Slowly they began to pull the two-hundred year old coffin up from the remaining dirt around its edges. Finally, it broke loose and began to rise as each man tugged with all his strength.

Suddenly, Duvall cried out, "I'm slipping."

April peeked around the corner and could see him sliding toward the edge of the grave as his feet tried to get a foothold.

"Stop!" Jean Pierre said. "Duvall, don't let go. We'll rest a moment while you find your feet. Put it back down, gently."

They did. Duvall was wringing wet. As was each of them.

"Use a shovel and each man dig a place for his feet," Duer said. "We cannot afford to drop it."

Each did. Finally, they were ready again.

Slowly they raised the casket out of the hole and slid it onto the wet grass.

Then, as if on cue, the clouds parted and a bright full moon peeked out casting an eerie blue hue over the graveyard. It was almost as if the sun had come out. April could easily make out the faces of each man. She could see the casket. She wanted to run over and open it, but she knew she couldn't. The rain was now a thin, fine mist, and ground fog was creeping over the entire graveyard.

Duer opened his umbrella and put it over the coffin. He told LeMieux to do the same with his umbrella. "We don't want it to get wet when we open it," he said.

Jean Pierre casually walked over to where his raincoat was and quickly put it on. He felt for his gun. It was there.

The coffin was made of heavy oak slats that were sealed with some sort of tar. It was shaped in the form of a coffin with a cross carved on the top.

As they brushed away the remaining dirt from the top, they could see that the wood seemed to be in good condition. "Get the crowbar," LeMieux said to Duvall.

"Hold the umbrella, and don't let any rain get on it," Duer commanded Duvall as he took the crowbar from him. Duvall held the umbrella in place. Duer got down on his knees beside the casket. He slid the crowbar under the top and began to pry. Everyone held their breath. To his surprise, the top loosened easily after the first few pries at each end. Duer put his chubby fingers under the top and pulled. The top came off.

All four men peered into the darkened box. Jean Pierre handed Duer a flashlight. He turned it on and pointed it inside the casket.

Each man gasped at the sight. Everything was covered with a fine dust. There were a few remnants of tattered cloth and the full skeleton of Ferdinand, except that his head was resting in his bony hands on his chest. The skull seemed to be smiling back at them. Aside from a few cobwebs in the corners, the interior of the casket seemed to be in perfect shape.

The beam of the flashlight bounced back and forth around the box. Finally, Duer asked, "The map, where is the map?"

Jean Pierre, who by now was standing behind Duer and looking over his shoulder, simply said, "It's in his crotch."

Duer looked back over his shoulder at Jean Pierre. "You must be joking."

"No. That's where she said it would be. In his crotch."

All three of the others began to laugh. Jean Pierre joined in.

April smirked.

Duer handed the flashlight to Jean Pierre and rubbed his hands together. "If you say so." Jean Pierre shined the light onto the pelvic area. Sure enough there was a large pile of dust between the hip bones. Duer reached down.

Jean Pierre coughed. "I would remind you that if the map is still in tact, it must be handled with great care. It will be very delicate. I wouldn't just grab it."

Duer pulled his hand back. "And just what would you suggest?"

"Blow on it."

"I beg your pardon."

"Blow on it. Blow the dust away so you can see it before you pick it up. So you won't drop it."

"I will not."

"Okay. It's your map."

Duer thought for a moment. Duvall and LeMieux could hardly contain their laughter.

253

April thought Jean Pierre's suggestion was a good one. I might not have thought of that she said to herself.

Duer turned back to the coffin, heaved a big sigh, bent down into it and blew. Dust flew everywhere. Especially in Duer's face. Dust clouded the light from the flashlight for a moment, but when it settled, there was a black, rounded object about the size of a fist resting right in the middle of the skeleton's crotch.

Duer reached down and carefully picked it up. He blew the last remaining dust off of it. He could see that it was oil cloth wrapped around something else. It was tied with a strip of leather.

"If I didn't know better," he said, "I'd say this was his cod piece." They all laughed.

Be careful with that, April wanted to scream out. It could disintegrate in this air!

Duer held out his hand, and Jean Pierre helped him up. He had to stifle a huge guffaw when he saw Duer's face. It was covered with dust! Finally, under control, he asked, "May I see?"

Duer held out his hand and showed Jean Pierre the lump. "This is perfect," Jean Pierre said in a loud voice.

Lizette, who had been watching the whole thing from her vantage point was mesmerized. She heard the signal, but didn't think a thing about it.

Jean Pierre glanced over his shoulder in her direction. Nothing. He clenched his teeth and said it again - louder, "This is perfect!"

Lizette suddenly realized it was her cue. She threw off the tarp, took off her rain coat, and stepped out beside the tombstone into the bright moonlight. She was totally naked!

"Hello, boys," she said as she walked toward the men. Each turned and gasped. "Mon dieu," Duvall said.

Jean Pierre knew this was the moment, he turned back to Duer and at the same time reached into his coat for his gun. But, when he pulled it out, he brushed Duer who was caught off balance and began stumbling backward toward the grave. His feet were slipping out from under him. Jean Pierre reached to stop him with his gun hand, but he also slipped, and his gun hand landed an uppercut to the hand in which Duer was holding the map. The force of the blow caused Duer's hand to release the map as he was falling backward into the grave. The map went flying skyward, and directly toward the corner of the caretaker's building where April was now standing. She saw the whole thing, and watched as the map arched its way toward her. She only had to move one step to catch it. She reached out and cradled it onto her hands.

At the same time, Duvall, LeMieux, Lizette and Jean Pierre watched in horror as Duer slipped and slid right into the grave and landed face down in the mud.

April ducked back into the shadows, pulled a plastic bag from her coat, slipped the map into the bag and sealed it. She peeked around the corner at the commotion, gave them all the finger and took off running toward her waiting taxi.

CHAPTER TWENTY-EIGHT

April ran to the waiting taxi on the Rue des Dames and jumped into the back seat. "75 Rue Danielle Casanova," she barked. "And step on it!"

"The other half please," the driver said calmly without moving the car an inch.

"What?"

"The other half of the one hundred-dollar bill."

"Oh." She reached in her coat pocket and handed it to the driver. "Now please hurry!"

"Now please hurry," the driver muttered to himself as he started the car and drove off.

April leaned back in her seat. She wasn't sure whether anyone had seen her. If they had, they'd be after her and the first place they'd look was her apartment. She had to get some things and get out as quickly as possible.

All four, Duvall, LeMieux, Jean Pierre and Lizette (still stark naked) peered down into the grave. Duer was struggling to get up out of the mud. "Don't just stand there, help me out of here," Duer said as he once again slipped and sat back in the mud.

"The map. Do you have the map?" Jean Pierre asked.

"No. It must have fallen out of my hand when you pushed me into this godforsaken pit!"

"I did not push you," Jean Pierre said. "I slipped and then you slipped in the mud."

"Perhaps it's down there with you," Paul said handing down a flashlight.

Duer carefully searched the bottom of the grave. Finally, in disgust he said, "It's not here it must be somewhere up there. Help me up."

Francois managed to get up the three temporary steps built into the grave and held up his hands. Jean Pierre took one hand and Duvall the other, but because Duer weighed nearly three hundred pounds, it was not easy. Each man kept slipping in the mud. Finally Paul put his arms around Duvall, and Lizette put her arms around Jean Pierre and they all pulled. It took nearly five minutes to get the struggling, mud-covered Duer out of the nearly eight foot deep hole.

All four men sat down exhausted. Lizette stood over them and announced that she was cold and was going home. They watched her shiny naked body glistening in the moonlight as she marched back to where her coat and boots were, put them on and strode off in the direction of the entrance.

Duer turned to Jean Pierre. "Why was she here?"

Jean Pierre said, "A diversion."

"Yes, I know that, but why was she here?"

Jean Pierre threw up his hands. "I just told you. Ah, it doesn't matter," he said "she's gone now."

By this time, the men had gotten their second wind. "Shall we look for the map now?" Paul asked.

"Yes. Yes, of course, you idiot," Duer said anxiously.

The first thing they found was the fourth flashlight that had fallen in the mud beside the grave. Now they spread out, the beams of their torches flitted about along the ground near the grave.

They had been searching for about ten minutes when Duvall suddenly whispered, "Quiet!"

They listened. They heard laughter coming from the direction of the entrance gate. They all turned out their flashlights and waited.

Coming along the path was a man and a woman arm in arm. He had obviously been drinking, and she was trying to steady him.

"Get down!" Paul whispered. All four laid down in the mud on their stomachs.

"The caretaker," Jean Pierre whispered louder. The other three shushed him.

They approached the caretaker's building and stopped. The caretaker and his woman were standing there in the moonlight and all four men could see them clearly.

"I can't find my keys," the man said with a slurring voice.

The woman laughed. "They are probably in your pocket."

He fumbled in his pockets, "Not here," he said. "You look."

She laughed. "In your pockets?"

"This is the one I usually carry them in," he said holding out one of his pants pockets. "See if they are in there."

The woman reached into his pocket. "I don't feel anything."

"Deeper."

"Oh, now I feel something."

"So do I," the man said holding up his keys and laughing.

The woman pulled her hand out, "You are a devil. A rather large one at that."

They laughed as Richard opened the door. They went inside and closed the door.

"We must be very quiet," Jean Pierre said. "He lives on the top floor."

"It's a good thing he wasn't home when we were digging, he would have surely heard the yells when you fell into the grave," Duvall said.

Just then the area was brightly lit as the lights in the apartment directly above them were turned on.

"Keep on searching. We must find the map before dawn," Duer whispered. They got up and began looking.

April ran into her apartment and took her overnight case from the armoire. She went into the bathroom and gathered up her make up and toiletries and threw them in the bag. She quickly got out of her wet clothes and threw them in the bath tub after carefully removing the map. She selected a couple of outfits from the armoire and put them in her small suitcase.

Once she was dressed, she took the map in its plastic wrapper and went into the kitchen where she wrapped it in several more layers of plastic wrap.

Then, she went to her desk. She wrapped up the book, the map, the maps Kevin had given her, and her notes and put them in her purse. She checked to see that she had her passport and money and was out of the apartment in less than ten minutes.

Her ever-faithful, for money, taxi driver was waiting in the courtyard.

"Where do you wish to go now?"

"London."

"London? At this time of night? There are no planes, no trains at three thirty in the morning."

"I know. Would you drive me?"

"Mon dieu, you are crazy."

"I know. Lots of people think that. But I have to get to London right away."

"I cannot drive to London, madame."

"But isn't there a tunnel under the English Channel?"

"Yes, but I am not licensed to drive in England."

"Oh," she said sounding very disappointed.

"There is one thing I can do. I can drive you to Le Havre. From there you can catch the boat train or a boat to England. But, it will be very expensive."

"How much?"

"In American dollars," he said, "five hundred."

"I can do that," she said. "Drive on."

Jean Pierre, Duer, LeMieux and Duvall were down on their hands and knees scouring every inch of the area around the grave. Jean Pierre looked at his watch. It was nearly four thirty in the morning. They had been searching for nearly two hours. Still no map. He knew that dawn would be in less than twenty minutes. He stood up. "I am leaving," he announced.

Duer looked up at him. "You will stay. We must find that map."

"No. It will be light in twenty minutes. If we are found here, we will be arrested. The map is not worth it to me. I have my reputation to protect."

"Then go," Duer said, "but you do not get any of the treasure."

Jean Pierre shrugged, turned on his flashlight and started toward the entrance, but just as he rounded the corner of the caretaker's building he stopped. He shined his flashlight around, scanning the area. There were footprints. They came to the spot then went back toward the gate. They looked fresh, and they were small. A woman's boots. He rolled his eyes. April. April was there. He knew it.

He knelt down to examine them more closely. But when he stood up, Duer was standing beside him. Duer was looking at the same footprints in the grass.

"Someone else was here tonight," Duer said. "Do you know anything about this?"

Jean Pierre could see the outline of a pistol in Duer's right hand. "No."

"No? I don't think you are telling the truth. You should you know it is very dangerous for you to lie to me."

"I didn't know anyone was here. I swear."

"But you have an idea who it was, don't you?" he said, raising the gun to Jean Pierre's head.

"Yes."

"Good. Now I will ask this only once. Was it Miss Mason?"

"I'm not sure, but it could have been her."

"And why would you think that?"

"Because she told me about the grave. She showed it to me this afternoon."

"And she doesn't trust you," Duer said in a matter of fact manner.

"Look, sir," Jean Pierre said, "I care about her, and I think she trusts me, but I can't be sure. Women are very difficult to read."

"Can you think of anyone else you may have told about the grave?"

"Lizette."

"The naked one?"

"Yes."

"Well, we all know she didn't find the map. She had no place to hide it. Anyone else?"

"No. No one."

"Then by deduction it must have been Miss Mason. Don't you agree?"

"It looks that way."

"Is it possible she has the map?"

"I suppose, if she were here when you dropped it, she could have picked it up," Jean Pierre admitted.

"I think she did," Duer said. "And furthermore, I think we should go and see her. Now."

Jean Pierre cursed under his breath. Of all the stupid things he could have done it was to implicate April. Well, she had gotten herself into this, she'd have to get herself out, he thought.

"Come on," Duer said to Duvall and LeMieux. "I think I know where to find the map."

The two men looked at each other, shrugged, got up off the ground and followed Duer and Jean Pierre out of the cemetery.

Suzette woke to the smell of fresh coffee brewing. Kevin was already up and dressed. "What time is it?"

"A little after seven."

"Oh, that's too early. Come on back to bed."

"I can't sleep. I want to call April."

"At this hour? She'll kill you. I know I would."

"I have to talk to her," he said as he picked up the phone and dialed. No answer. He frowned.

The phone in April's apartment rang. The four intruders looked at it. Duer motioned for them to let it ring. They nodded and continued their search. Duer lumbered from room to room. The entire place was trashed. Clothes were everywhere, the bedding was on the floor, in the kitchen all of the drawers were emptied. They had found nothing of interest except April's wet clothes in the bath tub. He was furious. Now, thoroughly convinced that April had the map, he wanted to find her, but there were no clues as to where she could be. An hour later he called off the search. As they started to leave, Duer saw the waste basket under the desk. He picked it up. There was a crumpled piece of paper stuck to the bottom. He pulled it out. It was April's "to do list". He carefully read each item then smiled. The last entry was a London telephone number with the notation "call Robert". Duer put the list with the telephone number in his pocket. They left April's apartment in shambles.

On their way back to Duer's apartment, Paul was worried that the Interpol stake out team would see them. Duer waved his hand. "Let them. They have no idea where we were. It will give them something to talk about."

Jean Pierre got into his car with Duer's warning ringing in his ears, "Don't say a word to anyone about this night or it will be the last time you tell anyone anything."

Paul drove straight to Duer's garage. The stakeout team, a man and a woman, saw the Mercedes in their rear view mirror and ducked down, but it was too late. The car was past them. She gasped. "What?" the man asked.

"How did they get out?"

"The question is, where have they been? Better call this in," the man said picking up his radio phone.

April slept most of the drive to Le Havre. When they arrived at the outskirts of the city, she woke. "What's the quickest way to get to London?" She asked.

"The boat train," the taxi driver said.

April nodded, "The boat train it is." Minutes later the cab pulled up to the terminal.

"I believe they run every hour. I'm not sure," the driver said as he opened the door for her.

April reached into her purse and pulled out the money and handed it to him.

He counted it and smiled. "I hope you have a pleasant journey, madame," he said as he helped her get her suitcase out. "I don't know what you were up to at the cemetery, and I don't want to, but you seem like a nice woman. Be careful," he said and tipped his hat.

April picked up her suitcase and started into the terminal.

CHAPTER TWENTY-NINE

April knocked on the glass door marked "Laboratory." A man in a white lab coat turned and waved to her.

He opened the door. "It's great to see you again, April."

April shook his hand then kissed him on the cheek. "It's good to see you, Robert. It's been a long time."

"About four years I think since I came to that seminar in Chicago."

"I want to thank you again for all your help with <u>Murder To A Fault</u>. That technical stuff you added was just the right touch. And, I might add, helped me get out of a bind."

"My pleasure. Now you said something about an old map?"

April told him about the map, and how long it had been buried and pulled it out of her purse.

"You kept it sealed and moist?"

"Yep, just like you told me."

"All right, I think the best way to examine this is in a vacuum. Air is probably the worst thing for it. Let's take it over here." He pointed to a large chamber. "This is actually a chamber within a chamber for maximum protection."

They walked inside a small room with a large pedestal in the center. On the pedestal was a glass enclosed, domed glass container about three feet in diameter. The outside enclosure was sitting on a chrome box. There were several dials and digital read outs on the chrome panel. There were also two rubberized gloves embedded in the glass dome with places to insert human hands.

Inside the smaller, domed glass were several small arms in various shapes. Above the domed glass cylinder was a camera mounted on a moveable base in the ceiling.

"This," Robert said with pride, "is our 'vacuum hut'. Here we can have a vacuum within a vacuum. It's one of five in the world. We can also maneuver whatever is inside by these handles which are like fingers and which move the arms just as if they were our hands."

"Fascinating," April said.

"So I guess you're ready to start."

April took the plastic wrapped map out of her purse and handed it to him. He slowly unwrapped it until he reached the oil cloth case around the map. "Feels good for a two-hundred year old ball."

April laughed.

"Here, hold it just one more minute," he said, handing it back to April.

The scientist went to another console filled with buttons and flashing lights. As he was busy setting up the vacuum unit, April wandered around the small glass enclosed room. It was only about ten feet by ten feet, and the vacuum unit took up most of the room.

April looked out through a large glass window at an expansive laboratory filled with state-of-the-art research equipment. There were several scientists at work at various projects.

April had met Robert Desmond in Chicago four years ago when she attended a seminar on the preservation of artifacts during the King Tut exhibit. He was a world-reknown expert in the restoration of antiquities from the British Museum. She had been fascinated with the exhibit and wanted to know how they had managed to keep artifacts from thousands of years ago in such perfect condition. She also needed some help for one of her books. Robert had volunteered to help her. They became friends during his visit.

April never expected to be in London, let alone the Museum, but now she was glad they were friends. Her map was in the hands of one of the world's foremost experts in the science of antique evaluation and restoration.

She loved the atmosphere. It was like being surrounded by history and yet in a sort of science fiction setting.

April heard a sudden whirring sound and then a rush of air. She turned as the exterior casing opened up automatically. Then the smaller glass domed receptacle opened on a hinge.

"Okay," Robert said getting up from the console, "I think we're ready for your map." April handed it to him. He examined it closely then placed it inside the smaller receptacle. Then he returned to the console and closed the smaller one first and then the larger outer case.

"This process takes some time," he said as he walked over to the "vac hut" and pointed to it. "First we have to seal the entire unit and check for any leaks. Then we pump all of the air out of the larger outer casing and again check for leaks, and finally we pump all the air out of the inner chamber and check for leaks. The process takes about an hour more or less. And, believe me, there is nothing to see. You can't see the air being pumped out, so I suggest you find something to do downstairs perhaps. We have an excellent exhibit of Egyptian weapons you might enjoy."

"That sounds fascinating, but right now I'm beat. Is there anywhere I could lie down?"

"Well, I didn't want to mention it, but you do look a bit frazzled. Come on, there's a lounge just down the hall."

Seconds after they left the lab the phone rang.

Duer listened intently as the phone rang several times. Finally, the operator came back on the line, "I'm afraid Mr. Robert Desmond has stepped out for a few minutes. Can I take a message?"

"Actually," Duer said, "I'm trying to confirm that this Robert Desmond is the person I'm looking for. I know he works there at the museum, but I'm not sure if he's the same one I'm looking for. The Mr. Desmond I'm looking for is an expert in fifteenth century painters."

"Oh, no sir, our Robert Desmond is a restoration expert for antiquities. He is involved in the recovery of specimens' from all over the world."

"I see," Duer said with a smile. "I'm terribly sorry to have bothered you. It's the wrong man. Thank you for your help," he said and hung up.

He looked at April's "to do list" and the notation he'd made at the bottom - British Museum. "Very clever, Miss Mason," he said aloud. "And I'll bet you're there this very moment." He grinned and pushed a button.

Momentarily LeMieux appeared. "Go to the public phone in the garage and call our man in London, give him a description of April Mason and have him follow her. She's at the British Museum, I believe it's on Montague Place, with a Mr. Robert Desmond. Tell him not to lose her and to report every two hours to the pay phone number."

LeMieux nodded and left. Duer wore a smug grin as he sat back in his chair and folded his hands. "I think this time I'll let you do the work, Miss Mason," he said and laughed loudly.

Kevin had called April's apartment ten times since seven o'clock and there still was no answer. He was getting worried. Suddenly the phone rang. It was Marcel. "Have you your television on?" he asked.

"No," Kevin replied, "Why?"

"Turn on the local news channel. I'll wait."

Kevin crossed the room and turned the TV on. He switched channels until he came to channel eight. There was a picture of several policemen gathered around an open grave. They seemed to be pointing at not one, but two coffins. He turned up the sound.

"And as you can see," the reporter was saying, "the grave robbers discovered not one but two caskets in the same hole. This, of course, is the same grave which has been dug up several times, not by robbers, but by people looking for a treasure map. This is, however, according to the caretaker, the first time two coffins have been found in this grave."

Kevin turned the sound down and returned to the phone. "Recit de la Revolution," he said into the phone.

"Precisely," Marcel said.

"And you think Duer is somehow involved?"

"Oh, yes. We know so. They returned early this morning to their garage."

"Hadn't our people been following them?"

"No. Unfortunately they pulled a switch last night with some woman who lived in another apartment and our people followed her for a few blocks. When they discovered their error, it was too late. But there is a bright side."

"And that is."

"One of our women went inside the garage after they returned and found mud all around the car they were using. A quick sample from the grave site was taken, they matched, and now we know where they were."

Just then Suzette came out of the bathroom where she had taken a shower. She was drying her hair and didn't have anything on. "Kevin? Who was that on the phone?" Her voice trailed off when she saw Kevin holding his finger to his lips to silence her. He mouthed "Marcel." She nodded and went back into the bathroom.

"So, why haven't you arrested them?" Kevin said into the phone.

"Ah, a very good question. Perhaps a bit more complicated than we should talk over the phone. And there are one or two more twists to this event that you will be interested in."

"I'll be down in thirty minutes," Kevin said. "I've got one stop to make."

After making his call, Paul LeMieux went back to his room. He was so tired he simply dropped his clothes on the floor and headed directly to his bed. He flopped down and his head was precisely three inches from hitting his pillow when his bedside phone rang jolting him into an upright position. He picked it up. "Hello?" he said half asleep.

"You must pick up the packages now," Snooky commanded in the phone so loudly he had to hold the receiver away from his ear.

"Ah, Miss Montedieu, so good of you to call."

"The packages are wrapped and waiting. You know I like to ship my merchandise out as soon as possible," she said through clenched teeth.

"Yes, well, there has been some difficulty arranging transportation."

"Fix the problem today or I will burn the merchandise," Snooky demanded and immediately hung up. Paul flopped back on the bed and stared at the ceiling. He was wide awake now.

The Interpol agent transcribed the conversation on his computer and immediately sent it by e-mail to headquarters, "Attention Marcel Le Pluete".

Jean Pierre went home, changed and went immediately to his office. He had to find April and warn her. He instructed his secretary to call every hotel in Paris on the off-chance that she had checked in a hotel rather than stay in her apartment. He racked his brain trying to figure out where she was.

April stood by the vacuum machine and watched Robert carefully manipulate the arms and fingers of the device inside the smaller vacuum unit. Slowly the fingers cut the leather strap holding the oil cloth pouch together. Then Robert lifted one edge of the oil cloth encasement. Then another until the oil cloth was flat on the bottom of the unit and the leather ball inside was fully exposed. "This is the delicate part," John said.

"I don't want to tear it. I don't see an edge so I'm going to turn the ball over." Slowly, delicately he turned the ball of leather over until he could see an edge. He gently peeled it off, and that revealed another edge. It was a slow, painstaking process.

It was nearly an hour later when the cloth was finally spread out flat on the bottom of the unit. Robert got up from the console and peered in at the crude map. April came along beside him and looked. The markings were faint, but readable.

"I'm going to take pictures of the map with the digital camera," he pointed to a huge camera suspended over the unit. "Once we get that, we can digitally enhance the map."

April just nodded and looked at Robert admiringly.

Fifteen minutes later, April was looking at the map on a computer screen. Robert stood beside the computer. A young man with horned-rimmed glasses sat at the keyboard. "Now, Lionel, we want to see the markings as clearly as possible."

"No problem," Lionel said in a slight cockney accent. "This will be a piece of cake." His fingers moved rapidly over the keyboard and the image became clearer and clearer until they could see every line. It was a crudely drawn, simple map with two lines for the street outside the bakery and two lines for the street which intersected that street. The names of the streets were also legible. The street in front of the bakery was Rue de Dauphin Est, and the intersecting street was Rue des Dame Marie. Underneath the map was written "13 Rue de Dauphin Est."

"We can print copies of this if you like," Robert said.

"Yes. Please."

"Comin' right up," Lionel said and his fingers again flew over the keyboard.

While Lionel was making the copies, April phoned and got a reservation at the Savoy Hotel.

Minutes later April had two copies of the map. "I know this sounds pushy, but is it possible to get a couple of copies on transparencies?"

"Sure." In minutes she had the map on both paper and transparencies.

"Thank you, Lionel," she said as he handed the maps to her.

"My pleasure, miss. Stop around anytime."

Robert led April out of the computer room and into the hallway. "Is there anything else I can do for you, April?" he asked.

"Well, since you asked, do you happen to know where I can get a map of Paris in 1790?"

"Trying to find this place, I see."

"Trying. I have one map but I'd like another, just to be on the safe side."

"Frankly I haven't the foggiest, but I know a man who will know."

April listened as Robert called one of the other curators of the Museum. He described what April was looking for. He listened then hung up the phone. "We don't have such a thing, but Samuel says that you might try Jenkin's Chart Shop on Kensington North West. It's his only suggestion. Anything else?"

"Oh, no. No you've done everything. You're a wizard."

"Thank you, but I prefer 'scientist'."

"How much do I owe you?"

"There's no charge. That's what we do here, deal with ancient things. I'm just very happy it all worked out."

"Me, too."

"Do you want to take the original back with you?"

"No. I'm afraid I might harm it. You can keep it if you like."

"Well, from the story you told me, that will depend on the French authorities I'm afraid. We'll notify them of your find."

"Must you?"

"Yes. It's only ethical. We have a joint agreement."

"I see," April said quietly. Then her eyes lit up. "Robert, could you wait a few days before you notify them?"

"Going to try and find this place?"

"Yes."

"Well, I don't suppose it would do any harm to wait, shall we say a week. After all, it has been around for two hundred years," he said with a smile.

"Thank you," April said. "If ever there's anything I can do for you, let me know."

Robert stopped her. "Actually, there is."

Is this a come on? April wondered. "What?"

"Could you write a mystery about antiquities? I rather liked being a technical consultant."

April laughed out loud and hugged him. "It'll be on the top of my list," she said and kissed him on the cheek. He blushed.

"I'll walk you out," Robert said, taking her arm. April put the maps in her bag, and they started down the long hallway. "By the way is there a post office nearby?" she asked.

CHAPTER THIRTY

April stood on the stone steps of the British Museum in the bright sunlight and yelled "Yahoo!" at the top of her lungs. Passersby stopped and stared at this crazy woman who was dancing a jig on the steps. April, who had been her own biggest critic, was now her biggest fan.

I did it, she said to herself as she danced around. I actually solved a mystery. A mystery I didn't create! A real life, honest to goodness mystery! Good girl!

Now, she told herself, all you have to do is go to the street where the bakery was, climb down into the sewer and recover the treasure. No Problem!

She headed down Great Russell Street toward the map store. Not far behind her was a slender man with wire-rimmed glasses, a small mustache and a scar on his left cheek. He didn't take his eyes off her.

Jean Pierre's secretary informed him that Miss April Mason was not registered in any hotel in Paris. He threw up his hands in frustration.

Snooky closed the sliding bookcase in her office at the back of the store, and went out into her shop to dust a bit. That always relieved her tension. She was furious. She had done her part. The counterfeit Dinars were all carefully wrapped for

Duer and in her secret laboratory piled up in a corner. She hated having incriminating evidence on the premises. There was always a chance the police would search the place. As she was steaming, the front door opened, and a handsome man walked in. "May I help you?" she asked.

Kevin looked at the woman. She was dressed in dowdy clothes, her hair was in a tight bun at the base of her neck and she wore tortoise-shelled glasses. She was young, in her mid-thirties he guessed, but there was something about her that was familiar. He stared at her.

"May I help you?" Snooky asked again.

"Oh, sorry. I'm looking for something special to give my wife. She loves antiques."

"What in particular did you have in mind?"

Kevin's eyes narrowed. Was she who he thought she was? There was a test. "Yes, a silver spoon serving set. Louis XIV."

Snooky frowned, trying to think whether or not there was one in the store. "A Louis XIV silver serving spoon set?"

The minute she spoke, Kevin knew it was Michelle Jardin. The sibilant 'esses' gave her away. It had been nine years since he'd seen her from behind a one-way glass at a police line-up in Nice. He recognized her and he knew she was much more attractive than she appeared. And, he reminded himself, she was an excellent forger. Come to think of it, he remembered, that case involved Duer also. Bingo!

"No," Snooky said, "I don't believe we have such a thing. Are you certain it was Louis XIV?"

"Yes. My wife's a stickler for authenticity. Well, I'm sorry to have bothered you."

"No trouble," she said.

Kevin walked out of the store and directly to his car. He reached under the dashboard and pulled out his radio phone and called Le Pluete. He gave him a report, and promised to stay there until a stakeout team arrived.

Suzette walked into the tiny bookstore on Rue Des Archives. It was dark and smelled of old paper and cigarettes. Seated behind a glass counter on a stool was Gilbert Lucase, an emaciated looking man in a well-worn brown suit. He was smoking a cigarette which dangled from his thin lips. There was an overflowing ashtray in front of him. He was intently reading a book.

When Suzette walked in, he ground out the cigarette and stood up. He was very short, less than five foot two Suzette guessed. He took off his reading glasses and she could see huge bags under his eyes. His hair, what little there was, was combed straight back. "Bonjour," he said in a raspy voice.

Suzette spoke in French and asked if he might have a copy of a very rare book, <u>Recit de la Revolution</u>. He coughed nervously and eyed her over the top of his glasses. "I don't believe I've heard of this book," he said.

"It's very old, and I'm told very rare. A friend, Monsieur Dure, suggested I come here."

"Dure? I'm sorry I never heard of this man."

"Really? He said he'd spoken to you this week."

"No. I think he must be mistaken. Besides, I don't know anything about such a book."

"Oh," Suzette said, looking as disappointed as she could, "My husband will be very upset. He is a collector you see. Francois Duer? He will be surprised you haven't heard of it."

Gilbert's face hardened when he heard Duer's real name.

"Did I tell you the name of the book?"

"Yes. <u>Recit de la Revolution</u>."

"Right. I believe the author is Charles Su Pypes."

"Su Pypes? I've never heard of him either."

"Or was it Du Pypes?"

Gilbert raised an eyebrow and gave a faint nod. Suzette saw the look of recognition and knew he was lying.

"I've never heard of either of these men. I've never heard of this book, and I never heard of your husband whom you say is a collector, and I know all of the book collectors in France. I am very busy. You should try some other place."

"Oh, dear. Well, sorry to have bothered you."

She went out the door and walked just out of sight, then she turned back and looked into the dirty window. Gilbert was on the phone talking excitedly. "I'll bet you're calling Duer," she said. "And the time is, she looked at her watch, three thirty-four."

April walked out of Jenkin's Chart Shop with two books under her arm. She was grinning ear to ear. She went to a copier store down the street and made copies of the maps in both books. Then she made two transparencies of those maps the same scale as the transparencies that Lionel had made for her.

She hailed a taxi and told the driver to take her to the Savoy Hotel. The man following her quickly hailed a cab also.

CHAPTER THIRTY-ONE

It was nearly six o'clock in the evening, and the small conference table in Le Pluete's office was very crowded. Seated around the table were Kevin, Suzette, Philippe Chartres, Inspector General of the Surete, August Mouthier, Le Pluete's second in command, Andre Goute, Special Investigator for the Paris police, and Le Pluete sat at the head of the table. Behind Le Pluete was a large blackboard with a list of the suspects: Duer, LeMieux, Duvall, Jean Pierre Demain, Snooky Montedieu, Gilbert Lucase and April Mason, with some notes scribbled beside each one.

They had been discussing the situation for more than two hours. Le Pluete summed up what they had so far, "So, we know that each one of the suspects is involved with Duer in one manner or the other. We believe that most of them are connected in some way with the rare book <u>Recit de la Revolution</u> and are looking for the map to the treasure reportedly in the book. We believe that April Mason led them to the grave site in order to find the elusive map, and that since the grave was dug up and two coffins were found, it is possible one of them has the map right now."

Kevin couldn't believe that April was involved with Duer, but every bit of evidence pointed to her involvement.

"So far they are only guilty of grave robbing, a minor offense. This Duvall person is wanted for questioning in regard to a murder in St. Tropez, but there is no direct evidence he committed the crime. The forger, Michelle 'Snooky' Jardin is also somehow connected to Duer, but we do not know either how or why. In short gentlemen and lady, we have our suspicions, but few facts to back them up. Certainly not enough to move against Duer our primary target. We must somehow connect him with a serious crime."

"What about this April Mason?" Andre asked. "Isn't she the key somehow?"

"Yes and no," Le Pluete said. "First, she has no history of association with Duer. In fact, our American counterparts tell us she has never been to Europe before. A search of her telephone records both in America and here in Paris fails to show any contact with Duer. Yet, we believe she has the book, how she got it, we do not know. We do not know how or why she led Duer to the grave site where the second coffin was found. The only fact we have is that the grave was dug up. We cannot even place Miss Mason at that scene last night. We need proof."

"Why not pull Miss Mason in for questioning?"

"Frankly we were hesitant up until the grave was robbed, but this afternoon I sent two men over to her apartment. She did not answer the door. We have since tried three other times to no avail, and no one in the apartment house has seen her today. Therefore, I asked Philippe to get a court order to search her apartment."

"I have it here," Philippe said holding up the document.

"I want to be there," Kevin said.

"Yes, I know, Kevin," Le Pluete said. "And so you shall. I suggest you and Philippe and a couple officers go there as soon as we conclude this meeting."

"Finally, we have surveillance teams outside all of the suspects' homes and offices. They will be on twenty-four hour stakeouts with rotating teams to avoid being detected. We know Duer has discovered our teams before, and we must be extraordinarily cautious. Are there any questions?"

No one spoke up.

"Very well," Le Pluete said. "Good luck to all of you."

Everyone got up and started out when Le Pluete called out, "Oh, Suzette. Would you mind staying for a minute?"

Suzette nodded and sat back down.

When the room was cleared, Marcel sat down beside Suzette. "I have a very special task for you."

"Yes?"

"We have a mole in our operation somewhere. Duer didn't discover our presence by accident. There were two phone calls to him from public phones. The first came just after we'd set up surveillance on his apartment, and the second yesterday before they eluded us to go to the graveyard. I want you to use all your skills to find this man."

"Where do I start?"

"I suggest you work with Goute. See if any of his informers know anything."

"I'll get right on it."

"Good." They both got up and went to the door. Le Pluete stopped and put his hand on Suzette's arm stopping her. "Looking for informers can be dangerous, Suzette. Be careful."

"I will be very careful," she said as she preceded him out the door.

Jean Pierre was going out of his mind worrying about April. He had no idea where she was. He'd called the apartment several times and gotten no answer. He decided to go there to see why she wasn't answering her phone.

Paul knocked and then entered Duer's office. "Our man in London found her right where you said she'd be. She's staying at the Savoy Hotel."

"Archie is very resourceful." Duer said.

"Yes. He said she went to a map store and purchased some books, then to a copier store and made some copies from the books."

"April Mason is very thorough," Duer mused. "She's doing her homework. She's becoming indispensable."

"What would you like Archie to do?"

"Tell Archie to stick to her. Not let her disappear again. We'll let her try and figure out where the vault is. After all, she found out where the map was hidden, perhaps, she can also find the vault."

Kevin knocked on April's door for the third time. No answer. Philippe and two policemen stood by his side.

"We have the court order. Do you want them to break down the door, Kevin?" Philippe asked.

"That won't be necessary," Kevin said pulling out a small black case containing his lock-pick set. They were inside in seconds. When he turned on the lights, he winced. The place had been completely trashed. They went in and shut the door. Carefully they began going over the apartment looking for any clues to April's whereabouts. "Mud," said one of the policemen.

"There's some over here, too," Philippe said.

"I've found some, too. It is on her wet clothes that were in the bath tub. And, unless I miss my guess, all this mud will match the mud at the grave site. "So, April Mason is involved," Philippe said.

"I'll admit, it looks bad for her," Kevin said as doubt of her innocence crept into his mind.

Jean Pierre got off the elevator a few minutes later and walked to April's door. He started to knock when he heard voices. He put his ear to the door and listened. He could hear men's voices on the other side. From what he heard, they sounded like the police. He turned and went back the way he had come.

Out in the courtyard, he got into his car and drove off. Paris undercover policemen followed at a discreet distance.

April, dressed in a hotel robe, studied the map of Paris in 1790. She was glad she'd bought a magnifying glass. She felt like Sherlock Holmes as she scanned the map looking for either Rue de Dauphin Est or Rue des Dames Marie. The street names weren't very legible. It took her over an hour to find it, but there it was, the intersection in Ferdinand's map.

She wrote down a list of all of the streets nearby before trying to find the same intersection in her modern street map of Paris.

She knew the general area to look, but the modern-day map was as different from the 1790 map as night is to day. She knew that Paris had undergone a renovation beginning in 1861, but it must have been massive, she thought. Nothing was familiar. None of the street names were the same. This was tedious business. She tapped her fingers. She got up and paced. Anything to clear her mind. She rubbed her eyes and even got a drink of water. She sat back down and began again. She'd been going at it for nearly three hours straight, and she was exhausted. It had to be there, but where?

She called down to room service for some more coffee and stretched out on the bed. She dropped off into a sound sleep.

Ten minutes later, the phone rang. April reached across the bed and picked it up. She yawned as she said, "Yes."

The voice on the other end said, "Miss April Mason, the author?"

She still wasn't awake when she said "Yes."

The caller hung up. April was still trying to clear the cobwebs from her mind when her doorbell rang. She opened it and a waiter brought in a service of fresh coffee.

She walked around her room trying to wake up. After a few minutes, the coffee took its effect. She had a new idea. At the copier place, she'd made the two transparencies of the maps so that they were approximately the same scale as the Ferdinand map. She brought the bed side lamp over to the desk and put it on the floor. Then she turned the lamp shade upside down and so she could lay the maps on top of it. She took the 1790 map and circled the area around the bakery shop. She laid the 1790 map over the lamp shade and put the modern day map on top of it. The strong light from under the maps made it possible to see both maps. She lined the two maps up as best she could. She saw that the circled area on the 1790 map was over a park!

No wonder she couldn't find the streets. She made a circle on the modern day map. The nearest streets to the small park were Rue Berger on the South and Rue du Louvre on the East. "Okay," she said aloud, "Tomorrow it's back to Paris and a visit to Les Gouts, the sewer museum." I should be able to get a map of the old sewer system there, she thought, then it's 'off to get the treasure'!

The next morning, Archie was seated in the lobby of the Savoy Hotel when April came downstairs. She checked out, and he followed her out to the taxi stand. He hailed the next cab and followed.

Suzette was up and dressed early. She had a hair appointment before they were to meet at Le Pluete's office at nine. She picked up her purse and stuck her head in the bathroom door. Kevin was shaving. "Don't worry, Kevin, I'm sure she's all right." He nodded and Suzette left.

Kevin was worried. No one knew where she was, or if she was even alive. There were no clues to her whereabouts in her apartment and no one had seen her during the past two days.

Duvall and LeMieux sat in Duer's library. "And the telephone arrangements?" Duer asked Duvall.

"The old man in the apartment upstairs was very cooperative," Duvall said with a smile.

"You didn't have to kill him," Paul said angrily.

"He was going to call the police. I had no choice," Duvall snapped back. "Now we have a secure phone. That is what Monsieur Duer wanted."

"I still say,"

Duer interrupted, "Paul, it's over and done. It was necessary. Now did you give Archie the new number?"

"Yes. An hour ago," Paul replied.

"Good."

"Archie said that April was boarding a plane to Paris and that he was boarding the same plane as soon as he hung up. He will follow her and report in using the new telephone number when the plane arrives in Paris."

"What are your instructions, Monsieur Duer when Miss Mason gets back?"

"We could intercept her and get the map from her," Duvall said flatly.

"Yes, Duvall, I know you could, but could you find the treasure, even with the map? I think not. No. We will let her do the footwork, and we shall be there when she finds it."

"We must make preparations if we are going down in those filthy sewers," Paul reminded Duer.

"Yes. See what we have in the storage room upstairs, then stay by the phone and await Archie's call. Tell him to call every fifteen minutes so we can move quickly if we have to."

Paul nodded and got up slowly. Duer watched him warily. As LeMieux opened the door, Francois called to him, "Paul. I know this thing with the old man wasn't to your liking. I, too, dislike violence, but sometimes it is the only alternative."

"I understand," Paul said and closed the door.

"Watch him," Duer ordered Duvall.

Duvall smiled. "Yes. I understand." Duvall got up and quickly followed LeMieux.

Suddenly, the phone rang. Duer frowned. No one was to call him at that number any longer. He let it ring four times before picking it up. The voice on the other end said, "Code three."

Duer squinted his eyes. That meant they were being watched very closely. He took a deep breath and said, "Go to telephone six."

The caller hung up. At least the mole had the good sense to use the old code, Duer thought. He would have to call back when the spy was in place. He looked at his watch. He would call in half an hour from the new phone upstairs.

April came out of the terminal at Orly Airport and hailed a cab. "Pont L'Alma," she said to the driver. Archie's cab was right behind her.

Kevin's phone rang at his office. "April Mason was spotted by one of the police at Orly Airport a few minutes ago," Le Pluete said. "We have the cab number."

A wave of relief washed over Kevin. She was alive! "Was she alone?"

"Yes. The officer said he just caught a glimpse of her as she got into the taxi. God knows where she's headed but there is an APB on the cab. Hopefully, they'll spot her."

"Tell them to follow only. She is not to be picked up. We want to see where she leads us."

"I already have given the order, Kevin."

"I'm coming over," Kevin said.

April's cab pulled up at the Pont L'Alma. She paid the driver and went to the entrance to the tours of the famous sewers, Les Gouts.

Archie's cab pulled up right after hers. He watched as she descended the steps. There's no way out of there but right here, little lady, Archie said to himself and asked the driver to wait.

She paid for her ticket and went down the stairs to the main exhibit. There were only a few people there. Inside the huge concrete tunnel were models of pumps, cutaway sections of the sewers in various years, and a big map on one wall. She stopped to look at it and tried to find the Forum les Halles.

When she finally pinpointed the spot, she saw that there was an old sewer line running right beneath the gardens. She looked closely at the map, but couldn't see any entrance to that part of the sewer. Was the old sewer still there? If so, how was she going to get down into it?

She looked around and saw an older man in a beret and smoking a pipe sitting on a stool near one of the models. She went to him. "Bonjour, monsieur."

"Bonjour," he said in a very bored tone of voice.

April tried to explain to the man that she was looking for an entrance to one of the old sewers in French. He just stared at her. She continued to try and explain, but he had no expression on his face. He just stared at her.

Finally, when she finished, he smiled. "Your French is very good. A bit confused perhaps, but you have a very good accent," he said in perfect English.

April sighed.

"Now, why don't you tell me what you are looking for?" he said.

April explained, this time in English, that she was a writer and she wanted to go down in one of the old sewers because she was writing a story about the French Revolution. She showed him her marked map and said that she wanted to see the sewers there because that was where her story was set. He laughed. "Madam."

"Mademoiselle," April replied.

He looked at her a moment and said, "Ah, you should be married by now."

April grinned, "Not yet. No one will take me."

"Men are fools," he said.

She held up the map again, and this time he took it and studied it. "I have worked here for nearly forty years, but I worked only on the modern sewers. There are very few left men who've even been in the old ones. I doubt that you will find anyone who knows that area anymore. They are all dead."

April's face sagged. She'd gotten this far only to run into a stone wall. "Is there no one?" she asked.

"I don't think so. I don't know anyone."

"It's very important to me."

"Yes. I can see. Alas, you are a century or so late," he said with a smile.

April couldn't help but like him. She let out a slow breath and said, "Well, thank you very much anyway. It was just a hunch."

The old man looked at her with his crinkly eyes that mirrored his smile. He rubbed his chin. "There is one possibility," he said slowly. "I'm not sure he's still alive, but there was a very old man, a veteran of the war. He used to tell us stories of how the Resistence used the sewers. He worked here until about ten years ago when he became ill. I used to visit him at the retirement home, but I haven't gone there in a couple of years. His name is Jacques Le Borsin."

April's face lit up. "Do you know which retirement home?" she asked anxiously.

"Yes. It is not far from here on the Rue Saint Dominique. It's only a few blocks. Here, I'll show you on your map." He pointed out the location of the home.

"As I said, I'd don't even know if Jacques is still alive. He would be very old now. But" he shrugged, "you can try. If he is still there, tell him Le Boot told you to come by."

April put her map away and thanked him.

"Oh, and if you are that seriously interested, there is a map at the gift shop you will want. It is number Q-11."

"Thank you so very much," she said and gave him a kiss on the cheek. "Au revoir."

Duer walked into the upstairs apartment and saw the dead man on the floor. "Duvall," he barked, "get rid of that body now."

Duvall grabbed the legs of the old man and dragged him into the bedroom.

Duer sat down by the phone, looked at his watch and waited.

April bought the map at the gift stand and walked out into the street.

Archie saw April come out of the sewer museum and walk across the street. She was walking South on the Avenue Bosquet. He got out of his taxi and started following her.

She turned left on Rue Saint Dominique and walked into a courtyard in the middle of the block which was the entrance to the retirement home.

He followed her to the front door, but did not go in, he watched. April was in the lobby talking with a grey-haired lady. The lady pointed to the elevators. April got on and pressed a button. Archie knew he had time. He pulled a cell phone and a note from his coat pocket. He looked at the note, then made his call.

"A retirement home? What is she doing there?"

Archie didn't have an answer. Duer told him not to lose April.

"The cab driver dropped April Mason off at Les Gouts," Le Pluete said, after hanging up the phone.

"I'm going after her," Kevin said as he picked up his coat and walked out of Le Pluete's office. Marcel smiled. "I hope this is nothing personal," said as he called after Kevin. Kevin was already gone.

April approached the third bed on the right in the crowded ward. The old man was asleep. She didn't want to wake him so she sat down on a stool beside his bed. The man in the bed next to Jacques' looked at her, then in a loud voice, he said, "Hey, Le Borsin, wake up. You have a visitor."

Jacques stirred then rolled over and saw April. "Am I dreaming?" he said quietly, "or are you the angel of death?"

"I'm certainly not the angel of death," April said smiling at him. April introduced herself and told him about her conversation with Le Boot.

"Help me to sit up, please," he said struggling to sit up.

April held him under the arms and boosted him up into a sitting position and fluffed the pillows behind his back. He asked to see the map. When she showed it to him, he nodded. "Yes, I remember that area well. It was heavily used by the Resistence during the war. We used to send couriers from one place to another by way of the sewers," he explained. "We used the old sections because the Bosch were afraid of the rats. They were such fools."

April explained what she was doing. The old man, with very few teeth, smiled and nodded as she told her story about the book and the vault, and the graveyard. He laughed many times during her description of what went on in the graveyard.

Then she showed him a picture of the map that Ferdinand had carried to his death. He studied the map for a few moments, then laid back on his pillow. "We used to look for that vault all during the war. We had all read the book, or at least heard about it. We dreamed about finding it, and about what we would do with the money. But we did not have the map, of course, so we had no idea where to look. So you think this vault is in this section of the city. The Forum. You know I supervised all of the work around that area. I suppose Le Boot told you all that."

April nodded. "When was that?"

"Oh, we began in the late 1950's."

"Were the old sewers still there?"

"Yes, at least the portion around the Forum and the park. We actually went down for a look, to see if it would support what was planned for above. It was in relatively good shape. Oh, there were lots of rats, and the smell was still there, but they built the walls very strong a long time ago. They should last for a long time to come."

"How can I get down in there?"

Jacques studied her for a few moments. "I know you think there is a treasure down there, lady, but, believe me, you don't want to go down there for any amount of money. It is worse than you can possibly imagine. No. You should not go."

April pulled her stool up close to the bed and leaned down so their faces nearly touched. "Jacques. How do I get down into this area of the old sewers?" she said forcefully, staring him straight in the eyes. "I'm going, but I need your help."

A wide grin infected his face, "All right, I'll tell you, but on one condition."

CHAPTER THIRTY-TWO

April winced when the needle was inserted into her arm. The nurse smirked. "This vaccination is to prevent Leptospirosis or rat bite. It will be sore for a few days, but, you'll live," she said, pulling the needle out and putting an adhesive bandage over the area.

April thanked her, got her things and walked down the corridor to the lobby.

After talking with Le Boot, Kevin raced out the door on his way to the retirement home. He was a half a block away from it when he saw April. She was standing on the street in front of the home. She was looking around. Kevin ducked into a doorway and watched from there. April made a decision. She turned right on Rue Dominique and began walking at a fast pace. Kevin was about to call to her, but stopped when he saw a man poke his head out of a doorway, look at April, and begin following her. Kevin decided to follow the man who was following April.

Archie pulled a cell phone from his coat pocket and dialed a number while trying to keep pace with April.

Duer answered the phone on the first ring. "She's on the move again," Archie said almost running to keep pace with her. "She's heading East along Rue Saint Dominique."

"Stay with her."

Archie hung up.

When April got to the next corner, she stopped and looked both ways down the street. This caused both followers to scramble so as not to be seen.

April was looking for a taxi. There were none in sight. Traffic was light. She looked at her watch. It was nearly eleven. She wanted to give herself plenty of time to look for the opening down into the old sewer which Jacques had told her about. She was excited. If she could find the opening, and Jacques wasn't sure it was still there since he'd been in the retirement home for almost five years, she could find the vault. April shivered when she thought about the rats and cockroaches Jacques had warned her about. She hated bugs, let alone rats! Frustrated at not seeing a taxi, she crossed the street determined to find one.

Archie followed her across the street. Kevin sensed that April was looking for a taxi. When Kevin reached the corner, a cab pulled up alongside him. He got in and immediately showed the driver his Interpol identification card. "See that woman in the red coat just up ahead?"

"Oui."

"I want you to follow her, not too close, by starting and stopping," Kevin said, in his very fluent French, "and if she gets a taxi, we follow. Got it?"

"Oui. Is this woman a fugitive?"

"Yes. Everyone wants her," Kevin said with a hint of irony.

"What has she done?"

"Oh, many terrible things."

April rounded the next corner and saw a taxi stand. There were several cabs. She climbed into the first one, gave the driver instructions, and they were off. Kevin watched as Archie jumped into the next cab and began to follow April. Kevin told his driver to follow both cabs.

April got out on the Boulevard Haussman at a Au Printemps department store. Archie followed her, and Kevin was right behind. After an hour of watching Archie watch April shop for everything from a flashlight to perfume to boots, Kevin was even more confused, especially since Archie seemed to understand what April was doing.

Then April went into a dressing room to try on some slacks.

Archie ducked around a corner and called Duer and reported.

Kevin split his time between watching the dressing room and watching Archie. When Archie moved around the corner to make his call, Kevin had to move out of sight. This meant he also lost sight of the dressing room.

"Just as I suspected," Duer said. "She's getting ready to go down into the sewers. Good work, Archie. Stay with her."

While Archie was on the phone, neither man saw April come out of the dressing room, throw the slacks over a chair and walk down the aisle away from them and completely out of their sight.

After his call, Archie peered at the dressing room door. Kevin had his eyes on Archie. They waited. And waited.

April came out of the department store with her arms loaded with packages. She was starved! She saw a sidewalk café just down the street and headed for it.

Twenty minutes later, Archie was getting anxious. April had been in the dressing room for a long time. Women, he said to himself, they do take their time shopping.

Kevin, too, was getting anxious. Could they have missed her? he asked himself.

A few minutes later, Archie could stand it no longer. He went to a sales lady at the counter near the dressing room and asked her to check to see if his wife was still in the dressing room. He described April. The sales lady went into the dressing room. She came right back out. She told Archie there was no one in the dressing room.

"Are you certain?"

"Positive, monsieur."

Archie slammed his fist down. He quickly scanned the area.

Kevin turned away from him, but he knew April was gone.

Suzette sat in Le Pluete's office. They were talking about the mole that seemed to be in their operation. Suzette filled him in on her findings, "And I've been through the personnel files of everyone who's worked on this case. I haven't found a thing."

Le Pluete scratched his forehead. "I have also had a man working on this internally, and he, too, reports no discrepancies. This is very serious. Somehow Duer knows what we are doing. Now he doesn't even use his phone. We know that LeMieux has gone to a public phone three times since we began monitoring his calls. I believe someone is giving him information, and that that someone is in our organization." He sat back and shook his head.

"I'll keep my eyes and ears open Marcel," Suzette said, "but frankly, I don't know where to turn."

"I understand. Our only hope is that the mole will make a mistake."

"They always do," she said, "sooner or later."

"I hope it's not too late," he said.

Suzette looked at her watch. "Well, I'd better get back to work," she said. "I have the watch on the antique shop this afternoon."

"Yes, well, I hope you can find something there," he said getting up from his desk.

Suzette stood up and went to the door. "I'll keep my eyes wide open," Suzette promised.

Suzette left the office, and just as she shut the door, a beeper in her purse went off. She pulled the pager out, looked at the message, put it back in her purse and walked out.

Seconds later, Le Pluete came out of his office and asked the secretary what that strange noise was. She told him it was Suzette's pager. He nodded and went back into his office and picked up the phone.

April finished her lunch and one last sip of her coffee. Her mind was filled with all the details of her venture down into the old sewer. She had all of the equipment, backpack, lantern, hatchet, camping shovel, waders, heavy boots, hat and clothes. She had everything that Jacques had told her to get.

She tried to visualize herself in the sewer, but all she saw were rats and cockroaches. Cold chills ran down her spine. She knew she was able to do it, but she finally had to admit to herself she didn't want to go alone. She needed someone else. She again thought of Kevin O'Connor, but he wouldn't understand. Besides, she thought, he thinks I'm crazy. The only other person was Jean Pierre. Even though he'd tried to cheat her out of the map, she had the advantage, she had the map! She thought of hiring someone, but who? Finally, she decided to call Jean Pierre.

Suzette pulled up a block away from the antique shop. She walked up to a car parked a few feet in front of hers. She knocked on the car window. It rolled down. The man inside recognized her. "Ah, Suzette. Are you my relief?"

"Yes. Cassell and I traded. He was bored here."

"Well, so am I, and so will you be. I've been here three times. The owner hasn't even come out of the store once."

"Good," Suzette said, "I need my rest."

"All yours," the man said as he started his car. "Adieu"

He drove off. Suzette smiled.

Jean Pierre had a room full of people in his office. He was explaining a recent trade agreement. His phone rang, and he picked it up quickly. "I told you I was not to be disturbed," he said sharply to his secretary.

"I wouldn't have bothered you, Monsieur Demain, but the young lady said it was urgent," she replied.

"What young lady?"

"She said her name was April Mason, an American I believe."

Jean Pierre's face flushed. He quickly glanced around the room his mind racing. "Tell her I'll be just a moment. Ask her to hold," he said hanging up the phone.

He turned to the assembled people. "I'm very sorry, but something urgent has come up. Why don't you all get some refreshment. We'll meet back here in ten minutes."

Jean Pierre waited impatiently as the group broke up and wandered out of his office. When the last one was out and had closed the door, he picked up the phone. "Put Miss Mason on, please."

"Hello? Jean Pierre?"

"April, my love, where have you been?" His heart was racing.

"It's a long story, Jean Pierre," she said. "But the good news is, I know where the treasure is."

"You do?" he said incredulously.

"But it's not easy to get to, and I need your help."

"Yes, of course," he said anxiously. "What can I do?"

"Go down into the sewers with me."

Jean Pierre felt a lump in his throat. It was one thing to dig up a grave, but go down into a sewer? His lip curled at the thought. "I don't think I can," he said honestly.

"I do. I talked with a man who explained it all to me, at least the part about getting down into the sewer. Jean Pierre, I can't do it alone."

Jean Pierre took a deep breath. Visions of gold floated in his mind. "Have you asked anyone else?"

"No, but if you can't, I suppose I'll try to talk Kevin into helping."

That did it! Kevin O'Connor! Never, he thought. "All right," he said reluctantly, "I'll help. What do I have to do?"

April explained everything to him, told him what equipment he'd need, and that he had to get a shot for the virus that some of the rats have. He winced at that thought. He was crazy, he knew, but the thought of all that money drove him. She suggested they meet at her apartment at six o'clock that evening.

"No!" Jean Pierre said abruptly. "They will have it watched."

"Who? The men at the grave?" she asked.

"So you were there."

"Yes. How do you think I got the map?"

"You have the map. Of course," Jean Pierre rubbed his face. "You know they suspected it was you."

"Oh? And who told them about me?"

Jean Pierre was caught and he knew it.

"All right. It was I, but...."

April interrupted. "All is forgiven, if you come down into the sewers with me."

"I said I would. Now, do not go back to your apartment. Take a hotel room and call me at home when you've checked in."

April agreed.

When he hung up, Jean Pierre told his secretary that urgent business would take him away for the rest of the day and to cancel the meeting and reset it for the next day. Then he left to get what he needed.

Archie, followed by Kevin, searched the department store for an hour to no avail. Finally, Archie made the phone call.

Snooky was sitting at her desk when Suzette walked into the antique store. As Suzette approached, Snooky got up and ran to her, "Suzette, it's so good to see you again," Snooky said, hugging her.

"It's been at least two years," Suzette said. "How are things?"

Snooky stepped back, "Well. I do a little of this, a little of that. The false passports and papers are a good business."

Suzette walked around the store. "You have a very good selection of goods."

"Thank you. Believe it or not, I even make money here, too."

"It's a great cover."

"Yes. Duer is a very good sponsor."

"Speaking of the man, I believe you have a delivery for him."

"Yes. It's all ready. Is LeMieux coming?"

"No. Actually I'm here to pick it up. Interpol is watching this place, and we decided this was the best way to move the goods."

"Oh, are you 'watching the store'?"

"Who else?"

"Let's go get it," Snooky said as she pressed a button under her desk. The bookcases opened revealing the staircase to her laboratory.

"How Victorian of you," Suzette quipped.

"The old 'hidden bookcase' trick. I saw it in the movies and had it made. It works like a charm."

They both laughed as they headed down the stairs.

Jean Pierre got off the elevator and walked out the revolving doors of his office building. He was followed by two Interpol operatives.

Paul watched as Duer paced frantically. "She's going down into the sewers, and we don't have the slightest clue as to where," Duer ranted. "Archie let us down at the worst possible time." He was furious!

"Did Archie say if she left any kind of clues as to where she would enter the sewers?"

"None," Duer snapped.

"She does have to change into her new clothes. Perhaps she'll go back to her apartment."

"She'd be a fool to go there, and the one thing I've learned about Miss Mason is that she is no fool."

"Where else would she go?" Paul asked.

"Straight to the treasure," Duer said in an annoyed bark.

LeMieux watched Duer, almost in a state of panic, pace around the old man's apartment. He rubbed his chin and thought about the sewers. He knew a little about them, and he, for one, wouldn't want to go down there alone. Perhaps April felt the same way. "Do you think she'd dare go into the sewers alone? They are very dangerous and filled with rats and vermin," Paul said.

Duer stopped pacing. "You have a good point, Paul. Who would she turn to?"

Paul thought about this question. Where would she go? Who would she turn to? "Would she go to the police?"

"No, I don't think so. She could have turned the map into the police. No, she's on a personal quest. She's out to prove to herself she can find the treasure. But I believe you are right about one thing. I don't think she'll go down there alone. The question is, who can she confide in?"

"I believe she'll at least try to talk Jean Pierre into going."

"For once we agree completely."

"On the other hand, I cannot see Jean Pierre going down into the sewers," Paul said candidly. "At heart he's a coward."

"You would be surprised what men will do for money," Duer said with a large grin on his face. "Let's find out if Monsieur Demain has talked with her," Duer said. He sat down at his desk and picked up the phone.

When he had finished talking with Jean Pierre's secretary, Duer said, "He talked to her this afternoon. And, whatever she said made him cancel all appointments for the rest of the day. I think it's time to go and see Jean Pierre."

"I think I should go," LeMieux said.

"Yes, I can understand you're wanting to go, but I think we should all go. She is not getting out of the sewers alive. Are the cars packed with the equipment we'll need?"

"Yes," Paul said, "everything is in order."

Just then the telephone rang. Duer answered, "Yes?"

Suzette handed the phone to Snooky. Snooky smiled at her and said, "It was wonderful of you to send my friend over."

"Just a bit of whimsey, my dear."

"Well, we're all loaded up, where shall we deliver?"

"Stay where you are until I call," Duer said and hung up the phone. He got up and headed for the door. As he passed by Paul he said, "And a little woman shall lead them,"

Kevin finished explaining how he lost track of April. Le Pluete patted him on the shoulder, "We all have our bad days, Kevin."

"She is going down into the sewers. I know it. But where? When?" Kevin said as he began to pace nervously.

Duer and LeMieux joined Duvall in the garage. Duer laid out the plan, "Since Interpol has doubled its watch, we will have to execute our escape plan. Do each of you remember your assignments? Duvall and LeMieux nodded. "Good. Prepare to leave immediately. LeMieux, put my things in your car. Duvall, put everything we'll need to go into the sewers in the Rolls. It's time to visit our friend Jean Pierre."

CHAPTER THIRTY-THREE

"I can't stand this! I've got to do something," Kevin said. He was pacing around Le Pluete's office like a cat in a cage.

Le Pluete just shook his head. "But what? There is no starting point, except of course her apartment, and neither you nor I believe she will go there."

"Starting point," Kevin said slowly. Then he snapped his fingers, "The museum, Les Gouts. She got her answer there, and I'm going back to find out what it was." He picked up his raincoat and left Le Pluete standing in his office shaking his head.

April tipped the bellman and closed the door to her hotel room. She began unwrapping the items she bought to go down into the sewer. She was very excited. Visions of gold and jewelry floated by in front of her eyes as she carefully laid out each of the things on the bed. When she finished, she took the phone number Jean Pierre had given her out of her purse and went to the phone. It had been about two hours since they talked. She hoped he was back from getting his things. The phone rang but there was no answer and no answering machine. Damn, she said to herself.

Duvall looked both ways as he drove out of the underground garage. On his left, he saw one of the Interpol cars. He pulled out onto the street and watched in his rear view mirror. Sure enough, the car was following him.

At the same time, Paul LeMieux pulled out of the garage two doors down the street. He watched as the other Interpol car began following him. It was now clear for Duer to escape without being followed.

Minutes later, Duer stopped at the entrance of the garage. He, too, looked both ways. Neither Interpol car was in sight. He grinned and gunned the engine of the car and pulled out into traffic.

The chase was on.

Kevin was in the retirement home talking to Jacques when his cell phone rang. "They're on the move," Le Pluete said. "They're using two cars."

"Watch out for a decoy," Kevin said.

"We know, but we only had two cars at the site. Another one is en route to the Duer apartment."

"I'm talking with someone who can help us find April, and unless I miss my guess, we'll find Duer's people near her."

"Let us know as soon as possible."

"I will," Kevin said as he hung up and put the phone in his pocket. "Now, Jacques, as I was saying, I talked with Le Boot. He told me to tell you that if you care for the young woman who came to see you today, you'll tell me everything you both talked about."

Jacques was tired and wary of the nice looking young man sitting on the stool beside his bed. He thought about it for a minute. Then said, "What's in it for me?"

Kevin bent down beside him and looked Jacques straight in the eye. "That woman is in grave danger. She is in deeper than she knows, and the people who are following her won't hesitate to kill her."

Jacques raised an eyebrow and cocked his head. "Kill her?"

"Yes. I've got to find her before they do. Now what did you tell her?"

LeMieux parked his car and went into the crowded department store. He walked as fast as he could, glancing behind him to see if he was being followed. He went immediately to the elevator and pressed the button for the basement. Once there, he walked to the shipping department and asked for Louis. A burly man in a leather apron came up behind him. "Are you ready?" he asked.

Paul nodded, and the man directed him to the back of a delivery truck. Paul got in and the man closed the doors. He got into the driver's seat and drove out the delivery truck entrance.

They passed right by the two Interpol men who were carefully watching the department store. Paul saw them out of the tiny window in the back doors of the truck. He was safe!

Duvall drove to the outdoor café and parked. He scanned the waiters and saw who he was looking for. A short, bald man with horned-rimmed glasses and a large, bushy moustache. He saw the Interpol car pull up and park in a "No Parking" zone. He got out of his car and walked inside the café. He waited for the waiter to see him, nodded to him and went into the men's room. The waiter followed. Once the waiter got there, he went to a stall and pulled out a large package with a waiter's coat.

Duvall quickly put it on, and the two left the men's room and walked back to the kitchen. Once there, the waiter led him past the cooks to a back door. Duvall took off the waiter's coat remembering to get the car keys out of the pocket and walked out into the alley where a car was parked. He got in and drove off down the alley and into a street far away from where the Interpol men were waiting.

Paul got out of the back of the truck a block from Jean
Pierre's apartment. There was a taxi waiting for him.

April called again and this time Jean Pierre answered. He
had what he needed and was just about ready. She told him to
meet her at the statue of the round head and hand by Henri de
Miller in the courtyard of the Church of St-Eustache as soon as
possible. Jean Pierre hung up the phone and put a black
leather jacket over his turtleneck sweater, picked up his
camping shovel and large flashlight. He was ready.

Duer was frustrated. He was hung up in traffic. He was
still blocks from Jean Pierre's apartment. He picked up his cell
phone on the first ring. LeMieux was at the apartment. He
told Duer he was going in to see Jean Pierre. Then, suddenly,
Paul stopped talking.

"Paul. Paul," Duer yelled into the phone.

"Jean Pierre is coming out of his apartment right now," he
said in a whisper. "He's dressed as if he's going into the sewer.
He's going to meet her," LeMieux said. "I'm going to follow
him." LeMieux hung up and got into the taxi.

"But where shall I meet you?" Duer yelled into his phone,
but there was no answer.

Jean Pierre got into his car and drove off with Paul was
right behind him.

Jean Pierre parked his car on the Rue Berger, took the tote
bag with all his stuff out of the trunk and began walking
toward the park.

Paul got out of the cab and followed him. There were a lot
of people on the street. Paul was afraid of losing him. He
decided to make his move.

When Jean Pierre stopped to get his bearings, Paul LeMieux
stepped up beside him and put his gun in Jean Pierre's ribs.
"Good afternoon, Jean Pierre," LeMieux said.

Jean Pierre turned with a look of both fear and astonishment, "Paul."

"Yes. And what you feel in your ribs is a gun. I'm very sorry you chose to get involved with this affair, Jean Pierre. I warned you."

"I know."

LeMieux interrupted, "Ah, but you do, Jean Pierre? Do you know what this is all about? The question is whether or not you're smart enough to do as I say."

"What do you want?"

"April Mason and the map to the baker's vault of course."

"Why do you think I know anything about where she is?"

"Because you are dressed to go down into the sewers. That is not your business suit you know."

Jean Pierre bowed his head. He knew the game was up.

"Now I don't want to shoot you, and I don't want my friends to either. But, unless you cooperate, I will be forced to do so to save my skin. You understand don't you?"

Beads of sweat covered Jean Pierre's forehead. His hands twitched and his knees felt weak. He just stared at LeMieux.

"What's the matter, Jean Pierre? I've never thought of you as one with nothing to say."

Jean Pierre looked into Paul's eyes. He was having trouble breathing and his heart was pounding. Panic was about to overcome him, and he wanted to scream. "I don't want to die," he finally said haltingly.

"You won't," Paul said trying to sound reassuring. But, in his heart Paul knew it would take every ounce of ingenuity he had to save Jean Pierre. Yet, he knew he would try. "Duer is only interested in getting the treasure. Once he has it, I believe both you and Miss Mason will be safe. But, if you both don't cooperate, he will kill you."

Resigned, he asked, "What do you want me to do?"

"Simple, take us to the vault in the sewer."

"But I don't know where it is."

"Ah, but Miss Mason does. You know it and so do we.
Let's go sit down in the park and talk."

Paul took Jean Pierre by the arm and led him to a park
bench near the Forum. They sat down.

"Here is what we want you to do. First of all, we don't
want to alarm Miss Mason. She might run. If that happened,
you'd die immediately. Then she'd die also."

Jean Pierre was numb. He heard Paul's words, but he was
too frightened to even acknowledge them. His eyes had tears
in them.

"Where are you to meet Miss Mason?" Paul asked.

Jean Pierre didn't want to tell Paul, but he also didn't want
to die. He hesitated. Then he felt the gun being jammed hard
into his ribs. He looked away and said, "By the sculpture of
the head by Henri de Miller, in the courtyard of the Church of
St-Eustache."

"When?"

"As soon as possible," he mumbled.

"Good, Jean Pierre. Good. Will she be alone?"

"I don't know."

"I believe you do."

"Yes. Alone."

"All right. Now just sit here like a good fellow while I
make a couple of phone calls." Paul LeMieux pulled his cell
phone from his coat pocket and punched a stored number.

Duer answered immediately. Paul told him where Jean
Pierre was to meet April and asked what he should do. Paul
listened carefully and looked at his watch. He nodded several
times. Jean Pierre watched Paul. He seemed so calm, so in
control, Jean Pierre thought. His brother-in-law, his friend, had
turned into a cold-blooded killer. Jean Pierre felt very sad.

"In fifteen minutes. Yes. We'll wait here for you." Paul
hung up.

Duer immediately dialed Snooky. "Both of you must meet me at the Bourse Du Commerce on the East side near the garden as quickly as you can get here."

"What do we do with the merchandise?"

"Put it in the boot of your car. I will pay you when we meet."

Snooky hung up.

Duer dialed another number. Duvall got his instructions where to meet.

April paced around the huge, round stone head and hand which Henri de Miller had sculpted. She looked at her watch. What was taking Jean Pierre so long she wondered? She felt a bit silly dressed in her boots and heavy coat. People were staring as they walked by her.

Neither Paul nor Jean Pierre heard Duer come up behind them. "Nice weather," Duer said.

Startled, both men turned at looked up at Duer. "I suppose you've told Monsieur Demain what we expect of him," Duer said calmly.

"I didn't give him the details. I waited for you."

"I see. Very well. I believe it is best that Miss Mason not know we are here until she reaches the sewer. Therefore, Jean Pierre, we want you to meet her. We'll be following closely, of course, and let her take you to the entrance to the sewer. When you get down inside, we will follow at a discreet distance. We wouldn't want her to know we're behind her. It is important that she use all of her talents and information from the map to find the vault. We'd rather she not feel she is working under, shall we say, duress. Is that understood?" he asked Jean Pierre.

"And if she finds the vault?"

"Oh, I believe she will, although there is a small possibility she won't. In which case, you and she will be allowed to continue on without interference from us. We shall remain in the background."

"But, if she finds it, we shall simply divide the treasure among all of us, including you, of course, and all go on our merry way richer for the experience," Duer said with a faint smile creeping across his stern face.

"You won't hurt her?"

"No. Why would we do that? After all, it isn't as if this treasure belongs to anyone. As the American's say, 'it's finder's keepers'. The only way either of you might get hurt is if you fail to keep our presence secret. I fear that if she knows we are nearby, she might cause a great deal of trouble. And, trouble, Jean Pierre, causes pain. A great deal of pain. Do I make myself clear?" Duer said with a sly smile.

Jean Pierre nodded. "Very clear."

"Good," Duer said, putting his hand on Jean Pierre's shoulder, "Let's do this right, shall we? Make no mention of us. No looking back over your shoulder. No mistakes," he said as he gripped Jean Pierre's shoulder in a vise like hold.

Jean Pierre felt as if his whole shoulder and arm were about to come off in Duer's hand. He winced with pain. Duer didn't let up for nearly a minute. When he did, he nodded to Duvall who came over and stood in front of Jean Pierre, opened his coat and brandished a Colt .45. Jean Pierre, now completely drained of energy, simply nodded at the gun and stood up. Paul also got up.

"Very good job, Paul," Duer said patting LeMieux's back.

"Now where is it you two are to meet?"

"At the sculpture of Henri de Miller."

"So? What are you waiting for? Good hunting," Duer said stepping out of Jean Pierre's way.

Jean Pierre wanted to look back, but he didn't dare. He trudged toward the cathedral. He had no doubt that his every move was being watched.

April broke out into a wide grin when she saw Jean Pierre coming toward her. Her heart was racing with eagerness. She couldn't wait to get into the sewer and find the treasure. "Over here, Jean Pierre," she called and ran toward him.

He looked up and saw her. Now was his last chance to warn her, but if he did he would write not only hers but his own death warrant. If she only knew, he thought, she'd run, and that would be the last time she ever ran.

April ran up to him and hugged him. She was excited, and happy to see him. She thought he looked tired. "Are you all right?" she asked.

He wasn't, but he vowed to himself to do as he was told. "I'm fine," he said holding her just a little too hard.

"Ooh," she said as his grip was squeezing the breath out of her.

"Sorry," he said, relaxing his grip on her.

"Did you bring everything?"

"I think so," he said pointing to his tote bag. "But I don't understand why I had to get paint masks."

"You will," she said pulling on his arm. "Let's go. I know just where it is. I scouted it out on my way over here." She began leading him into the park.

Duer and LeMieux followed Jean Pierre and stopped behind some bushes when he walked out into the open courtyard and headed toward the sculpture. They saw April greet Jean Pierre. Duer was all smiles. Just then, he felt a tap on his shoulder. He looked up to see Duvall. He had brought Suzette and Snooky with him. Now they were all together. He shook Snooky's hand and hugged Suzette. "My little mole," he said with a grin.

Suzette returned the hug. "It's been a long time."

"Yes, since the Loire Valley job. You're looking marvelous as usual."

"Why thank you, sir. And thank you for the monetary aid."

"One good turn deserves another," he said. They both laughed.

"Speaking of monetary aid," Snooky broke in.

"Ah, yes. I have it in my car. We'll get it just as soon as we do a little other business."

"You found the vault," Suzette said.

"April Mason found the vault," Duer said. "At least I think she has. I have a treat for both of you. A trip down into the sewers."

Both women frowned. "What?" they said in unison.

"It's just a necessary side trip. Come. This should be fun," he said looking at LeMieux as he was motioning for them to follow. "I'll explain as we go."

April and Jean Pierre arrived at a large area of tall bushes in the middle of the huge garden area. "It's in here," she said as she walked right into the bushes.

Jean Pierre shrugged and followed her. The bushes surrounded a modern iron sewer main. It was padlocked.

"This is it," April said as she knelt down beside the iron lid.

"How did you find it?"

"A foreman who worked on the renewal of this area in the 1950's, told me."

"I, I don't understand."

"Well, this area was part of a renovation project. He worked for the sanitation department and was an expert on the old sewer system. When they began digging this area up to make the garden, they didn't want to have to tear up the old sewer because it would have been both costly and time consuming, so they asked him to go down and see if the old sewer was in good enough shape so they could leave it alone. He went down and saw that it was still intact and told them they did not have to dig it up. They were happy to save the time and money. He built this entrance to the sewer just in case anyone needed to go down there. It is also a way of draining off the methane gas that sometimes builds up in these old sewers. Although he said when he went down he didn't have any indication of any methane gas, it serves as a combination emergency entrance and relief valve.

"But how did you?"

"The map." April said opening her purse and pulling out the copy of Ferdinand's map. "I took it to London to a friend of mine, and he opened it and made this picture of it. Then I got this map of Paris in 1790," she said spreading out the map on the sewer lid. "I overlaid Ferdinand's map like this," she put the transparency of Ferdinand's map over the 1790 map. She had drawn a circle on the 1790's map to indicate where Ferdinand's map matched. "Now I simply lay this modern day transparent map over the 1790's map and voila! This is the area where the old bakery must have stood," she said proudly.

Jean Pierre examined the maps. The area of Ferdinand's map was squarely over the Forum. "You're amazing," Jean Pierre said truly in awe of her.

"Thank you. Now all we have to do is go down inside and find the vault."

"But the sewer lid is locked."

"So it is," April said with a wry smile. She reached into her coat and pulled out a small leather case. "You know that when you write mystery novels, you have to learn a lot of crazy stuff. One of them is how to pick a lock." She opened the case and took out several small wire-like devices and began picking the lock. It opened in less than a minute. "Hey, before we pull this thing up, look around to see if anyone is watching us."

Jean Pierre nodded and peeked out through the branches of the tall bushes. He saw Duer leaning on a tree not far away. Duer tipped his hat.

Jean Pierre came back to where April was tugging at the sewer lid. "Anyone?"

"Not a soul," Jean Pierre lied.

April had a can of oil and oiled the hinges that held one end of the lid in place. She saw Jean Pierre looking at her. "Jacques told me a lot of things - like bring oil." She laughed and he did too.

"Help me with this thing," April said, grunting as she tried to pull the heavy iron cover up. Jean Pierre reached down and pulled on it. Slowly, creaking with every inch it gave, the lid came up. Finally, with one last tug the sewer lid fell open revealing the entrance to the sewers.

Both were greeted by a stench that was overpowering. It was like nothing either of them had ever smelled. "Ugh!" April said, drawing back and wrinkling her face.

"Ah, this is too much," Jean Pierre said and started to stand up.

"No. Wait!" April said. "Did you bring the paint masks?"

Jean Pierre reached into his coat pocket and pulled out several white cloth paint masks with elastic bands to hold them in place.

"Great," April said. "Another trick Jacques taught me. She reached in her purse and pulled out a bottle of cologne. "Just pour a little on the mask and that's all you smell. No sewer odor," she said as she put the cologne on both masks and put hers on. Jean Pierre did the same.

April studied Ferdinand's map and looked around to get her bearings. "The ladder faces south. This is the tricky part. Which way we should turn when we get to the bottom. I think it's to the right."

"After you," Jean Pierre said in a mock bow.

"Okay, but stay right behind me," April said as she put her foot on the first rung of the steel ladder that led down to the floor of the sewer. She turned on her flashlight and shined it down into the hole. It looked dry. She slowly began climbing down the ladder.

CHAPTER THIRTY-FOUR

After her head was below the level of the ground, Jean Pierre went back through the bushes and waved to Duer. He motioned in the direction April had told him they would go. Then he returned and climbed down the ladder.

April was waiting for him at the bottom. She shined her light around. She saw a few rats skittering about and a lot of cobwebs. The stone walls were seeping a little water, but the floor of the sewer was only damp. The walls were only about six feet high with an arched ceiling. She was surprised to see that there wasn't a trench down one side as she'd seen in books. About three feet from the bottom was a black water line where the water probably ran most of the time. She faced the ladder and pointed to her right. "Let's try this way," she said, shining her light ahead of her. Jean Pierre shined his light ahead of them weaving the light up and down the walls. They began to walk slowly, deliberately. "According to the story and the map, Ferdinand scratched two crosses on the wall near the vault at a bend in the tunnel. It's been a long time, and they're probably gone, but it's worth a try. Let's see if we can find them. You take the left side and I'll take the right." They trained their lights on the walls and slowly moved ahead.

Duer looked at his watch. It had been ten minutes since Jean Pierre had given him the signal. He motioned for his cohorts to follow him. When they were all gathered near the sewer lid, he pointed to the entrance. "The door to riches," he said.

"I hope you don't want me to go down there," Suzette said.

"No," Duer said with a chuckle. "I don't think you'd fare well down there in high heels. I want you and Snooky to be our lookouts. Stay near the bushes and keep a sharp eye out. If you see anyone who might be curious, try your best to dissuade them. If you cannot, one of you will have to climb down and signal us with this whistle." He gave a police whistle to Suzette. "But try not to resort to that unless it is an emergency. We don't want Jean Pierre and Miss Mason to know we're near until they find the vault."

Suzette took the whistle. She and Snooky climbed back out of the bushes and began their watch.

"Duvall, I want you to take the lead. Use only your pen light if possible. I don't want her to know she's being followed. And do not, I repeat, do not talk or even whisper. The sound may carry much further than we think."

Duvall nodded and began climbing down the ladder followed by LeMieux then Duer.

Kevin and Le Pluete were both pacing in Marcel's office. Kevin had lost track of April, and now, no word from any of the people on stakeout. Suzette didn't answer the three calls Marcel had put in for her, and she was supposed to be watching the antique shop. "She's reliable," Kevin said after no answer the third time.

Le Pluete looked at Kevin over the top of his eyes. "Do you really think so?"

"Sure. Why?"

"Because I am not so sure. In fact, I have a hunch she is our mole."

"Suzette? Are you crazy, Marcel? She's been with us for years. She's saved my life."

"Really? I thought she shot you."

"No it was Steven Harret."

"Ah, you are sure?"

"Sure. She pushed me out of the way. Remember?"

"Yes. But what you do not know, is that we ran a ballistics test on that bullet. It was Suzette's gun that shot you."

Kevin frowned. He turned and faced Marcel. "Why didn't you say anything to me?"

"We had suspected her for some time, but we could not get enough evidence to hold her. This last assignment in Marseilles confirmed it for us. All we had to do was set a trap for her. It worked. She was the one who warned Duer about the stakeout, and the phones. We had her followed, and her phone calls to Duer match the time and the public phone numbers of the calls she made to him. Our people watched her make the calls and noted everything very specifically. She took over the stakeout of the antique shop without our knowledge, but the man on duty reported her 'relieving him'." And finally, our man reported that she entered the shop and hugged the owner, whom you confirmed as Michelle "Snooky" Jardin. They acted as if they were long lost friends. I'd say we have a very good case now, because, as you know, "Snooky" is a forger and counterfeiter. They were seen loading bundles of paper in her car. Unfortunately, our people lost their car in the crowded traffic."

"I thought she was too slick."

"And, right you were, Kevin. But, not slick enough."

Just then the phone on Le Pluete's office rang. He picked it up and listened. As the caller talked, Marcel's face began to light up. A grin crept slowly across his face, and he made a note on the pad on his desk and showed it to Kevin as he listened. The note said, "Found them!"

There were wet spots on the sewer floor, and those wet areas seemed to breed rats. Several times April and Jean Pierre shuddered as rats raced over their boots. April brushed away the cobwebs as best she could, but they still got on her clothes and her black watch cap.

They walked side by side which made it cozy since the sewer was only about five feet wide most of the time.

They came to a fork in the tunnel. "Which way?" Jean Pierre asked.

"You got me," April said. She shined her light on Ferdinand's map and studied it. Suddenly she gave out with a scream. "What's on me? What's on me?" she yelled as she danced around.

Jean Pierre shined his light on her and saw a large, long centipede crawling on the back of her neck. He flicked it away.

"It was only a bug," he said. She shuddered and so did he.

All three men heard April scream. They stopped. Duvall turned off his light. Several yards ahead of them they could see a dim flickering light. They slowed down their pace.

April and Jean Pierre stood at the fork in the tunnel and shined their flashlights down each. There were two different kinds of tunnels. The one with the flat floor that they had been walking on, and a larger tunnel with an eight inch wide drain running down the middle of the floor. The intersection was flooded with about six inches of water.

April tried to think back to the story in the book. Which kind of tunnel was Ferdinand in? She shook her head. She couldn't remember. She shined her light first down one tunnel then the other.

The one they'd been walking in kept going in a straight line, but the other curved several feet ahead of them. Then she remembered that Ferdinand had said that he hid at a bend so as not to be seen. "We'll go that way," she said, shining the light in the direction of the curved tunnel.

The further they went, the slimier the floor seemed to get. Water was seeping out of the walls more frequently. The footing was more difficult.

April slipped and had to catch herself by trying to hold on to the slippery walls. There were a lot more bugs crawling on the walls now, and she began to feel itchy all over. As they were about to round the bend, April slipped again and fell on her knees. Jean Pierre helped her up and held her for a moment.

"You know that this is really silly. We have no idea where this vault is, it could be miles away. We don't even know if we're in the right sewer line."

"I know I'm right, Jean Pierre," April said, brushing her self off. "Something tells me we're going to find it."

"Ah, yes. Your intuition again."

"It worked before," she said defensively.

"All right. I was just trying to be practical."

She shined her light in his face. "I know I'm right."

Jean Pierre threw up his hands. "Okay, I'm willing to go on if you are."

"Let's go," she said and slipped again and Jean Pierre caught her. He held her up until she could get her footing in the slimy mud.

"I love the feel of you in my arms," he said.

"I love the feel of your arms holding me up, but I still want to go on."

"Well, at least do me a favor. Let's change sides. You can walk on my left and I can hold you up better."

"Deal," April said as she was slipping once again. Jean Pierre held on to her, put his flashlight under his arm, and using both hands helped her stand up and get her footing. April tested her feet and the ground under them seemed more solid. "Okay. I'm fine now," she said. Jean Pierre kept on holding her and not letting go.

April turned her flashlight on Jean Pierre. "Let go, I'm fine."

Jean Pierre kept holding on. His eyes were wide as saucers. "Tell me again how this Ferdinand marked the vault," he said haltingly.

"With two crosses," April said quietly.

"Turn your head to the left and look on the wall"

April slowly turned her head and saw that the beam from Jean Pierre's flashlight was fixed on two crosses etched in the stones. They were black and faint, but they were definitely two crosses.

CHAPTER THIRTY-FIVE

April stared at the two crosses for a long time. Slowly Jean Pierre let go of her and stepped back. "I can't believe it," he said slowly. "It's unreal." "I know. I just hope Ferdinand made them." "Ah, so do I," he said a smile growing on his face.

Duvall stopped the other two men when they came to the fork in the tunnel. He turned off his light and looked down each of the tunnels. The second direction he looked, he could see Jean Pierre's and April's flashlights shining on the wall.

Suddenly April let out a whoop! "We did it! We did it!" she cried out. She flew into Jean Pierre's arms. "I know it's here!"

Duer, LeMieux and Duvall heard her clear as a bell! They stifled their laughter. "Shall we take them?" Duvall whispered to Duer as April was still shouting.

"No. Not yet. They haven't found the vault. And even if they have, they haven't opened it yet. Let them do the work," Duer whispered.

April and Jean Pierre began tapping on the wall just past the crosses with the handles of their camping shovels. They

318

were looking for a hollow sound. They moved slowly, carefully.

"Are you sure it's on this side?" Jean Pierre asked.

April stopped. She wasn't sure. She tried to remember what it said in the book, but she couldn't remember the specifics. "I want to play a game," she said.

Astonished, Jean Pierre stopped and gave her an incredulous look. "What? Now?"

"I want to act out what it said in the book as if I'm Ferdinand." She shined her light around the tunnel. Then she took her backpack off and reached in for the book. She opened it to the story and began reading. Jean Pierre leaned against the wall and waited.

"What are they doing?" Duer whispered to Duvall. "It's very quiet."

"Reading," Duvall said flatly.

Duer rolled his eyes and leaned back against the wall.

"Here it is," April said. "Look."

Jean Pierre looked over her shoulder.

"Read this to see if I'm right," April asked, holding the book closer to Jean Pierre's face.

"Where?"

April pointed to the passage.

Jean Pierre began to read - silently.

"No. Out loud."

"Ah, yes," he said playfully. "'Curious, Ferdinand went to the curve in the tunnel."

"This has to be it," April interrupted.

Jean Pierre nodded and continued, "'and looked down the long sewer opening.'"

Both of them flashed their lights toward the curve, then past it. The tunnel was long and straight. They nodded to each other. "'Not far away, a few meters or so, he saw a light coming from a hole in the sewer wall. It was shining on the opposite wall.'"

"Wait," April interrupted. "Go back to when he first sees the light."

Jean Pierre found it and read, "'He saw light coming from a hole in the sewer wall. It was shining on the opposite wall'."

"Right. That means that from here the glow was on that side of the tunnel," she said pointing across the tunnel to the opposite side.

"And the cellar was on this side."

"You got it," April said excitedly. "Now, how far is a dozen meters?"

"About fourteen yards."

"Okay," April said, crossing to the other side of the tunnel and moving toward where she thought the vault might be. She began pacing, "One, two, three, four, five."

She stopped. "Let's start looking here," she said as she pulled out her camping shovel from her backpack.

They tapped on the walls. Thud, thud, thud. No hollow sound. They tapped for nearly fifteen minutes with no results.

"Maybe we were wrong," April said. "Let's try the other side.

They crossed the tunnel and began tapping. Suddenly April stopped. "There's a loose stone here."

Jean Pierre shined his light where April was pointing. She tapped on the stone and it moved. She opened the blade of the shovel and began working it into the crevice. The stone moved. She pulled it out. The stone next to it fell out. Then she pulled out three more stones. She peered in with her flashlight. There was a stone wall on the other side of the tunnel wall. Frowning, she pulled out a few more stones and looked in again. This time she could see something different. She shined her light more and more to the left and saw a piece of board standing upright. It looked like the edge of a door. She pulled out more stones and now the outline of a doorway was evident. It was filled with dirt. She stepped back. "This has to be the baker's cellar," she said.

"Yes. It is a door," Jean Pierre said as he joined her with his flashlight and looked inside the hole in the wall. "I believe you're right."

"So?"

"So the vault is on the other side of the tunnel," they both said together.

"Right."

They crossed back to the other side of the tunnel. Once again they began tapping. Thud, thud, thunk!

April tried again. Thud, thud, thunk! She was getting very nervous. Her hands were shaking as she tapped some more. Thunk, thunk, thunk.

"You try," she insisted.

Jean Pierre, using the handle of his camping shovel tapped. Thud, thunk, thunk, thunk.! His hands were shaking now. "I think this is it," he said quietly. "You have the honor." He stepped back to allow April to work. Jean Pierre held the light on the wall.

April took a deep breath and shoved the blade of the shovel between two of the stones. One moved slightly as she wiggled the shovel. She tried another side of the stone. It loosened. She pushed the shovel deeper in the crack and pushed. The stone fell inward away from her. They heard it drop. She tried the next stone. It was easier and it, too, dropped inside.

As she made the hole bigger and bigger, she became more and more anxious. Her heart was racing, and her hands were shaking so much that when she touched the next stone it fell in. Startled, she stepped back for a moment to try and get her breath.

As she stood there, she noticed the beam from Jean Pierre's flashlight was bouncing around everywhere. She glanced at Jean Pierre. He was sweating profusely and nervously twitching. He looked silly, and April began to laugh. "What?" Jean Pierre said.

"Look at the light from your flashlight."

He did and slowly he began to chuckle. As he did, the beam seemed to settle down as he became more relaxed.

Steeling herself, April bent down and removed a stone. Suddenly she screamed and jumped back as five rats, screeching their heads off, came scampering out of the hole. One was ran up her arm! She tried to get it off, but it was as scared as she was and clung to her. Jean Pierre saw it, grabbed it, and threw it off her. April was still screaming. Jean Pierre held her. Finally, after a minute or so, she calmed down.

"Don't you think you'd better look inside?" he said.

Still shaking, April drew herself up again and pulled away from him. She picked up her flashlight off the floor and walked over to the hole. Her mind was racing, her body was quivering, and she was breathing hard. She held the flashlight with both hands to keep from shaking, bent down, and shined it inside the hole in the wall. Rats. A lot of them were milling around inside the vault. The light frightened them, and they scurried around looking for places to hide among the piles of dust-covered golden candlesticks, trinkets, and jewels on the floor of the vault. "Oh, Jean Pierre. It's there. The treasure's there."

Jean Pierre came up beside her and shined his light into the cavern. He let out a long, low whistle. "Mon dieu."

The vault was approximately ten feet deep and eight feet wide. It was only about five feet high. There were all sorts of riches from golden vases and candlesticks to jade vases and other objects of art and jewelry lying on the floor.

April stood there mesmerized. She was in a state of complete astonishment. She just stared at the vault. She couldn't talk. She was dumbfounded at the thought that she had solved this two hundred year-old mystery.

Jean Pierre also stood there. He was mentally counting his millions. When he had finished, he said, "I can be so happy with all of this."

Finally, April came out of her reverie. She turned and hugged Jean Pierre, "I did it! I did it," she said softly, as if by rote.

"Yes, April," Jean Pierre shouted, "you've found the vault!"

April nodded absent-mindedly. Then, as if waking from a dream, she walked over to the hole and began removing more stones.

Jean Pierre watched April for a moment, then the excitement hit him, and he began removing stones. "You're very quiet, my dear, for having made such an outstanding discovery," he said.

April was almost in a trance. She heard Jean Pierre talking, but she couldn't talk. She just kept staring inside the vault and working slowly, methodically removing the stones one by one. The lights from their flashlights cast eerie shadows inside.

As they began removing the stones from the bottom, the rats sensed a way out. They came at April and Jean Pierre en mass. They both jumped back. April was screaming now, but she couldn't hear herself. She was shaking violently. Jean Pierre held her and waited for the rats to leave.

Then, almost as suddenly as she had gone into her trance, April came out of it. She began laughing and crying at the same time. "It's here, Jean Pierre," she kept repeating.

"I know," he said gently trying to calm her down. Finally she pulled away from him, picked up her flashlight and started inside the vault. "It's just like in the book," she said. "Just as I imagined it."

Peeking around the bend, Duer watched and waited. He and LeMieux and Duvall had moved closer to the vault when they heard the sound of the stones being removed. All three had grins a mile wide.

"Apres vous," Jean Pierre said as he bowed and indicated that April should be the first to step inside the vault.

Once inside, April knelt down and picked up one of the golden vases and brushed the dirt from it. "It's real."

"Very," Jean Pierre said as he, too, climbed inside.

"It must all be worth a fortune."

"Several fortunes."

April shined her light on Jean Pierre's face. "Thank you for helping," she said quietly.

Jean Pierre picked up a jeweled necklace. "Nice diamonds," he said. "It would look wonderful around your neck."

April smiled.

"So, what do we do now?" Jean Pierre said.

"I think I can answer that," Duer said standing just outside the entrance to the vault. Duvall's light was shining on the gun in Duer's hand.

CHAPTER THIRTY-SIX

Kevin, Le Pluete, Inspector Antoine and several policemen approached the garden in the Forum. Suddenly, Kevin stopped, held out his arms and backed the group up around the corner of a building. "Suzette," he said quietly.

"Where?" Le Pluete asked.

Kevin guided Le Pluete to the corner and pointed at Suzette and Snooky standing near the bushes guarding the sewer entrance. They were laughing and having a good time as they scanned the park.

Le Pluete stepped back. "I believe that confirms my theory."

"Yep. I've got to hand it to you, Marcel. She definitely is our mole." Kevin said with a hint of sadness. "See the woman she is talking with?"

"Yes," Le Pluete said. "I believe I've seen her somewhere before."

"She's the woman I spoke within the antique store. Snooky Jardin."

At Marcel's beckon, Inspector Antoine came up and peered around the corner then turned back smiling. "Ah, yes, that is Michelle Jardin also known as 'Snooky'. I remember her," Inspector Antoine said. "I helped put her away five years ago for forgery."

"She was released from prison a year ago," Le Pluete said. "We have suspected that she may have had something to do with Duer, but couldn't prove it. However, when her name turned up on the phone list of Duer's callers, we decided to watch her. She helped uncover our mole."

"Shall I arrest her, Inspector Le Pluete?" Antoine asked.

Kevin stopped Antoine. "Don't go out there. You'll spook both of them." Kevin peered around the corner again. "From the way they're behaving, I'd say they are lookouts. And I'll bet Duer isn't far away."

"He's right," Antoine said.

"The question is, why are they there? Where is Duer?"

"Down in the sewer," one of the officer's said. "There is an entrance to the old sewers there. I followed Miss Mason. She was dressed to go down there with a backpack and everything."

"And Jean Pierre was dressed the same," said another.

"And Duer's man, LeMieux was also dressed to go down into the sewers."

"Do you suppose Miss Mason found the baker's vault?" Marcel asked Kevin.

"Oh, yeah, I think she did it," Kevin said with a hint of admiration. "And if I'm right, Duer's down there with her."

"Shall we take a look for ourselves?" Le Pluete asked.

"We can't let them warn him," Kevin said indicating Suzette and Snooky. "Let me handle this."

Seconds later Kevin, all alone, walked toward the two women. He raised his hand. "Suzette!" he called.

She spun around and saw Kevin approaching. What the hell was he doing here, she wondered. Suzette raised her hand and called to him. "Kevin. What a surprise." Then she whispered to Snooky, "I can handle him. Watch this."

"I just came over to get some peace and quiet," he said as he sidled up to the two women.

Snooky looked at Suzette anxiously. It was the man who came to her store. She started to move, but Suzette grabbed her arm. She didn't like this at all.

"Oh, Kevin, have you met my friend Michelle?" Suzette asked pulling Snooky toward Kevin.

"No, I don't think I've had the pleasure. Wait. Don't you run a small antique shop?"

Snooky nodded, not sure what to do.

"I went in there to find an antique to surprise you with," he said to Suzette. "Nice to see you again," Kevin held out his hand, and they shook hands. "Hey, Suzette, you never told me about her. She's a beauty."

Snooky demurred. Suzette laughed. "You never change," she said.

"So what are you two beautiful women doing in the park?"

"Like you, we just like to come here and talk. It's so peaceful."

"That it is," Kevin said moving so that the two women had their backs to the nearby building. "Hey, I've got an idea, why don't we all go get a cup of coffee? Or maybe a drink?"

"Oh, I don't think so, Kevin," Suzette said. "We just want to have a little 'girl talk'. Michelle is having man trouble, and...."

Suzette suddenly stopped talking. She felt the barrel of a gun pressing against the back of her head. Snooky felt the same sensation.

"I wouldn't move if I were you two," Kevin said looking over the women's shoulders at Le Pluete and Antoine and three policemen standing behind the women.

"What is going on?" Suzette asked. She looked around and saw the policemen.

"I could ask you the same question, Suzette," Kevin said, "but, frankly, I think I know the answer. Now, isn't that the opening to the sewer somewhere in those bushes behind you? And isn't your friend Duer down there? With April?"

Suzette turned ashen. Then she stared daggers at Kevin. Slowly she reached into her shoulder handbag, but she didn't get the whistle. Kevin grabbed her arm in a vicelike grip. "Looking for something?" he asked, wrenching the handbag from her shoulder and looking inside. "What's this? A police whistle? How appropriate."

Le Pluete instructed the three policemen to take the two women into custody. Kevin started into the bushes.

Duvall climbed into the vault and pushed April and Jean Pierre back into a corner. He motioned with his gun for them to sit.

"What is going on?" April demanded.

"Nothing important," Duer said with an ugly grin on his face. "We just want to thank you for finding all of this for us," he said, indicating the bounty on the floor.

"For you?"

"Yes. I must admire your ingenuity, Miss Mason. You have solved an age-old mystery all by yourself. Unfortunately, I'm afraid you won't be able to take advantage of it."

April finally saw Duer's face in the dim glow of the flashlights. It was the man she'd seen before. "The graveyard. Mr. Duer," she said quietly.

"Precisely, my dear," Duer said. "And it seems you got what we went there for. But, but the looks of things, we'll let bygones be bygones. After all, you did all the really hard work."

Jean Pierre started to get up.

"Sit down, Jean Pierre," Duer commanded.

April turned to Jean Pierre. "You're in this with him. I knew it. What an idiot I am."

"Au contraire, Miss Mason. It is Jean Pierre who is the idiot. He led us to you, and thus to the treasure as well."

"How could you?" April asked Jean Pierre.

"I didn't want to see you get hurt."

328

"He's got a gun trained on us and you don't think he'll use it?" she said, throwing her head back in disgust.

Jean Pierre looked up at Duer. "You promised no one would get hurt."

Duer smiled down at him. He shrugged. "Perhaps I misstated the situation. I meant I would not get hurt."

"What are you going to do with us?" Jean Pierre asked.

"I believe the saying is 'dead men tell no tales'."

"But you can't shoot me! What about my wife and children? Paul help me!"

April was shocked. "Your wife and children!" April screamed. "You're married? You son of a bitch!" April started pounding on Jean Pierre with both fists furiously. "How could you? You bastard!"

Duer, Duvall and LeMieux watched as April attacked with all her might. They laughed as Jean Pierre tried to protect himself from her blows.

"You son of a bitch!" April kept screaming until she broke out in tears and rolled over on the floor sobbing.

"I told you women would be the death of you, Jean Pierre," LeMieux said. "You never listen."

Jean Pierre looked up at Paul with tears in his eyes. "Please, Paul, I beg of you. Don't let them kill me. What would my sister say if she knew you were involved?"

"She won't know, Jean Pierre. No one will know."

"Please, Paul, help me!"

"Shut up," Duvall said as he slammed his pistol into Jean Pierre's face. Jean Pierre went down holding his head and curled up into a ball. He was softly sobbing.

April raised her head. She looked at Jean Pierre then at Duvall. "You son of a bitch!"

"Shut up or you'll get the same treatment," Duvall said.

"What's worse than killing me?" April said. Her leg shot out from beneath her and her foot slammed into Duvall's crotch. He let out a yell, dropped his gun, and bent over. The gun bounced off a vase and fell near April.

She dove for the gun, but Duer quickly kicked the gun away from April and picked it up. "You asked what would be worse? Pain, Miss Mason. Pain," Duer said quietly. "Now kindly move over to the corner."

Duvall straightened up and kicked Jean Pierre. "You, move!" he shouted. Duer handed Duvall his gun back.

Suddenly, Jean Pierre grabbed Duvall's legs and pulled, but Duvall was too strong. Duvall spun and shot Jean Pierre in the head. The sound of the gunshot was deafening. Jean Pierre slumped over in a heap.

April screamed. Duer grabbed Duvall's arm. "Enough."

Paul LeMieux knelt down beside Jean Pierre. He was suddenly very sad, very angry. He rolled Jean Pierre over. April was in shock. She fought to keep her composure, but everything inside her head was whirling.

Jean Pierre's head was covered with blood. Paul bowed his head, then in one swift, fluid movement, turned his gun on Duvall and fired.

Duvall was thrown back by the force of the bullet entering his chest, and he fell out of the vault and onto the sewer floor. He was very dead.

Duer was shocked, and quickly turned his gun on Paul and fired. Paul staggered back, then bounced against the wall and fell forward his arms extended toward Duer. Duer fired again which caused Paul to spin and fall at Duer's feet.

April was screaming. She was completely out of control as she rocked back and forth on the floor. "Why?" she screamed. "Why?"

Duer raised his gun to kill April, but that would be all he'd remember as the butt of Kevin's gun slammed down on Duer's head with all the force Kevin could muster. Duer fell forward and April had to skitter to get out of the way of the huge bulk as it hit the floor.

Kevin quickly grabbed Duer's gun. The vault was quickly flooded with light from the big flashlights held by the police and Le Pluete. April was blinded by the light and curled up in

330

a ball against the wall of the vault shaking violently and screaming. Kevin put his arms around her. "It's all right. You're safe now," he said over and over as he held her closely and rocked with her. April felt nothing. Her body and mind were numb.

CHAPTER THIRTY-SEVEN

Kevin, the stubble of a three-day beard showing prominently on his weary face, sat in a straight-backed chair beside April's bed in the hospital. He hadn't slept much because each time she screamed as she drifted in and out of nightmares, he was instantly awake and at her bedside holding her hand and whispering, "It's all right. You're safe."

He held her hand and comforted her until she calmed down and slept again. She was under the heavy sedation and never really woke up, but she wasn't in a coma either.

Kevin often wondered if she would ever be the same. He felt responsible. If he'd gotten there sooner, he chided himself, if he'd been closer to her, if he hadn't tried to...the list went on and on. His guilt was tremendous.

He was on the verge of falling asleep once again when April stirred. He sat up quickly and watched her intently. Her head slowly rolled back and forth on the pillow. Then, her eyes fluttered and opened. She looked at him. At first, she seemed not to recognize him, then April cracked a smile. "Kevin," she said weakly.

"I'm here. You're safe," he said reassuringly.

"Where am I?"

"In the hospital. You're safe," he repeated.

"I feel so, so out of it," she murmured.

"It's all right," he said as he patted her hand.

"I'm thirsty."

Kevin reached for the pitcher of water, poured some in a glass and put in the glass straw. He put it in front of her. She raised her head slightly, sipped and fell back on the pillow. She drifted back to sleep.

Kevin got up and walked to the door. He looked back at her, smiled, and went out to the nurses' station. He told the head nurse that April had wakened. She called the doctor. Kevin went back to April's room.

An hour later, April was sitting up in bed. The doctor had just left. He gave her a clean bill of physical health, although he confided to Kevin that she might need some psychological therapy.

"You look like hell," she said to Kevin.

"I feel great," he said with a warm smile.

"I must be a mess," she said.

"Well, I have to say you've looked better."

She nodded. "I hope so." She hesitated then said, "I want to know what happened."

"In Duer time. The doctor wants you to get some rest."

"You could use some yourself."

Kevin yawned. "Yeah, that might be good."

April talked him into going home and getting some rest. He promised he would and told her he'd be back that evening.

At seven that evening, Kevin knocked on her open door with flowers in hand. He had shaved, slept, and talked with Le Pluete. He felt terrific, especially when he saw April sitting up in bed. Her bright shining hair flowed over the pillow. She had a little make up on and looked beautiful. She was smiling.

"Come in," she said cheerfully. "My, aren't you the page out of GQ! A tie and all."

Kevin handed her the flowers which she dutifully sniffed and handed back to him. He put the vase on the window sill. "Thank you. You didn't have to."

333

"True. Shall I take them back?"

"Oh, you can't. They're perishable goods. Non-returnable."

Kevin laughed. "I see you got your sense of humor back."

"It comes and goes. Where is Suzette?"

"She won't be coming."

"Oh?"

"Not for a long time," he said.

April sensed the serious tone and frowned. "Did I say something wrong?"

"No," Kevin looked down at the floor.

Once again, April thought he looked like a little boy who'd just been caught doing something wrong. "Do you want to tell me about it?" she asked in her best maternal tone.

"Do you mind if I sit down?"

"Don't be silly, sit down."

"I'm not sure whether I should tell you this after all you've been through," he said as he pulled up a stool and sat next to her bed.

"It's over, Kevin. I realize it. I had a long talk this afternoon with a psychiatrist that Julian recommended."

"Julian?"

"He's here in Paris. George called him. He'll be here a little later," she said cheerfully.

Kevin wasn't sure whether that was good news or not.

"How long has he been here?"

"Since the day before yesterday. He wanted to see me, but he didn't want to disturb you."

"Oh?" he said thinking that was a good sign. "He's very thoughtful."

"Yes. I dearly love him," she said wistfully. "And, my parents arrived this afternoon, came to see me, and are coming back soon."

"They found out?"

"George called them, too. Now, you were about to say?"

Kevin hesitated looking for the right way to tell her. He couldn't think of one, so he plunged right in, "Suzette is not my wife."

April cocked her head. Did she hear him right? "Suzette is not your wife?"

"No. Our marriage was a cover."

"And what was it to cover?" she asked now thoroughly intrigued.

"My other job."

"Am I going to have to drag everything out of you piece by piece?" she asked. She sat up and looked more than a little annoyed.

"Okay. Sit back. Relax. Here goes. I am an undercover agent for Interpol. I have been since 1991, just after 'Operation Desert Storm'. I was in the Criminal Investigation Division of the Army. I came here on assignment to find some Iraqi terrorists. My cover was working on the Paris Gazette as a reporter. When I completed my mission six months later, I had fallen in love with Paris. Are you following me so far?"

April just stared at him and nodded.

"Anyway, after we caught the bad guys, I was Duer to get out of the Army, and I was offered the undercover job by a man I'd worked with on the terrorist assignment. He was an inspector in Interpol. We kept my cover at the paper, and I've been doing both jobs since." He sat back, folded his arms and raised his eyebrows. "That's it."

April sat up. "That's what? It? That's not 'it'. That doesn't explain Suzette or why you lied to me," April said growing more and more angry each minute.

Kevin held up his hands to stop her. She was getting too upset. He knew that wasn't good for her. "Hold it. Hold it" he said trying to calm her down.

April collapsed back on her pillow looking like fire was coming out of her eyes.

"Okay. The whole story. Like I said, I was an undercover agent. Well, this assignment came up in Marseilles four years ago. It was a drug thing and involved parties and officials who where high up. They, my bosses, decided that I should work with another agent, Suzette."

"Suzette is an agent, too?" April interrupted.

"Yes. I mean, was."

"Was?"

"She was then, she's no longer an agent."

"But she's still your wife."

"No. We merely posed as man and wife to build a better deep cover. We were never married."

"So you've never been married?"

"Nope. Engaged six times," he said playfully.

"Funny," April said flatly. She looked at him out of the corner of her eyes, "So you told me you were married to protect your cover?" she asked hesitantly.

"Right."

"You didn't trust me."

"I didn't know you," he said with a hint of frustration.

"You didn't try."

"I couldn't, I was in the middle of a job."

"With Suzette?"

"Yes, with Suzette."

"But you said Suzette wasn't in Interpol any longer."

"She was then. She's not now!"

"What happened? You two have a fight?"

"No. She turned out to be a double agent."

April pondered this for a moment. "Suzette was a double agent? And you didn't know?"

"Nobody did!" Kevin was beginning to get defensive. She was getting to him. He caught himself just in time. "Sorry," he said calmly. "I didn't mean to yell."

April looked at him. She wanted to hug him. He looked so hurt and frustrated.

He heaved a great sigh and began, "Suzette had been a double agent for a long time. She was working for Duer. We knew there was a mole in our operation, but we could never pin down who it was," he explained slowly. "It wasn't until she tried to protect Duer this time that we finally were able to catch her. Now she's in jail for a long time."

"And you feel?"

"Frankly, a bit sad. It wasn't easy seeing her behind bars. And bit betrayed. But otherwise, she was a friend that turned out to be an enemy."

"She doesn't mean more?"

"No. She was just an agent I worked with."

"So you never...loved her?"

"Nope. Never."

"Never made love to her?"

"Well, one does have to keep up appearances. It was just part of the job."

"Just part of the job?"

Holding three fingers up, he said, "Scout's honor." Then he quickly added, "But I was never in love with her. I swear," he said looking her straight in the eye.

April sighed. "Well, I guess I can understand that."

"Can we start over?"

"You want to?"

"Yes. Very much."

"Okay," she said a smile creeping over her face. She held out her hand. "Hello. I'm April Mason."

He took her hand and held it for a long time, then he said, "Hello, I'm Kevin Morrison, and I love you."

"Morrison? What happened to O'Connor?"

"It's a long story."

THE END

EPILOGUE

The Rest of the Story

Where they are now:

Michelle "Snooky" Montedieu Jardin is now serving a sentence of ten years for counterfeiting and aiding and abetting Duer. Her car was recovered but the counterfeit money in the boot, was never found. Rumor has it there are three Paris teenage street punks living like millionaires in Algeria.

Francois Duer was sentenced to life imprisonment for the attempted murder of Paul LeMieux. His escape plans are all but complete.

Paul LeMieux is in prison, serving a 20-year sentence for the second degree murder of Pepe Duvall. He wants to escape with Duer, but there's no chance.

Jean Pierre Demain recovered from his head wound, and is on probation. He was the key witness against Duer and LeMieux. He's back at the Tourist Bureau. His divorce was made final the day after he was tried and found guilty of grave robbery.

Suzette managed to escape by selling her favors to seven policemen, three judges, and a locksmith.

Julian Maxwell has just finished reading a new novel from George LaValle entitled, <u>A Spy in My Office</u>. He loves it!

Marcel Le Pluete is still trying to think of a way to get Kevin back into Interpol.

Kevin O'Connor, aka Morrison, is finally writing his first book, <u>The Mole and I</u>.

April Morrison, nee Mason, is sitting in her Paris apartment, in her white bikini, admiring her new wedding ring and working on the final chapter of her new mystery novel, <u>The Baker's Vault</u>.

ABOUT THE AUTHOR

THE BAKER'S VAULT is John K. Potter's second novel. His first, THE WAREHOUSE, will soon be republished. John is a graduate of Indiana University and has been a television writer and producer for more than thirty years. He has also written and produced several comedy revues for nightclubs. John is currently the Supervising Producer of CBS's *The People's Choice Awards* which airs each January.

John, and his wife Lynn, recently celebrated their thirtieth wedding anniversary. His two children, John, his son, and his daughter, Meredith are off pursuing their own individual careers.

Printed in the United States
1529200002B/118-198